Charles G

Iran, Saudi Arabia, and the Law of the Sea

POLITICAL INTERACTION AND LEGAL DEVELOPMENT IN THE PERSIAN GULF

CONTRIBUTIONS IN POLITICAL SCIENCE, NUMBER 48

Greenwood Press
WESTPORT CONNECTICUT • LONDON, ENGLAND

Grateful acknowledgment is made to the following source:

Journal of South Asian and Middle Eastern Studies for permission to reprint "The Roles of Iran and Saudi Arabia in the Development of the Law of the Sea" by Charles G. MacDonald 1 (Spring 1978): 3–10.

Library of Congress Cataloging in Publication Data

MacDonald, Charles G
    Iran, Saudi Arabia, and the law of the sea.

    (Contributions in political science ; no. 48
ISSN 0147-1066)
      Bibliography: p.
      Includes index.
      1. Maritime law—Persian Gulf region. 2. Maritime
law—Iran. 3. Maritime law—Saudi Arabia.
4. Persian Gulf. I. Title. II. Series.
JX4422.P44M3   341.4'5'09536   79-6186
ISBN 0-313-20768-2 lib. bdg.

Library of Congress Catalog Card Number: 79-6186
ISBN: 0-313-20768-2
ISSN: 0147-1066

First published in 1980

Greenwood Press
A division of Congressional Information Service, Inc.
88 Post Road West, Westport, Connecticut 06881
Printed in the United States of America

10 9 8 7 6 5 4 3 2 1

To the memory of Roscoe R. Oglesby

Contents

Maps

Tables

Preface

As we move into the 1980s the world has become increasingly dependent on the oceans for the supply and transportation of food, petroleum, and other natural resources. Traditional international law does not deal adequately with this new dependence. The basic lack of legal guidance relating to the delimitation of national jurisdiction in offshore areas, the allocation of offshore resources, and the regulation of international access has been compounded by the emergence of developing states as active participants in the international legal order. A plethora of conflicting claims has exacerbated political rivalries and has become a potential threat to world order. This study focuses upon the approaches of two developing states, Iran and Saudi Arabia, to the law of the sea in the Persian Gulf as a study of the development of the law of the sea in general. Special attention is given to the relationship between specific legal developments (claims and treaties) and the underlying political interests that influence the substance and timing of such developments. The claims of Iran and Saudi Arabia to offshore jurisdiction and their various treaties delimiting offshore boundaries are evaluated according to prevailing international legal standards with a view to understanding their effects on basic community policies within the Persian Gulf and their contributions to the development of the international law of the sea. The implications of the Iranian and Saudi offshore claims, agreements, and policy statements not only offer insights into the approach of developing states to international law but suggest future steps that could lead to the resolution of many current disputes.

The research for this study began at the University of Virginia; it was revised and updated while I was teaching in the Department of International Relations at Florida International University in Miami, Florida; final revisions were made in the fall of 1979 after I returned to the University of Virginia with a visiting appointment in the Woodrow Wilson Department of Government and Foreign Affairs. I wish to acknowledge with gratitude the following individuals for their suggestions and encouragement during my initial research: Professor Richard B. Bilder, Mr. Nasser Ghoushbeigui, Mr. Christopher C. Joyner, Mr. Fahim Al-Qasimi, Mr. Frederick S. Tipson, and Mr. William Hays Parks. I would like to express my sincere thanks to Ambassador Ezedin Kazemi for the opportunity to talk with him. I also wish to thank Mr. Richard Young for sharing some of his Persian Gulf experiences with me. Moreover, my special thanks are extended to Professor Rouhollah K. Ramazani and Ambassador John Norton Moore for their advice and direction.

My subsequent research and the completion of my manuscript were funded in part by the Faculty Development Funds from the College of Arts and Sciences and from the International Affairs Center at Florida International University. My gratitude is extended to my colleagues in the Department of International Relations at Florida International, especially to Dr. Ken I. Boodhoo and Ivan C. Harnanan, Esquire, for their helpful discussions on developing states. I wish to express my appreciation to Dean K. William Leffland and Dean James A. Mau for their encouragement and interest in my work. I also wish to thank Mr. Gordon E. Jessee, Ms. Allison Fisher, and Mr. Bahman Bakhtiari for their assistance in my research.

I wish to thank the Cartographic Division of the Central Intelligence Agency for maps one and two, which come from the *Indian Ocean Atlas*. I also thank the Office of the Geographer in the Department of State for the international boundary studies from which maps three through eight were drawn.

I wish to thank the staffs at Florida International University and the University of Virginia for their assistance in the preparation of the manuscript. I am especially grateful to Mrs. Roberta Comfort and Mrs. Bunny Stinnett for their typing. I wish to express my sincere thanks to the staff at Greenwood Press for their always friendly assistance. I am greatly indebted for the support and patience of my wife, Jane, and my family. I especially wish to thank my mother, Mrs. Gordon H. MacDonald, for drawing maps three through eight.

By dedicating this work to the memory of Mr. Roscoe R. Oglesby I wish to acknowledge my deep gratitude to the professor and Virginia gentleman who introduced me to the study of international law and to the possibilities of using international law to resolve or limit conflict.

The assistance of all the individuals and institutions that I have mentioned is greatly appreciated, but responsibility for any errors of fact or interpretation is solely mine.

Charles G. MacDonald

Iran,
Saudi Arabia,
and the
Law of the Sea

Introduction: The Role of Developing States in the Law of the Sea as a Major Public Order Concern

Previously wars were fought for the control of territory and land resources. Today disputes over the control of the oceans and their resources create new possibilities for armed conflict. The new and dynamic extension of land-boundary conflicts can threaten access to adequate supplies of food, fuel, and raw materials.

During the last decade the nuclear arms race, the war in Vietnam, and the Arab-Israeli conflict have held public attention. Meanwhile seemingly insignificant events involving the offshore use of coercion, as in the North Atlantic, the Mediterranean Sea, the Aegean Sea, and the Persian Gulf,[1] quietly presaged the coming of a new era of uncertainty in which the rivalries and claims of developing states could have repercussions throughout the changing international system.

The increasing world population and the revolution of rising expectations have resulted in an unprecedented demand on the oceans for supplies of food, fuel, and raw materials.[2] Advances in technology have made the exploitation of the oceans possible but at the cost of new environmental dangers and new political problems associated with the delimitation of offshore areas, the allocation of offshore resources, and the regulation of international access. Furthermore, the increased world population, coupled with technological advances, has undermined the traditional principle of "freedom of the seas" because the premise that the ocean and its resources are infinite has proved invalid.

The emergence of developing states as active participants in the international legal order has compounded the inadequacy of the traditional international law of the sea. The basic lack of normative guidance has resulted in a plethora of unilateral claims, which have been aptly termed an "ocean rush," to expanded national jurisdictions.[3] Between 1 January 1967 and 1 March 1973 there were as many as seventy-six extensions of national jurisdiction, twenty-eight of which were for distances ranging from 12 to 200 miles.[4] Many other claims followed the unilateral United States claim to a 200-mile fishery conservation zone in 1976. Whether the "ocean rush" is the response of developing states to the exploitations of the oceans by the technologically advanced states or a basic assertion of nationalism, a growing number of claims to expanded national jurisdiction is evident. These claims clash with other claims and threaten broader community policies, such as rights of free access.

Four major threats to world order emanate from expanded ocean claims. First is the threat of an outbreak of hostilities over conflicting claims to exclusive control of offshore areas or resources. Second, conflict could result from a destabilization of regional and global equilibrium brought about by the limiting of international access and a resultant altering of tactical and strategic military balances. Third, conflict could result from any disturbance to the freedom of the ocean arteries through which vital supplies of oil must pass. Fourth, conflict could stem from an interference with or detention of foreign ships in order to enforce a unilateral claim to a pollution control zone or a fishery conservation zone.

The first and most obvious threat of an outbreak of hostilities involves assertions of exclusive jurisdiction that clash with the claims of other states. The danger of conflicting claims is most serious where hostilities have previously existed. Where distrust and rivalry are present, the assertion of an exclusive claim could easily precipitate armed conflict. The Arab-Israeli War of 1967— touched off by Arab claims concerning the Strait of Tiran and the Gulf of Aqaba and the preclusion of Israeli access—is an obvious example.[5] Conflicting claims to offshore resources have also proved to be potentially volatile, especially between recognized adversaries. Conflicts over the unilateral extension of fishing limits have brought about the use of force on a limited scale, such as in the "Cod War" between Britain and Iceland[6] and in the "Sardine War" between Spain and Morocco.[7] Conflicting claims to ownership of offshore oil resources have also contributed to a heightening of tensions and a threatened use of force between Greece and Turkey,[8] and to a lesser degree between Iran and Saudi Arabia.[9]

While the use of force might result from expanding claims of exclusive national jurisdiction, an indirect effect of limiting international access might prove to be a greater threat to world order by destabilizing previous regional and global balances of power. A potentially dangerous instability might result if the mobility of the United States armed forces were restricted or if there were an elimination of the United States military presence from various regions of the world. The presence of the United States fleet in many areas has served as a stabilizing force, deterring aggression by radical regimes and protecting against violent actions aimed at changes of regime.[10] Limiting of international access might also have a dangerous destabilizing effect on the strategic doctrine concerning submarine warfare, since such limitation would make the detection of submarines more difficult and would increase the possibility of a surprise attack.[11]

The current trend of a general downgrading of power has enabled developing states to enjoy far more freedom of action than previously experienced,[12] but has also encouraged developing states to be critical of a superpower presence. Similarly, developing states have sought the formation of nuclear-free zones to avoid possible involvement in any East-West conflict and to eschew superpower influence. However, such a posture may prove a fatal delusion and simply result in the creation of new power vacuums and a recrudescence of conflict.[13]

A third major threat to world order involves the limitation of access for commercial vessels. The threat of a closing of international straits to shipping, such as the vital artery represented by the Strait of Hormuz, might have an unprecedented and disastrous effect on the oil-dependent free-world economy.[14] A closing of such straits for radical political or economic reasons, which would cause massive economic dislocations and shortages, could easily produce a violent international struggle to secure needed resources.[15]

A fourth threat to world order comes from the possibility of armed clashes over interference with international shipping in such areas as pollution control zones and fishery conservation zones. Interference with shipping could easily bring about open conflict where there were preexisting tensions. For example, interference with American shipping by the British contributed significantly to the causes of the War of 1812 between the United States and Britain.[16] Such a threat would be increased where state control over economic activities existed.

In light of these potential dangers to world order, it is apparent that the attitudes and roles of developing states are an essential component in the development of an effective law of the sea. Furthermore, the convoking of the Third United Nations Conference on the Law of the Sea (which had the direct participation by some 150 states in an attempt to formulate and codify a new international law of the sea) underlines the importance of the roles of the developing states. Thus to understand better the problems besetting attempts to develop universal norms governing international maritime behavior, it is necessary to examine the nature of the parts played by the developing states and to evaluate their contributions to the development of the international law of the sea.

PROBLEMS OF THEORY

TERMINOLOGICAL CONFUSION

"Terminological confusion"[17] is a major stumbling block to any intellectual pursuit involving widely used concepts. Two related problems are usually involved. First, the content of a term often is not sufficiently clear to distinguish its usage from that of other similar terms. Second, if the term is used in a number of ways, there is the risk that an acquired usage might be contrary to the intended usage. To avoid such confusions and to achieve the desired meaning, it is necessary to recognize possible ambiguities and to establish an operational usage.

While the concept of "developing state" is often used in U. S. Department of State publications pertaining to the law of the sea,[18] a number of terms are used more or less interchangeably with it in the study of international law. For example, Jorge Castañeda has chosen the concept of "underdeveloped countries"[19] and G. Abi-Saab uses the phrase "the newly independent states."[20] Richard Falk utilizes the category of "new states" and formulates eight classifications expressly to "identify the phenomenon of the 'new states.'"[21] Similarly, A. A. Fatouros, drawing upon the work of Pierre Hassner,[22] employs the expression "new states" and cites five overlapping groupings.[23] Taking a slightly different approach, Oliver Lissitzyn discusses the appearance of "newly independent nations" and then uses the more inclusive "less-developed countries" for the subject of his analysis.[24]

From the uses of these various terms, it is apparent that there is widespread interest in determining the role in the development of international law of a certain heterogeneous group of states that have come to participate in the international system. Two distinct emphases can be discerned. The first is the phenomenon of "newness," the second a relatively low level of economic development.

While these two phenomena represent potentially useful parameters, they have been primarily used descriptively, often interchangeably.[25] For the purposes of this study, however, the concept of "newness" is not restricted to newly independent states, but represents a new international participation and influence by states that previously acted or were forced to act at the behest of a great power, even though they might have been "sovereign states."[26] Coupled with this new participation is a relative lack of economic development and a relatively low level of technology. Moreover, with this new participation has come a conscious desire for development and a revolution of rising expectations.

While an attempt has been made to distinguish the use of "developing state" from similar concepts, the concept may still have a number of usages. For example, it has been suggested that all states are developing states, especially the technologically advanced states, which continue to develop. While the validity of such a statement is a matter of semantics, it underlines the importance of the specified operational usage of a term in a given work. "Developing states" in this work refers to technologically less developed states that are experiencing a *new* level of international influence.

CONTEXTUAL FALLACY

The second problem of theorizing about the role of developing states in international law is "contextual fallacy." For the problem of intervention, John Norton Moore views contextual fallacy as

the failure clearly to recognize the diversity of issues and contexts in which intervention is alleged, and to formulate a framework for inquiry which organizes these diverse claims according to features of the context which raise common issues of policy and are shaped by common conditioning factors.[27]

Both parts of Moore's definition are applicable to theorizing about the role of developing states. First, it is essential to recognize the *diversity* of issues and contexts involved. Second, it is important to recognize the *relationship* between given claims and the context in which they are made.

In examining the diversity of issues and contexts with which developing states are involved, the variety of such states becomes important. For example, developing states may be old or new, large or small, rich or poor, conservative or radical, capitalist or communist; policy issues vary according to the interests of the given situation. Similarly, the broader regional and global contexts, with their respective political interactions, provide additional complexity for policy formulations. For instance, the East-West rivalry, as well as regional rivalries such as the Arab-Israeli conflict, are important factors affecting given policy decisions. Thrust into the midst of these broader contexts are the narrower, and often competing, national interests reflecting religious leanings, racial orientations, historical experience, economic pressures, and special minority interests.

In exploring the relationship between claims and contexts, a wide array of competing interests becomes apparent. For example, developing states may present claims based on geographical criteria, such as whether they are coastal, land-locked, or shelf-locked; whether they border on a strait, have a broad continental shelf, or an irregular coastline; or represent an archipelago. Claims might also be made according to a specific economic interest or historical experience, as those relating to coastal and distant-water fishing, the presence of offshore petroleum resources or land-based natural resources, or balance of payments problems.

When all these special interests are placed in larger regional and global contexts, the importance of having a means to organize diverse claims, identify conditioning factors, and determine common policies becomes apparent. Furthermore, in the study of international law the need to avoid contextual fallacy is underlined by the propensity of lawyers to reason by analogy (in terms of a given precedent) without realizing the complexity of a given international situation.[28] Such an oversimplification of a complex situation could result in irrelevant conclusions.

MOTIVATIONAL OBSCURITY

The third problem concerns the "Why" of a state's policy and the nature of the policymaking process. Motivational obscurity involves a multiplicity of internal factors that affect the formation of national policy. As the level of bureaucracy and vested interests rises, the complexity of the problem of linking a given policy with a state's interest increases. It may not be possible to determine what position a state should take on an issue because of the competing interests within the state, such as coastal versus distant-water fishing interests. Although compromises may be made, the possibility exists that neither interest will be satisfied, instead of both interests being satisfied.[29]

In addition to conflicting special interests, a state's motivations may be obscure because of political maneuvers aimed at achieving an unrelated goal. A state may increase its offshore jurisdiction to provoke another state's response, or as a ploy relating to a fundamentally different matter. Such a ploy is sometimes the nature of international logrolling in the United Nations and at international conferences (such as the Third United Nations Conference on the Law of the Sea).[30] Thus when the decision on a state's policy is finally made, it is impossible to identify the most significant conditioning factor involved. One can only attempt to identify the role of conditioning factors in any policy formulation. A consideration of motivational obscurity is essential in recognizing that causes of national policy decisions, although systematically analyzed, can be only imperfectly determined.

A POLICY-RESPONSIVE APPROACH

Only after the problems in theorizing about developing states in international law have been taken into consideration is it possible to adopt an approach that responds to the changing community needs yet is sensitive to the complexity of global, regional, and national interactions. Because the primary interest here pertains to community needs involving the law of the sea, it is necessary to set forth the central issues of the law of the sea before the role of the developing state can be assessed.

THE CHANGING LAW OF THE SEA: CENTRAL ISSUES

The central issues of the changing law of the sea stem from the extended claims to national jurisdiction, and involve the determination of offshore jurisdictional boundaries, the allocation of offshore resources, and the regulation of international community access. Each of the three areas of contention involve fundamentally different questions that, if left unresolved, could lead to armed conflict.

Claims to Authority over Offshore Areas

How should offshore areas be delimited? How should offshore jurisdictional boundaries be determined? How should offshore areas be parceled for purposes of exclusive, inclusive, and functional (limited) jurisdictions? These are basic questions without universal norms. Offshore areas are divided roughly into three basic jurisdictional areas: an area of exclusive national jurisdiction (the territorial sea), an area of limited or functional national jurisdiction, and an area beyond the limits of national jurisdiction. While the broad areas of jurisdiction are acknowledged in principle, offshore boundaries are normatively indeterminate, and problems of realizing exact boundaries continue, the efforts of the United Nations Third Conference on the Law of the Sea notwithstanding.[31]

The first jurisdictional area, the territorial sea, is a commonly recognized offshore extension of a state's sovereignty. However, there is a recurring debate over the breadth of the territorial sea, the method by which it is measured, and its relationship to international waterways. Of special importance are questions involving claims to a comprehensive authority to deny passage through international straits.

The second jurisdictional area, the area of limited or functional jurisdiction, includes contiguous zones, exclusive economic zones, and environmental protection zones. The contiguous zone refers to an area extending beyond the territorial sea in which the coastal state may exercise control to "prevent infringement of its customs, fiscal, immigration or sanitary regulations within its territory or territorial sea."[32] In the Convention on the Territorial Sea and Contiguous Zone the zone was formally limited to twelve miles (twenty-four are proposed in the ICNT/Rev. 1) from the baseline from which the breadth of the territorial sea is measured. Although the contiguous zone has been so delimited by international convention, fundamental differences exist pertaining to its nature and method of measure.

The second type of functional zone, the exclusive economic zone, provides for the control of offshore resources by the coastal state. An exclusive economic zone of 200 miles has been proposed at the Third United Nations Conference on the Law of the Sea,[33] but there has not been agreement on its composition. Currently, offshore resource jurisdiction is essentially in the form of exclusive fishing zones, regional fishing regimes, and continental shelf claims. While the limits and types of jurisdiction over fishing zones vary, coastal states have been granted resource jurisdiction over continental shelf resources "to a depth of 200 meters, or beyond that limit, to where the depth of the superjacent waters admits of the exploitation of the natural resources."[34] With technology steadily advancing, such a limit as "depth of exploitation" has proved meaningless. Resource zones face continuous problems relating to their method of measurement and degree of jurisdiction, as well as to their breadth. Interrelated with the delimitation of resource jurisdiction are the broader questions of resource allocation.

A third type of functional zone is an environmental protection zone. Pollution control zones and fishery conservation zones also exist, but are not widely accepted. The problems leading to the establishment of such zones have been acknowledged, but the assumption of a limited national jurisdiction to deal with the respective problems remains controversial.

The third jurisdictional area is the area beyond the limits of national jurisdiction, the inclusive nature of which has been accepted in principle. The area, though vaguely delimited, has been reserved as "the common heritage of mankind." The United Nations General Assembly declared that "no claim to any part of that area (beyond the limits of national jurisdiction) or its resources shall be recognized."[35] Despite this reservation, which is not legally binding, the area has continued to shrink as the limits of national jurisdiction expand. The failure of the international community to establish a viable seabed authority raises the question of whether a community authority can be realized in a heterogeneous community.

How the offshore jurisdictional boundaries are to be determined remains open to question. But it is clear that any comprehensive legal regime for the oceans must provide a framework for negotiating acceptable and identifiable offshore boundaries. The problems of delineating offshore areas and the disagreements over the nature of functional jurisdictions are interrelated with the allocation of offshore resources and the regulation of international access.

Claims to Authority over Offshore Resources

Who should have authority over offshore resources in areas not previously subject to the jurisdiction of any state? How should ocean resources be allocated? Technology has been responsible, in part, for such questions and may play an integral part in their solution. First, the use of technologically advanced fishing techniques threatens fishing stocks that were previously thought to be limitless. Second, the mineral resources of many previously inaccessible areas are now the subject of competitive exploitation by the technologically advanced states, much to the chagrin of the developing states. Since ocean resources are not limitless, some means of resource control and allocation is necessary. Developing an acceptable and workable system, however, involves dealing with a variety of claims that differ according to the type of resource involved.

The first broad group of resource claims relates to the control of living resources, the very presence of which is dependent upon some form of conservation. Questions arise such as: How can the various species of fish be preserved? How can a functional jurisdiction be established when fish recognize no fixed boundaries? In approaching such questions there are two possibilities—exclusive control or a shared control (which implies a resource allocation). Which type of control should be established in a given area remains open to question and might depend on the species involved as well as the geographical configuration of the area.

The three general types of species—coastal, anadromous, and migratory—pose different problems and suggest different methods of control. The coastal species would be more susceptible to coastal state management, but the distance from shore where such species might be found could vary greatly with the water depth. In the case of anadromous species, the host state might be responsible for the spawning environment, and would thus exercise a greater claim to the species throughout their range of travel. The highly migratory species, such as the tuna, present even greater problems in that the broad range of the species would dictate some form of international regulation. Current jurisdictional delimitations, whether left to the coastal state or assumed by regional organizations, have not proved successful, and disputes over fishing zones have resulted in hostilities. International agreement on an exclusive economic zone of a given breadth would solve some problems, but problems of allocation within the zone as well as problems related to the status of fish swimming beyond the zone might continue.

One major problem of allocation that is yet to be resolved concerns the inequality of states and is related to historical experience. The disparate methods of fishing used by developing states underline the fundamental advantages of the advanced states. Many developing states, especially former colonies, do not have modern fishing fleets to take full advantage of the fish off their coasts. Should the advanced states be permitted to exploit the fish stocks in these waters? What is the role of historic fishing rights off the coasts of developing states that were the subject of colonial exploitation? Should the allocation of living resources compensate developing states for their inequalities? If one state extends its fishing jurisdiction into an area that historically has been fished by others, should the

coastal state compensate the other states even if they are technologically advanced and much richer? Should a state make an exclusive
claim to resources that were previously shared by the international
community? If coastal states expand their fishing limits, should there
be any compensation for land-locked states that previously shared
the right to fish in the given offshore area? Such questions of control
and allocation abound and are pertinent to mineral resources as
well as to living resources.

The second broad group of resource claims relates to the control
of mineral resources. How will offshore mineral resources be allocated? What should determine the extent of exclusive national
resource jurisdiction? How will resource boundaries be delimited
between adjacent and opposite states? How might offshore resources
be shared? Such questions, while similar to those concerning living
resources, differ in that mineral resource boundaries can conceivably
be fixed.

However, the delimitation of fixed boundaries for the exclusive
control of mineral resources faces various problems. While offshore
mineral resource jurisdiction has been tied to the continental shelf
doctrine, claims have extended jurisdiction to the continental margin
and have brought to light additional questions of resource sharing
for areas extending beyond the continental shelf.

Basically the claims to mineral resources can be divided into
claims to an exclusive control and claims to a shared use of mineral
resources. Most problems encountered pertain to contending claims
to resources of a given area by opposite or adjacent states and involve
disagreement over methods of measurement. Irregular geography
and offshore islands serve to complicate measurement schemes.

Where a shared resource use has been recognized in principle, as
in the area beyond the limits of national jurisdiction, there remains
the problem of actually devising a system of allocation that can bring
about an equitable distribution of resources to the various members
of the community. In the absence of an acceptable community
authority and a system of resource allocation, some advanced
states have recognized a freedom to exploit deep-sea minerals until
such time as a community authority is established. This has raised
questions of the technological advantages that would enable advanced
states to reap a disproportionate share of resources beyond the

limits of national jurisdiction.

Questions relating to the control and allocation of offshore re-sources are complicated not only by the technological gap between the advanced and developing states, but also by the historical memories of colonial exploitations. Thus, some form of technology transfer has been suggested as a possible compensating factor in the allocation puzzle.

Claims to Regulate International Access

Can international access be preserved for purposes of transit through straits, for scientific research, and for the laying and main-tenance of submarine cables and pipelines? Are the security interests of developing states compatible with the commercial and strategic interests of the major sea powers? Such questions represent a third area of contention: the regulation of international access.

This question is often associated with the transit through straits of commercial and military vessels, especially large tankers and nuclear-powered and -armed military vessels. The major sea powers fear that local and strategic power balances, as well as world economic stability, might be seriously threatened without some guarantee of unimpeded passage. Claims of developing states concerning straits are usually based on security interests, just as the claims of the major sea powers are.

The questions of access for scientific research or the laying and maintenance of submarine cables and pipelines are usually based on distrust and inequality between states. Developing states tend to be sensitive to the activities of the more advanced states. They fear that technical information about their offshore areas might be used to their disadvantage by advanced states, such as in negotiations involving offshore resource concessions. There is also the fear of espionage and surveillance by the advanced states, as alleged in the case of the U.S.S. *Pueblo.* Juxtaposed to these security and economic interests are the broader community interests in the benefits to be received by the identification of environmental dangers, the deter-mination of fish populations, or the notice of current changes in addition to the functional benefits received from submarine pipe-lines and cables. Thus claims restricting international access affect broader community interests shared by developing and advanced states. How the coastal state security interests and the broader community interests in free access can be reconciled remains to be seen, and represents a formidable problem in the realization of a new comprehensive law of the sea.

The central issues of the law of the sea are: How will offshore areas be delimited? How will offshore resources be allocated? In what manner will international access be preserved or limited? It should be remembered that there is an underlying conflict of interest between the developing and the technologically advanced states over resource exploitation and allocation, as well as over their respective security interests.

THE METHODOLOGY

To determine the role of the developing states in the changing law of the sea and to evaluate their contribution to international legal development, an examination of their roles in a given situation is required. The roles of Iran and Saudi Arabia in the development of the law of the sea within the Persian Gulf are examined as a "case study" in the development of the law of the sea in general.[36]

In this study the policy-oriented approach to international law is utilized; it selectively draws upon the analytical framework suggested by Myres McDougal and Harold Lasswell. This approach allows analysis of the changing law of the sea in terms of political interaction and social change while reflecting the decision-making aspects of international legal development. In this exercise international law is viewed not only in terms of what the law is taken to be at a given time, but also in terms of the interests and principles upon which it is based. As such, law is not analyzed as a rigid set of rules, but rather as a flexible ordering device through which the members of the system seek to obtain their goals, whether exclusive or inclusive (community-oriented).

This approach allows law to be viewed both as an instrument of and a constraint on policy. The functions of law are therefore examined along an instrument-constraint continuum. The notion of continuum is based on the assumption that state actions involve in varying degrees a combination of national and community interests— thereby avoiding the controversy over the national interest—

community interest dichotomy.

The study, while presenting the development of the law of the sea in the case of two developing states, stresses the relationship of political interaction and social change to legal development. The emphasis of the study is on the effect of interactions within the Persian Gulf subsystem, but the interplay between the subsystem and the international system is considered as well. The Persian Gulf practice is approached in part from a historical-analytical stand-point, and the adoption of specific laws is examined chronologically in order to demonstrate the impact of political factors on the timing of significant legal changes.

The Persian Gulf context is examined according to its physical characteristics, historical perspective, and ongoing process of inter-action, which together provide the setting in which the law of the sea in the Persian Gulf is developing. Next, the basic community policies at stake in the changing law of the sea in the Persian Gulf are assessed. In addition, the actions of Iran and Saudi Arabia at the United Nations conferences on the law of the sea are considered. Finally, the trends are evaluated in terms of their effects on the basic community policies within the Persian Gulf, their contributions to the international law of the sea, and the insights into the role of the developing state in international law that they produce.

The significance of this study is twofold. Empirically, it attempts to contribute to a better understanding of the problems experienced in the pursuit of new universal norms for the governing of inter-national maritime behavior. Theoretically, it seeks to provide bases for generalizations regarding the attitudes of developing states toward international law. It is also hoped that the findings of this study will be of interest not only to students of international law, but also to area specialists interested in the Middle East.

NOTES

1. International incidents involving maritime disputes have been increasing as the number of claims to expanded jurisdiction increases. The incidents in the North Atlantic between Britain and Iceland, in the Mediterranean between Morocco and Spain, in the Aegean between Greece and Turkey, and in the Persian Gulf between Iran and Saudi Arabia are representative

of types of offshore conflict that might occur (see notes 6-9).

2. While the revolution of rising expectations is usually associated with developing countries, the continuing desire to achieve a higher standard of living in the developed countries appears to be as insatiable. The question of greed, or whether a human can ever achieve satisfaction is at the root of the problem facing a world with an expanding population and a limited resource supply.

3. *See* Anthony D'Amato and John Lawrence Hargrove, *Environment and the Law of the Sea*, Studies in Transnational Legal Policy, no. 5, (Washington, D. C.: American Society of International Law, 1974), p. 28.

4. U. S., Department of State, *International Boundary Study, Series A—Limits in the Seas*, no. 36, "National Claims to Maritime Jurisdictions," rev. 1 March 1973.

5. *See* "Speech by President Nasser on Closing of the Gulf of Aqaba, May 22, 1967," in *The Arab-Israeli Conflict*, ed. John Norton Moore, 3 vols. (Princeton, N.J.: Princeton University Press, 1974), 3:725-29. For a discussion of the opposing claims, *see* Carl F. Salons, "Gulf of Aqaba and Strait of Tiran: Troubled Waters," *U.S. Naval Institute Proceedings*, 94 (December 1968): 54-62.

6. The "Cod War" was the result of Iceland's unilateral extension of its fishing limits, and at one time involved West Germany as well as Britain. For an international legal examination, *see* Richard B. Bilder, "The Anglo-Icelandic Fisheries Dispute," 1973 *Wisconsin Law Review* 37 (1973). *See also* "Judgment of the Fisheries Jurisdiction Case," 13 *International Legal Materials* 1049 (1974).

7. The "Sardine War" followed Morocco's unilateral extension of its fishing limits from twelve to seventy miles in March 1973. For details *see Arab Report and Record* (London), 1-15 March 1973, p. 108; 16-31 March 1973, p. 135; and 1-15 January 1974, p. 9.

8. The dispute between Greece and Turkey involves oil exploitation rights in the Aegean Sea. Turkey's claim to the continental shelf conflicts with Greek claims to the continental shelf and territorial sea around more than 350 Greek islands off the Turkish coast. *See* Clyde H. Farnsworth, "Greek-Turkish Oil-Field Dispute Remains Unresolved," *New York Times*, 23 July 1974.

9. For details of the offshore oil dispute between Iran and Saudi Arabia, *see* "Offshore Demarcation: Top Problem in the Gulf," *Middle East Economic Survey* (Beirut) 11 (16 February 1968): 1-5.

10. *See* J. C. Wylie, "The Sixth Fleet and American Diplomacy," in *Soviet-American Rivalry in the Middle East*, ed. J. C. Hurewitz (New

York: Praeger, 1969), pp. 55-60.

11. Arthur H. Dean, "Freedom of the Seas," *Foreign Affairs* 37 (October 1958): 90. *See also* statements by John Norton Moore and Charles N. Bower on "Free Transit of International Straits," in *Digest of United States Practice in International Law 1973,* ed. Arthur W. Rovine (Washington, D. C.: Government Printing Office, 1974), pp. 271-73.

12. A. A. Fatouros, "The Participation of the 'New States' in the International Legal Order of the Future," in *The Future of the International Legal Order*, ed. Richard A. Falk and Cyril E. Black, 4 vols. (Princeton, N.J.: Princeton University Press, 1969), 1:344.

13. The quixotic belief in the currency of a nonuse of force doctrine that emanates from the United Nations is reminiscent of the Kellogg-Briand Pact era sentiment in the League of Nations, especially with major powers seeking arms limitation as well as access to additional oil supplies.

14. *See* Charles A. Heller, "The Strait of Hormuz—Critical in Oil's Future," *World Petroleum* 40 (October 1967): 24-26.

15. Such a possibility brings to mind Lenin's interpretation of imperialist capitalism and the inevitability of capitalist nations going to war over the exploitation of limited resources.

16. *See* "Madison's War Message, June 1, 1812," in *Ideas and Diplomacy*, ed. Norman A. Graebner (New York: Oxford University Press, 1964), pp. 112-15.

17. John Norton Moore has identified terminological confusion and contextual fallacy as two intellectual traps encountered in theorizing about intervention. These tools are also applicable to other conceptual studies in international law. *See* John Norton Moore, "The Control of Foreign Intervention in Internal Conflict," 9 *Virginia Journal of International Law* 205 (1969).

18. In addition to the Department of State, the Law of the Sea Institute also employs the concept of "developing states" or "developing countries." *See The Law of the Sea: Needs and Interests of Developing Countries, Proceedings of the Seventh Annual Conference of the Law of the Sea Institute,* ed. Lewis M. Alexander (Kingston, R. I.: University of Rhode Island, 1973).

19. Jorge Castañeda, "The Underdeveloped Countries and the Development of International Law," *International Organization* 15 (Winter 1961): 38-48.

20. Georges Abi-Saab, "The Newly Independent States and the Rules of International Law: An Outline," 8 *Howard Law Journal* 95 (1962).

21. *See* Richard A. Falk, "The New States and International Legal Order," Hague Academy of International Law, 118 *Recueil des cours* 1 (1966).

22. *See* Pierre Hassner, "Le système international et les nouveaux états,"

in *La communauté internationale face aux jeunes états*, ed. J. B. Duroselle and J. Meyriot (Paris: Librairie Armand Colin, 1964), pp. 11-59.

23. Fatouros, "Participation of 'New States,' " p. 319.

24. *See* Oliver J. Lissitzyn, *International Law Today and Tomorrow* (Dobbs Ferry, N. Y.: Oceana, 1965).

25. Richard Falk, after formulating eight classifications to identify the phenomenon of the "new states," suggests that "no one of these factors operates as an indispensable prerequisite for membership, nor does its absence disqualify a state as 'new.' " *See* Falk, "The New States," p. 12. Similarly, A. A. Fatouros, after identifying five overlapping categories, indicates that he "shall use interchangeably most of the five terms." *See* Fatouros, "Participation of 'New States,' " p. 320.

26. The move toward a lessening of East-West tensions and the expansion of the United Nations—providing new outlets for smaller states—have contributed to a new freedom of action on the part of many less-powerful states.

27. Moore, "Control of Foreign Intervention," p. 217.

28. Stanley Hoffmann has criticized the tendency to *"oversimplify* complicated situations" and to *"reason by analogy."* *See* Stanley Hoffman, *Gulliver's Troubles, or the Setting of American Foreign Policy* (New York: McGraw-Hill, 1968), pp. 129, 135.

29. *See* Ann L. Hollick, "Seabeds Make Strange Politics," *Foreign Policy* 9 (Winter 1972-73): 148-70; and Ann L. Hollick and Robert E. Osgood, *New Era of Ocean Politics*, Studies in International Affairs, no. 22 (Baltimore, Md.: Johns Hopkins University Press, 1974).

30. The United States Delegation Report of the Third United Nations Conference of the Law of the Sea (Caracas) indicated that at the conference "tactics, rather than negotiation, was the rule." *See also* Charles Maechling, Jr., "The Politics of the Ocean," *Virginia Quarterly Review* 47 (Autumn 1971): 505-17; and Louis Henkin, "Politics and the Changing Law of the Sea," *Political Science Quarterly* 89 (March 1974): 46-67.

31. Although there has been no comprehensive law of the sea treaty, negotiations so far have resulted in a Revised Informal Composite Negotiating Text (ICNT/Rev. 1). This is not international law as such, but reflects ongoing negotiations. For text of ICNT/Rev. 1, *see* 18 *International Legal Materials* 686 (1979).

32. *See* Article 24 of the Convention on the Territorial Sea and Contiguous Zone (U. N. Doc. A/CONF.13/L.52). *See also* Article 33 of the ICNT/Rev. 1 in 18 *International Legal Materials 686, 709 (1979).*

33. *See* ICNT/Rev. 1, Part 5, "Exclusive Economic Zone."

34. *See* Article 1 of the Convention on the Continental Shelf (U. N. Doc.A/CONF.13/L.55). *See also* ICNT/Rev. 1, Article 76, which provides

for the breadth to extend 200 miles or to the outer edge of the continental margin.

35. *See* General Assembly Resolution 2574D (24).

36. The selection of these two developing states is influenced by several considerations. First, the Persian Gulf represents a microcosm of the major issues of the international law of the sea, and possesses the characteristics of a subsystem within the international system. Iran and Saudi Arabia are the major actors of the Persian Gulf subsystem. Also, as the principal oil producers of the Persian Gulf, Iran and Saudi Arabia exert far-reaching influence in the international system. Finally, as the largest coastal states of the Persian Gulf, Iran and Saudi Arabia have been in the forefront of change in the law of the sea in the area.

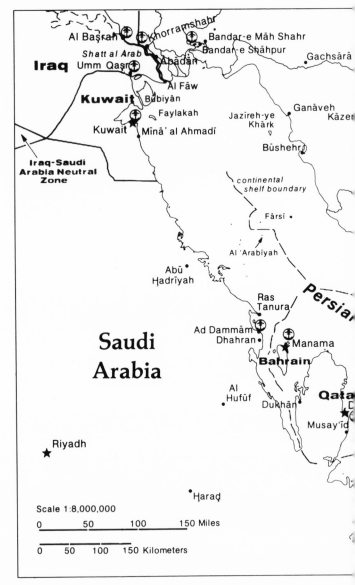

Map 1. The Persian Gulf. Enlargement of inset of the Strait of Horm found on p. 27. *Courtesy of the Cartographic Division of the Cen Intelligence Agency.*

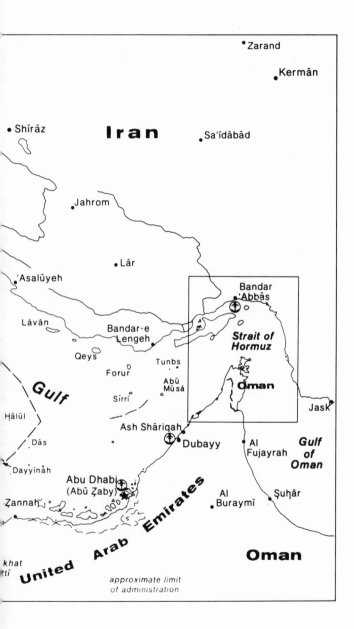

Zarand

Kermân

Shīrāz

Iran

Sa'īdābād

Jahrom

Lār

'Asalūyeh

Lāvān

Bandar-e Lengeh

Bandar 'Abbās

Qeys

Strait of Hormuz

Forur

Tunbs

Abū Mūsá

Sirrī

Oman

Gulf

Jask

Hālūl

Dās

Ash Shāriqah

Dubayy

Al Fujayrah

Gulf of Oman

Dayyināh

Abu Dhabi (Abū Ẓaby)

Al Buraymī

Şuḩār

Zannah

khat tī

United Arab Emirates

Oman

approximate limit of administration

23

CHAPTER 1

The Persian Gulf Context

Understanding the political context in which legal development takes place enables law to be viewed in a broader perspective of events, shifting interests, and national goals. Here the context is examined according to physical characteristics, historical perspective, and the process of political interaction.

THE PHYSICAL CHARACTERISTICS OF THE PERSIAN GULF

The Persian Gulf is a semi-enclosed sea situated between the Arabian peninsula and Iran (*see* Map 1). It is approximately 70,000 square nautical miles in size, or about one-tenth the size of the Gulf of Mexico, and has 97 percent of its periphery occupied by land.[1] The Persian Gulf is joined to the Gulf of Oman, the northernmost arm of the Indian Ocean, by the Strait of Hormuz (see Map 2). The length of the Persian Gulf from the Shatt al-Arab to the Strait of Hormuz is approximately 430 nautical miles; its maximum width is about 160 nautical miles.[2] The narrowest part of the gulf is in the Strait of Hormuz, which is the only outlet, 20.75 nautical miles wide.[3]

The gulf is a relatively shallow basin with an average depth of less than 40 meters and a maximum depth of about 100 meters.[4] The deeper waters run along the Iranian coast and off the Musandam Peninsula. Scattered throughout the gulf, particularly along the Arabian shore, are numerous islands. These islands contribute to the irregular configuration of the coastline and complicate efforts at establishing offshore boundaries. Three of these islands, Abu Musa, Greater Tumb, and Lesser Tumb, are of strategic importance because of their position relative to the shipping lanes within the gulf at the approach to the Strait of Hormuz.

The Persian Gulf has seven littoral states—Iran, Iraq, Kuwait, Saudi Arabia, Qatar, the United Arab Emirates, and Oman. There is one island state in the gulf: Bahrain. Coastline measurements within the gulf vary from 635 nautical miles for Iran and 296 nautical miles for Saudi Arabia to 10 nautical miles for Iraq.[5] Oman's only gulf coastline is on the Musandam Peninsula, which borders the Strait of Hormuz on the south. The strait is bordered on the north and northwest by Iran.

Apart from its physical dimensions, the Persian Gulf has been important for its resources and its geographic position. Historically, the gulf was noted for its pearls. Emerich de Vattel, an international legal scholar, made special mention of these offshore resources in his *Le droit des gens, ou principes de la loi naturelle* in 1758.[6] Currently, the gulf is valued for its vast oil resources, upon which the industrial nations of the West depend for energy. Less significant, but growing in importance, is the gulf's fishing potential.

Juxtaposed to interest in Persian Gulf resources is political-strategic interest in the gulf for its geographic position. Historically the gulf has been viewed not only as an important crossroads of trade and communication, but also as strategically important for the defense of India and the British Empire in the East.[7] After World War II, the gulf was still seen as a British sphere of influence, but with its strategic importance now lying in the containment of the Soviet Union.[8] More recently, as the political-strategic interest in the gulf has come to merge with the growing economic interest in its oil reserves, the so-called energy crises of the 1970s have made it apparent that the Persian Gulf has itself become the subject of strategic concern.

THE PERSIAN GULF IN HISTORICAL PERSPECTIVE

The Persian Gulf as a political subsystem has made a full circle in its form since the beginning of the nineteenth century.[9] In Ramazani's terms, the subsystem has changed from a "pre-pluralistic

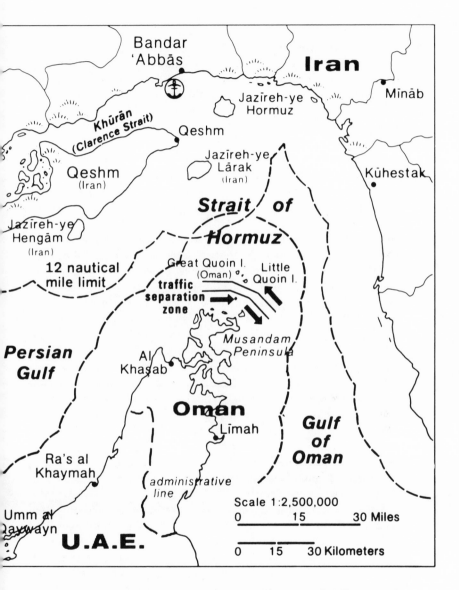

Map 2. The Strait of Hormuz. *Courtesy of the Cartographic Division of the Central Intelligence Agency.*

system" in the early nineteenth century, to a "hegemonic system" of British control around 1820, to a "quasi-hegemonic system" following the relative decline of British authority after World War I, and finally to an emerging pluralistic system with the announcement in January 1968 of the forthcoming British withdrawal.[10]

The European traders of the eighteenth and early nineteenth century found a prepluralistic system in the Persian Gulf based, *inter alia*, on pearling, maritime trade, and piracy. This system also included an ideological dimension, as the revolutionary zeal of Wahhabism was extended to the gulf littoral by the Saudis. At the turn of the nineteenth century the gulf experienced ongoing maritime strife among the border entities; piracy and plunder were the order of the day.

Disturbed by the continuing maritime disorder in the gulf and concerned with broader geopolitical interests, such as the defense of India, the British asserted their power and diplomatic influence. By using their superior naval power in the gulf, the British were able to establish a predominant position, which brought about the signing of the "General Treaty with the Arab Shaikhs for the Cessation of Plunder and Piracy by Land and by Sea"[11] in 1820. However, maritime warfare continued because the treaty outlawed only piracy, and did not apply to the "legitimate" maritime wars between the littoral tribes. But British diplomacy was again successful: an annual truce was achieved that coincided with the pearl-diving season. These truces proved successful and were renewed each year until 1843, when a ten-year truce was signed.[12] This 1843 treaty was followed by a "Treaty of Peace in Perpetuity" in 1853.[13] The pluralistic system in the gulf had thus evolved into a hegemonic system of British predominance brought about by the British navy and the diplomacy of the British resident.

The preponderant position of the British in the gulf did not wane until after World War I, when the states of the gulf littoral reasserted their interests. Most significant was Iran's rising nationalism under Reza Shah.[14] The realization of an independent Iraq also had important overtones. The system in the gulf following World War I can be described as a quasi-hegemonic one in which the superior British power faced an awakening nationalism.[15]

Within this system the rapid development of the oil industry gave the gulf area new significance. Accordingly, when World War II broke out and the British reestablished their control over the area by invading Iraq and Iran, they did so to ensure that these oil areas did not fall under the influence of hostile nations.

Following World War II there was a resurgence of nationalism in the Persian Gulf that eventually led to the announcement in January 1968 of British withdrawal from the area. Since no other external power moved to fill the resulting power vacuum, the new pluralistic system of independent littoral states that had begun to emerge in the immediate postwar period became the order of the day. The circle was completed. The Persian Gulf subsystem had evolved into a pluralistic system of independent littoral actors, similar in form to the prepluralistic system of the early nineteenth century.

THE PROCESS OF INTERACTION IN THE PERSIAN GULF

For the purpose of providing a broader context in which to view legal developments and national claims pertaining to the law of the sea, the process of interaction in the gulf area is analyzed here. The term *process* refers to a "complex of interacting variable factors moving through time; its principal connotation is that of continual change in the relationships over a time period."[16] Since the new law of the sea in the Persian Gulf did not begin to develop until the assertion of national claims following World War II, the study of the process of interaction is limited to the postwar era.

Phase analysis has been selected to analyze the process of interaction in the Persian Gulf. This method of analysis, borrowed from the work of Myres McDougal and Harold Lasswell, breaks the process of interaction into the participants, the situations encountered, the objectives or goals of the participants, the base values or capabilities of the participants, and the strategies chosen by the participants to accomplish their goals in the given situations with their given capabilities.[17] This method is adopted for its utility in explaining context; it is hoped that its use will provide insight into the dynamic nature of the Persian Gulf system. Since this study is primarily

concerned with the roles of Iran and Saudi Arabia, only those interactions involving or affecting their roles are considered.

PARTICIPANTS

The participants within the Persian Gulf subsystem include the
independent states of Iran, Saudi Arabia, Iraq, Kuwait, Bahrain,
Qatar, the United Arab Emirates, and Oman.[18] Before its withdrawal in 1971 Britain was also a major participant in that it was
responsible for the protection and foreign relations of the gulf
protected states prior to their independence. The gulf states that
became independent in the postwar period are Kuwait (19 June
1961), Bahrain (15 August 1971), Qatar (3 September 1971), and
the states of the United Arab Emirates—Abu Dhabi, Dubai Sharjah,
Ajman, Umm al-Qaiwain, Ras al-Khaimah, and, on the Gulf of
Oman, Fujairah—(all on 1 December 1971). The emergence of these
independent states represented a significant change because they
assumed responsibility for their own foreign relations.[19] Thus their
relations with Iran, Saudi Arabia, and Iraq could be direct rather
than through the British.

Also participating in the gulf subsystem are various national
liberation organizations and national groups that are seeking autonomy, secession, and, sometimes, social revolution. The Kurds and
the Dhofari rebels have been significant. Minorities in areas such as
Baluchistan, Khuzistan, and Pashtunistan have also been important
as potentially destabilizing elements, especially after Iran's revolution.

The presence of multinational corporations represents a different,
and not unimportant, dimension. While such corporations are
usually considered extensions of the influence of larger industrial
states, it might be argued that some corporations could be considered
participants in their own right. Such a contrast is offered by the
actions of the Anglo-Iranian Oil Company and Aramco, operating
in Iran and Saudi Arabia respectively. The Anglo-Iranian Oil Company was partly owned by the British government and relied on
that government to engage in relations with the Iranian government
on its behalf.[20] On the other hand, Aramco represents a privately
owned corporation that not only has granted loans to the govern-

ment of Saudi Arabia, but also has carried out development projects in Saudi Arabia by building railroads, hospitals, schools, and other projects.[21]

In addition to the participants within the Persian Gulf subsystem there are external powers that have penetrated the gulf through various military, commercial, and agricultural agreements. Such states as the United States, the Soviet Union, Egypt, and South Yemen (People's Democratic Republic of Yemen or Democratic Yemen) have actively sought to influence the gulf subsystem. More recently, with the availability of gulf oil becoming crucial to Europe and Japan, their involvement has increased. India and Pakistan, as well as Israel and the Palestinians, have also been external influences in the gulf. Cuban and East German involvement, especially in South Yemen, increased significantly in the middle 1970s.[22]

SITUATIONS

The situations in which the interactions of the gulf participants have taken place can be expressed in geographic, temporal, and political dimensions. The geography is that of the Persian Gulf proper and its littoral states; the time is the postwar period; and the political situations are those patterns of interaction through which the continuing underlying political rivalries can be envisioned.

In the postwar period the gulf subsystem was a quasi-hegemonic system; it evolved into an emergent pluralistic system. Within the system there have been four general patterns of political conflict, which can be examined in terms of nationalism versus imperialism; nationalism versus nationalism; traditionalism versus revolution; and national interest versus national interest. These underlying political conflicts are further tangled by the political rivalries resulting from the Arab-Israeli conflict, the American-Soviet rivalry, the Indian-Pakistani conflict, and the rivalry between the oil-exporting and oil-importing countries.[23]

First is the ever-present struggle between nationalism and imperialism. For Iran the struggle has had several external forms: Iran versus British influence; Iran versus Russian influence; and, beginning in the 1970s, Iran versus American influence. For Saudi Arabia the struggle has assumed two primary forms: Saudi Arabia versus British influence and the broader Arab nationalism versus British influence. Since the British withdrawal from the gulf in 1971, both Iran and Saudi Arabia have opposed the entry of any great power, including the United States, into the power vacuum left by the British.

The nationalistic quest for self-determination and autonomy also has internal dimensions. First, the multinational oil companies in the past have had control over production decisions for oil output. Because of the importance of the oil revenues to governmental policy, the gulf states have moved to put the control of the oil operations into their own hands. Second, many of the minorities of the area have sought autonomy or self-determination. For example, the Azeris, the Kurds, the Turkomans, the Baluchis, the Pashtuns, the Dhofaris, and the Arabs of Khuzistan all have had elements that have called for a greater autonomy or self-determination.

The second underlying political conflict is between Iranian and Arab nationalism. This conflict is partly historical and cultural in nature; it also has racial overtones. It predates Islam but has assumed, especially since the Iranian revolution, a religious dimension because of the differences between Sunni and Shiite Muslims. While surfacing periodically with various expressions of distrust and suspicion, it was largely responsible for what has been termed the "Arab-Iranian Cold War" prior to the announcement of the British withdrawal.[24]

The third underlying political conflict is between traditionalism and revolution. Although the conflict is usually represented in the gulf by a monarchist-antimonarchist conflict—the antimonarchists usually being the more radical Nasserist, Baathist, and Communist elements—more recently Islamic revolutionaries have challenged traditional governments.

The Iraqi coup of 1958 introduced to the Persian Gulf a revolutionary ideology that alarmed the conservative Arab states and Iran. Saudi Arabia also has faced radicalism within the Arab world, as the ongoing Arab Cold War has displayed. Saudi Arabia has been repeatedly menaced by radicals in the Yemen Arab Republic and South Yemen. Under the Shah Iran became directly involved in the attempt to put down the Popular Front for the Liberation of Oman and the Arab Gulf (PFLOAG) in Oman.[25] Generally speaking,

Iran, Saudi Arabia, and the Arab sheikhdoms usually find themselves aligned against leftist groups attempting to foment revolution in the region. After the Iranian revolution, however, certain Shiite extremists supported by Iran have become a destabilizing force on the Arab side of the gulf, especially in Iraq, Kuwait, and Bahrain.

The fourth type of political conflict present is more substantive in nature and involves the conflict of national interests. This type of conflict is often issue-oriented and usually involves territorial disputes. Dynastic and tribal rivalries might also be included when they involve a conflict of interests between states, as opposed to being solely within states.[26] These issue-oriented disputes are often the points of contention that bring the other underlying political conflicts and rivalries to the fore.

In the postwar period territorial disputes have been widespread. They often have resulted from the fact that many borders in sparsely populated and nomadic areas have never been delimited or demarcated. Similarly, many relatively unpopulated islands have been disputed. However, since the British withdrawal from the area was announced, there has been a continuing effort on the part of the littoral states to establish borders and resolve some of the lingering border problems. Moves have also been made to resolve new disputes, such as those over offshore boundaries.

Of the territorial disputes, two have stood out as especially significant: Iraq's claim to Kuwait and Iran's claim to Bahrain. First, the Iraqi claim to Kuwait stirred a major controversy in the gulf in 1961, as Iraq tried to annex Kuwait. A settlement was eventually reached in October 1963. Iraq recognized Kuwait's independence, but some border questions still remain.[27] Second, Iran's long-standing claim to Bahrain (which had been under British control for some 150 years) was a major point of contention in the gulf after the British announced their withdrawal. The dispute was apparently settled when Iran, amidst considerable political maneuvering, relinquished its claim to Bahrain in May 1970 and supported the Bahraini desire for independence in accord with the principle of self-determination.[28] While many disputes have been settled, many remain as potential foci of conflict.[29] Traveling around the gulf from the Strait of Hormuz and Iran, significant territorial disputes and settlements are as follows.

1. Iran–Oman, offshore boundary—accord delineating the continental shelf boundaries signed 25 July 1974; agreement for joint naval operations in the Strait of Hormuz announced in January 1975.
2. Iran–Ras al-Khaimah, Greater and Lesser Tumb Islands—occupied by Iran 30 November 1971; revolutionary Iran has maintained its claim.
3. Iran–Sharjah, Abu Musa Island—occupied by Iran 30 November 1971 following announcement of agreement on Abu Musa between Iran and Sharjah 29 November 1971, but agreement disputed; revolutionary Iran continues to control Abu Musa.
4. Iran–Sharjah–Umm al-Qaiwain—offshore oil rights off Abu Musa.
5. Iran–Sharjah, Sirri and Sir Abu Nuʾayr (islands)—agreement signed between Iran and Dubai 31 August 1974 identified Sirri as Iranian and Sir Abu Nuʾayr as belonging to Sharjah.
6. Iran–Abu Dhabi, offshore boundary—agreement initialed demarcating continental shelf 7 September 1971.
7. Iran–Qatar, offshore boundary—agreement on continental shelf boundary signed 20 September 1969; entered into force 10 May 1970.
8. Iran–Bahrain, offshore boundary—agreement on continental shelf boundary signed 17 June 1971; entered into force 14 May 1972.
9. Iran–Saudi Arabia, al-Arabiyah and Farsi (islands)—agreement signed 24 October 1968 recognizing Iranian sovereignty over Farsi and Saudi sovereignty over al-Arabiyah; came into force 29 January 1969.
10. Iran–Saudi Arabia, offshore boundary—agreement delimiting the boundary line separating the submarine areas between Iran and Saudi Arabia signed 24 October 1968; came into force 29 January 1969.
11. Iran–Kuwait–Saudi Arabia, Neutral Zone offshore boundary.
12. Iran–Kuwait, offshore boundary—agreement on the delimitation of the continental shelf signed 13 January 1968; did not come into force.
13. Iran–Iraq, offshore boundary.
14. Iran–Iraq, Shatt al-Arab boundary—1937 Irano-Iraqi Boundary Treaty governing the status of the Shatt al-Arab declared null and void by Iran 19 April 1969; new, comprehensive treaty delimiting river frontier according to *thalweg* line signed 13 June 1975. Iraq indicated desire to withdraw from treaty in October 1979.
15. Iran–Iraq, land boundary—comprehensive treaty signed 13 June 1975 delineated 670 disputed areas.
16. Iraq–Kuwait, land boundary—delimited in 1922 treaty and further defined in exchange of letters in 1923 and 1932, but remains undemarcated; major dispute arose over Iraqi claim to all Kuwait in period

from 1961 to 1963; Iraq recognized Kuwait independence but boundary dispute flared in March 1973 and December 1974.

17. Iraq-Kuwait, offshore boundary.
18. Iraq-Kuwait, Bubiyan and Warbah (islands).
19. Iraq-Saudi Arabia, land boundary—agreement delineating disputed diamond-shaped Neutral Zone by a simple line drawn through the middle signed 2 July 1975.
20. Saudi Arabia-Kuwait, land boundary—Kuwait-Saudi Arabia Neutral Zone established in Uqair Convention 2 December 1922; agreement relating to the partition of the Neutral Zone signed 7 July 1965 and entered into force 25 July 1966; agreement formally dividing the Neutral Zone signed 18 December 1969; agreement reached in December 1978 on measures to be taken to demarcate the median line of the Neutral Zone.
21. Saudi Arabia-Kuwait, Kubbar, Umm al-Maradim, and Qaru (islands).
22. Saudi Arabia-Kuwait, offshore boundary of Neutral Zone—agreement relating to the partition of the Neutral Zone signed 7 July 1965 (entered into force 25 July 1966) included provisions for offshore areas, but some questions remain; agreement on a set of general principles for partitioning the Neutral Zone offshore area announced in December 1978.
23. Saudi Arabia-Bahrain, offshore boundary—agreement delimiting submarine boundaries signed 22 February 1958; entered into force 26 February 1958.
24. Saudi Arabia-Bahrain, Lubaynah al-Kabirah and Lubaynah al-Saghirah (islands)—agreement signed 22 February 1958 assigned the first to Saudi Arabia and the second to Bahrain, but without either having a territorial sea.
25. Saudi Arabia-Qatar, offshore boundary—agreement delimiting submarine boundaries signed 27 June 1965; entered into force in December 1965, but status is in question.
26. Bahrain-Qatar, Hawar (island)—long-standing dispute over Hawar revived in 1978 following Bahraini military maneuvers near Hawar and the detention of Bahraini fishermen by Qatar.
27. Bahrain-Qatar, offshore boundary.
28. Bahrain-Qatar, Zubarah (part of the Qatar peninsula).
29. Qatar-Abu Dhabi-Saudi Arabia, Khaur al-Udaid (strip of land at base of Qatar peninsula)—agreement between Saudi Arabia and Qatar signed in December 1965, but contested by Abu Dhabi and Britain; temporarily resolved in 1974 but border still undefined.
30. Qatar-Abu Dhabi, Halul (island)—two British experts examined dispute in early 1962 and awarded Halul to Qatar, some smaller islands to

Abu Dhabi, and left question of two other islands undecided; ruler of Qatar issued a decree 10 March 1962 concurring with the award.

31. Qatar-Abu Dhabi, offshore boundary—agreement signed 20 March 1969; entered into force 20 March 1969.

32. Abu Dhabi-Dubai, offshore boundary—agreement delimiting the submarine boundaries signed 18 February 1968.

33. Abu Dhabi-Saudi Arabia-Oman, Buraimi Oasis—dispute first arose over oil concession in 1933; negotiations held between Saudi Arabia and Britain 1934-38 and 1948-52 included London Conference in 1951 and Dammam Conference in 1952; Standstill Agreement signed October 1952; Arbitration Agreement signed 30 July 1954; Buraimi Arbitration Tribunal proceedings ended *sine die* 15 September 1955; British Forces seized Buraimi 26 October 1955; United Nations fact-finding mission in September 1960; announcement 16 January 1963 that Saudi-British efforts to settle dispute would continue; agreement in principle announced 29 July 1974 on border dispute between Saudi Arabia and Abu Dhabi for several hundred kilometer border and territory that includes Shaybah and Zararah oil field, also reported that Saudi Arabia ceded six of the Buraimi oases to Abu Dhabi, leaving three in question with Oman.

34. Saudi Arabia-Oman, land boundary.

35. United Arab Emirates-Oman, land boundary—agreement announced December 1979.

36. United Arab Emirates-Oman, offshore boundaries.

37. United Arab Emirates, internal land boundaries.

38. United Arab Emirates, internal offshore boundaries (with the exception of the Abu Dhabi-Dubai offshore boundary).

In addition to these various territorial disputes there are a number of tribal and dynastic rivalries that over time became manifest as rivalries between states. The foremost example in the Persian Gulf has been the rivalry between the ruling families of Saudi Arabia and Iraq,[30] which resulted from the earlier struggle in the Arabian peninsula between ibn-Saud and Sharif Husein. When ibn-Saud was victorious in Arabia (Hejaz) and Husein was forced to flee, the stage was set for a continuing rivalry between ibn-Saud and Husein's son, Faisal, who had become king of Iraq.[31] (A similar rivalry existed between ibn-Saud and Husein's son Abdullah, who became king of Transjordan.)

Such rivalries often continued from generation to generation with suspicion and distrust characterizing the relations between the various Arab states—a suspicion and distrust not unlike that present in the broader conflict between Iranian and Arab nationalism. Often the family or tribal rivalries derived from or were closely involved with the numerous territorial disputes. Yet regardless of the source of the distrust, the rivalries often became manifest as conflicts of national interest between states. These conflicts of national interest add another dimension to the three basic political conflicts present in the Persian Gulf subsystem and further complicate any analysis of policy decisions.

In addition to the four basic political conflicts underlying interaction within the gulf subsystem, there are four other political conflicts that complicate policy decisions. These involve external influence and have had a continuing effect on the process of interaction in the area.

First, the Arab-Israeli conflict has aligned Saudi Arabia with the more radical Arab states against Israel. In light of this, Iran's relations with Israel have proved a point of contention with the Arab states in the gulf. This was especially true following the Iranian reference to the recognition of Israel in 1960. However, in January 1975 the Shah indicated that Iranian sympathies were with the Arabs. Revolutionary Iran went much further with the Ayatollah Khomeini's reception of the PLO leader Yasir Arafat following the Ayatollah's return to Iran. The Arab-Israeli conflict has tended to align the gulf states against the United States and its allies because of American support of Israel. Prior to a final Middle East peace settlement, the Arab-Israeli conflict undoubtedly will offer numerous maneuvering possibilities for the United States and its close allies and the gulf states, including Iran.

Second, East-West relations have had a major influence on the gulf subsystem, especially in relation to the United States policy perspectives and American aid to the region. In the immediate postwar period Iran feared Soviet aggression and looked to the United States for assistance. Iran later joined the Baghdad Pact and relied on American protection from Communist aggression and subversion. However, beginning in the early 1960s Iran, though anti-Communist, sought a more independent stance and worked to better its relations with the Soviet Union. Just as Iran had previously maneuvered to play Russia and Britain against each other, it came to balance the

United States and the Soviet Union, receiving benefits from each. Even with the anti-American rhetoric of the Iranian revolution, the balancing of the United States against the Soviet Union is likely to continue.

Saudi Arabia, similarly anti-Communist, sought American aid in the early postwar period, but later chose a more independent policy. In the early 1950s the United States attempted to ally the Arab states against the Soviet Union, but they were more concerned with the British. Both Saudi Arabia and Iran welcomed détente and the increased freedom of action that it brought. Both are opposed to either the United States or the Soviet Union assuming the former British position in the gulf.

Third, the Indian-Pakistani conflict has affected the Persian Gulf subsystem. Because they are Muslim, the Arab states of the gulf and Iran have sympathized with the Pakistanis against India. Moreover some minorities in Pakistan, such as the Baluchis, extend into Iran. Therefore Iran has a strong interest in seeing the Pakistani government maintain control of its various minorities, since any disintegration could adversely affect Iran.

Fourth, the rivalry between the oil-exporting and oil-importing countries following the 1973 oil embargo and price rise has added new pressures to the gulf subsystem. The problem initially concerned the embargo, but the relative price and supply of oil have also become points of political contention. The jockeying of the various industrial states to secure oil supplies has caused an apparent loosening of the Western (Cold War) alliance. The additional oil revenues realized by the gulf states appear to have altered fundamentally the global view of the availability of scarce natural resources and commodities. A result of the ensuing rivalry has been the attempt of the oil-exporting countries to tie the price of oil to the price of raw materials and commodities. Especially significant to the gulf states have been certain proposals by some oil-importing states. For example, American officials went so far as to suggest the possibility of the use of force to prevent a "strangulation of the industrialized world."[32]

OBJECTIVES

In the postwar period the objectives and aspirations of Iran and

Saudi Arabia have varied according to the given situation encountered. However, the objectives of the two states roughly fall into
three categories: security and freedom of action, economic and
social development, and regional security. These categories are
interrelated and can only be disassociated analytically.[33]

The objectives of Iran have been directed essentially toward
defense and securing a freedom of action.[34] Iran, once partitioned
by Britain and Russia and occupied by external powers during
World War II, is very conscious of potential threats to its sovereignty
and national security from both external and internal sources.
Under the Shah Iran sought to establish internal stability or domestic
tranquility, to secure internal and external freedom of action, and
to protect itself from external attack. In revolutionary Iran internal
stability remains a goal to be realized, as does the desire for balancing
defense and freedom of action.

Also prominent, especially since the early 1960s, has been Iran's
interest in economic and social development. Not only has Iran
sought to exploit its oil resources, but also has moved to diversify
its industrial base to ensure economic viability and success for the
time when its oil reserves are depleted. To industrialize, Iran sought
technological assistance from abroad and purported to undertake
an ambitious educational program at home. It has worked to establish
economic justice internally and to provide a share of the wealth
for its people. The official name for much of the Shah's program of
economic and social development was the "White Revolution."
Revolutionary Iran challenged the Shah's sincerity in seeking such
goals. Moreover, the goal of establishing an Islamic Republic was
adopted as the ideal for economic and social development.

To insure that development could continue, the Shah's Iran asserted
its interests in stability both domestically and regionally. Iran's
interest in regional stability—tied to the vulnerability of its oil
arteries to the outbreak of hostilities in the region or to the presence
of a hostile power bordering on a strategic shipping lane—has continued with revolutionary Iran, despite disclaimers of continuing
a regional security role. Obviously, a decision to export revolution
would contradict this.

In addition to Iran's awareness of the necessity of security, economic and social development, and regional stability there exists
the historically rooted aspiration for Iranian greatness. Under the

Shah, Iran sought to achieve a modern great-power status, and it aspired to the "Era of Great Civilization." Revolutionary Iran has voiced the desire of being a leader of a broader Islamic revival (which has worried its Sunni neighbors).

The objectives of Saudi Arabia in the postwar period have generally run parallel to those of Iran; they can be readily examined in terms of interests in security, economic and social development, and regional peace and stability. There are, however, some differences in the Saudi objectives.

Whereas Iran has had a legacy of foreign influence and domination, Saudi Arabia has been relatively isolated and able to avoid foreign control. Nevertheless, Saudi Arabia has not been unaware of the British presence in the Persian Gulf. Since the Saudi security interests have been vulnerable to the vicissitudes of inter-Arab politics, Saudi policy has fluctuated. Relations with Egypt, Britain, and Iraq in the postwar period illustrate such fluctuations.

Although often differing in direction, Saudi security interests are similar to Iran's in that both have internal and external dimensions. The Saudi defense interests have had to deal not only with the effects of modernizing pressures and the danger of Communist or radical subversion, but also with the threat of external attack. Saudi Arabia, concerned with the broader and abstract interest of "Arab security," has faced a variety of external adversaries as determined, *inter alia,* by the Saudi and Arab search for a solution to the Palestinian problem and for a "restoration of the rights of the people of Palestine."[35] Saudi defense objectives, while varying with the political conflicts encountered, have been primarily concerned with Israel and Iraq in the north.[36] In the south Saudi Arabia has had to contend with Egypt in the Yemen civil war[37] and more recently with the activities of South Yemen in its support of the Dhofari rebels and actions against the Yemen Arab Republic and Saudi Arabia.

The Saudi objectives of economic and social development are similar to those of Iran in that Saudi Arabia has sought to diversify and modernize its industrial base, not only for that time when oil revenues begin to decline, but also in light of the fluctuation of oil income. Following a severe financial crisis that began in 1956 and extended into 1958, Saudi Arabia undertook major financial reforms. Then in the early 1960s it initiated economic and social development programs to "broaden the industrial base" and to "increase education and literacy."[38] Saudi Arabia approved its first five-year plan for development in September 1970 under the guidance of the Stanford Research Institute of California. The second Saudi development plan represents a continuing emphasis on economic and social development, calling for the unprecedented expenditure of almost $150 billion.[39]

The Saudi objective of regional stability and tranquility stems from its very size. Any disturbance in the gulf represents a potential threat to its territory and could affect the outflow of Saudi oil. The Saudi objective of regional stability coincides, in principle, with that of Iran: neither Saudi Arabia nor Iran wishes to have its oil flow disrupted or oil revenues adversely affected. Saudi Arabia, however, has been suspicious of Iranian actions under both the Shah and the Ayatollah. Saudi security objectives also extend to the Red Sea and Gulf of Aqaba, especially with the presence of a hostile Israel in the Gulf of Aqaba.

BASE VALUES

Base values are those capabilities or bases of power at the disposal of the participants that may be utilized to attain desired objectives. Base values of states may vary in degree and kind, but for this analysis of the Persian Gulf context the following three categories have been chosen: military power, economic resources, and human resources.

In examining these base values for Iran and Saudi Arabia, several considerations will be made. First, military power capabilities will be examined in terms of expenditure for defense, with special notice taken of weapon sophistication and flexibility. Second, economic power will be viewed according to oil revenues and the availability of real and potential resources. Also to be considered are the relative level of technology and the availability of financial reserves. Third, human resources will be analyzed according to number, ability (education and skill), and attitudes (degree of solidarity). Associated with human resources is the quality of leadership. In considering these base values it should be remembered that statistics for developing states often lack reliability as well as completeness. Nevertheless the general trends, relative strengths, and specific landmarks encountered do serve to provide a significant insight into the process of interaction.

The base values of Iran increased dramatically in the postwar period, especially in terms of military and economic bases of power. The human element not only proved to be problematic for the Shah but resulted in his fall from power and an uncertain stability in revolutionary Iran. Iran's policy decisions and actions within the gulf context have been dramatically influenced by these base values.

First, Iran's military power increased significantly, and Iran transformed itself from an occupied nation in World War II to the predominant military power in the Persian Gulf in 1976.[40] In 1979, however, Iran's military seemed to evaporate in the domestic chaos. In viewing Iran's military growth five distinct phases can be discerned: end of World War II to 1953; 1953 to 1964; 1964 to 1971; 1971 to 1978; and 1978 to present. Each phase represents a change in the rate of military expenditure and capability, and is characterized by some change in the nature or purpose of the military power base.

Following World War II Iran's military was relatively weak and primarily concerned with internal matters. In the late 1940s and early 1950s the main purpose of Iranian forces was internal stability. Iran relied on the United States for protection from external attack. Iran's defense expenditures increased slowly during this period.[41] Iran repeatedly sought expanded aid from the United States, but was unsuccessful.[42] During the period from 1947 to 1953 Iran received $16.6 million in aid from the United States.[43]

The second period, 1953-64, began with the reestablishment of the Shah's control in Iran. Iran's military continued its internal stabilization role but with greatly expanded American assistance. Membership in the Baghdad Pact (and later CENTO) accorded Iran a new role in America's Cold War defense posture and brought significant increases in American military assistance. In contrast to the 1949-53 figure of $16.6 million, American aid between 1953 and 1960 increased to $386.9 million.[44] Iranian defense expenditure rose steadily during the period, moving from about $32.8 million in the 1953-54 budget to nearly $212.7 million in the 1964-65 budget.[45] During the 1953-64 period, Iran began to expand its naval strength with the addition of vessels from Italy, the United States, and Britain.

The 1964-71 period marked Iran's move to acquire sophisticated weapons and to diversify its suppliers. Iranian defense expenditures grew, rising from the 1964-65 figure of nearly $212.7 million to over $1.02 billion in 1971.[46] After receiving the Raytheon Hawk missile in 1964, Iran received its first sophisticated aircraft in 1965, the Northrop F-5A (and F-5B) Freedom Fighters.[47] Following Iran's announcement in July 1966 of negotiations with the Soviet Union for arms, the United States agreed in September 1966 to supply the much-wanted McDonnell-Douglas Phantoms. Receipt of the Phantoms began in September 1968. In February 1967 Iran announced the conclusion of its arms deal with the Soviet Union, in which it puchased $110 million worth of "nonsensitive" military equipment. During this time period the sophistication of Iran's naval power increased significantly with the acquisition of a destroyer from Britain in 1967 and its first hovercraft in 1969.[48]

Accompanying the sophistication of weapons, the diversification of suppliers, and the rapidly rising defense expenditures were Iran's assumption of a regional defense role and a move toward self-reliance. At the opening of the Majlis in 1966 the Shah stressed that "in spite of all existing pacts and friendship accords we [Iran] must above all, rely upon ourselves."[49] This movement toward self-reliance came to correspond with the American policy, enunciated in November 1969, known as the Nixon Doctrine.

The next phase, 1971-78, began with Iran assuming a stabilizing role in the region in contrast to its previous defensive role. This phase was set off by Iran's move to secure control over Abu Musa and the two Tumbs on the eve of the British departure from the Persian Gulf. Iran's active stabilizing role was further exemplified by sending troops into Oman. In order to support this policman role, Iran increased the rate of its military buildup. Military expenditures soared in the 1971-76 period, moving from $779 million in the 1970-71 budget to $1.023 billion in the 1971-72 budget.[50]

After rising slightly to $1.189 billion in the 1972-73 budget, military expenditures reached $2.096 billion in the 1973-74 budget and $5.5 billion in the 1974-75 budget.[51] After 1975 defense expenditures were exorbitant until the Shah's government began to fall in 1978. Expenditures for the years from 1975 to 1978 were $8.8 billion,

$9.5 billion, $7.89 billion, and $9.9 billion respectively[52] (see Table 1).

During this fourth phase, the Shah emphasized flexibility and mobility as well as sophistication in Iran's weapon procurement; he acquired additional hovercraft and advanced attack helicopters.[53] The Shah also moved to increase his armor with the order of 800 additional British-made Chieftain tanks.[54] Iran moved to establish what has been called a "gulf-wide quick reaction capability," and it was reported that Iran was capable "of landing a battalion of troops on the opposite shores of the gulf."[55]

Although Iran had developed a regional superiority in conventional military forces, there were soundings of still further military expansion.[56] As early as November 1972 the Shah included the Indian Ocean as an Iranian defense concern, which suggests a continued expansion of Iran's naval capability. In light of the Indian

Table 1   DEFENSE EXPENDITURES: IRAN AND SAUDI ARABIA, 1966–1978 (*in millions of dollars*)

Years	Iran	Saudi Arabia
1966	255	138
1967	389	286
1968	495	321
1969	594	343
1970	779	387
1971	1,023	383
1972	1,189	941
1973	2,096	1,478
1974	5,500	1,808
1975	8,800	6,771
1976	9,500	9,038
1977	7,894	7,539
1978	9,942	13,170

SOURCE: Adapted from International Institute for Strategic Studies, *The Military Balance* (1967-68 through 1978-79) (London: Chatto and Windus, 1967-79).

nuclear explosion of May 1974 it appeared that Iran might seek to acquire a nuclear capability. Iran's move to acquire nuclear power plants, together with reports of a proposed purchase of from $700 million to $1 billion worth of uranium from South Africa and joint development of a uranium enrichment plant in South Africa, suggest that Iran (at least under the Shah) left the option open for a nuclear weapon capability.[57]

After 1978 Iran's defense expenditures dropped abruptly with the departure of the Shah. The skyrocketing arms purchases during the preceding eight years served, in part, to undermine the legitimacy of the Shah. Moreover when the Shah's government fell, many of the arms deals it had negotiated came unglued; orders were cancelled and contracts were broken. The earlier "policeman's role" in the gulf as assumed by the Shah was disclaimed by an inward-looking revolutionary Iran.

The Iranian economy saw dramatic growth during much of the postwar period, but its successes were qualified. Final cost of the Iranian revolution to Iran's economic system remains to be seen, but the economy promises to be chaotic for the foreseeable future. In retrospect Iran's economic power grew steadily and continually throughout the period (following the resolution of the Anglo-Iranian oil crisis) starting in 1953. Iran's production of crude petroleum supported this advance, rising from 1.342 million metric tons in 1953 to 251.930 million metric tons in 1972[58] (*see* Table 2). The oil revenues (*see* Table 3) in turn were responsible for supporting Iran's growing budget. Oil revenues resulted, *inter alia*, in broad increases in Iran's international monetary reserves, especially after 1973 (*see* Table 4). In 1971 reserves were placed at $621 million; they rose to $1.237 billion in December 1973 and to $8.383 billion in December 1974.[59] The Arab oil embargo and ongoing price rise following the October War in 1973 resulted in a major increase in Iran's economic power.

Though Iran was attempting to expand its economic power base (see Table 5), it lacked the broad-based technological sophistication of the industrialized countries. Accordingly Iran, under the Shah, emphasized its education programs and the acquisition of technical assistance from the West. Its move to industrialize was hampered by an uncertain oil market. The failure of Iran's dynamic develop-

Table 2   PRODUCTION OF CRUDE PETROLEUM:
IRAN AND SAUDI ARABIA, 1950–1975
(*in millions of metric tons*)

Years	Iran		Saudi Arabia	
	Total	*Offshore*	*Total*	*Offshore*
1950	32.259		26.649	na
1951	16.844		37.122	na
1952	1.360		40.313	na
1953	1.342		41.172	na
1954	3.502		46.881	0.850 *
1955	16.431		47.664	0.700 *
1956	26.335		49.037	0.780 *
1957	35.989		50.024	3.380 *
1958	41.275		51.586	2.330 *
1959	46.379		56.432	4.150 *
1960	53.491		64.524	9.350 *
1961	59.305	na	73.437	12.950 *
1962	65.809	na	81.535	16.760 *
1963	73.557	na	88.729	19.220 *
1964	84.612	na	94.566	24.550 *
1965	94.126	na	109.550	28.920 *
1966	105.455	na	129.241	37.040 *
1967	130.578	na	139.202	32.490 *
1968	142.372	6.716	151.374	32.500 *
1969	168.293	13.244	159.546	35.600 *
1970	191.296	16.101	188.417	54.200 *
1971	226.819	19.146	238.678	69.536 *
1972	251.930	23.434	299.867	84.604 *
1973	292.840	22.604	377.503	108.788 *
1974	300.852	22.860	421.397	113.953 *
1975	268.035*		349.740*	

SOURCE: Adapted from United Nations Statistical Office, Department of Economic and Social Affairs, *World Energy Supplies 1950-1974* (New York: United Nations, 1976), pp. 210, 212 (ST/ESA/STAT/SER.J/19).

*Statistical office estimate
na = not available

Table 3   OIL REVENUES: IRAN AND SAUDI ARABIA,
1966–1976 (*in millions of dollars*)

Years	Iran	Saudi Arabia
1966	81.0	789.1
1967	710.1	909.1
1968	803.9	926.8
1969	1,378.6	949.0
1970	1,226.1	1,214.0
1971	1,902.7	1,884.9
1972	2,430.5	2,744.6
1973	4,000.0*	4,340.0
1974	20,000.0*	22,573.5
1975	18,900.0*	25,676.2
1976	22,000.0*	30,747.5

SOURCE: Adapted from *The Middle East and North Africa* (1971-72 through 1978-79) (London: Europa Publications, 1971-79).

* = estimate

Table 4 INTERNATIONAL MONETARY RESERVES:
IRAN AND SAUDI ARABIA, 1961–1978
(*in millions of dollars*)

Years	Iran	Saudi Arabia
1961	208	239
1962	224	268
1963	246	514
1964	199	585
1965	236	726
1966	255	747
1967	305	761
1968	291	662
1969	310	607
1970	208	662
1971	621	1,444
1972	960	2,500
1973	1,236	3,877
1974	8,383	14,285
1975	8,697	23,319
1976	8,833	27,025
1977	12,266	30,034
1978	12,152	19,407

SOURCE: Adapted from United Nations, Statistical Office, Department of Economic
and Social Affairs, *Monthly Bulletin of Statistics* (December 1968, December
1976, December 1979, and June 1979).

Table 5   IRAN'S FIFTH DEVELOPMENT PLAN 1973–1978
         (*in millions of rials*)

	Original March 1973	Revised August 1974
Agriculture	121	239.6
Water	106	160.0
Industry	180	352.1
Mining	46	62.0
Oil	130	333.0
Gas	24	51.0
Power	53	240.0
Communication	177	404.0
Telecommunication	36	91.4
Rural development	36	60.0
Urban development	32	45.0
Government building	91	320.0
Housing	90	230.0
Education	127	130.0
Arts and culture	5	10.0
Tourism	7	11.0
Health	24	43.0
Welfare	5	9.0
Sports	9	15.0
Provincial development	0	10.0
Public affairs	0	32.0
Total Government Expenditure	1,299	2,848.1
Expenditure by government companies		445.0
Expenditure by private sector (estimated)		1,570.0
Less government loans to private sector		- 229.0
Total (Net)		4,364.0

SOURCE: *The Royal Road to Progress,* Ministry of Information, Tehran, 1974, p. 24.
The Middle East and North Africa 1978-1979, 25th ed. (London: Europa Publications, 1978), p. 353.

ment plans to meet projections under the Revised Fifth Plan[60] contributed, in part, to the fall of the Shah's government.

Iran's human resources contrast sharply with those of other gulf states. Iran is the most heavily populated state in the gulf. Its population, placed at 36.365 million in 1978,[61] has provided Iran with the manpower potential for its development programs and the potential to absorb large oil revenues.[62] However, Iran has suffered from problems associated with developing states. The low level of education and high illiteracy rate, accompanied by a "brain drain," has created shortages of the managers and skilled personnel needed for development. Iran has also faced problems of internal pressures of modernization. Although the Shah emphasized the importance of domestic solidarity, and worked to influence the attitudes of the masses by asserting that they had a vested interest in the state's progress, he was not successful in stabilizing the domestic situation. Revolutionary Iran under the Ayatollah continues to face desperate domestic pressures, both economic and political.

Saudi base values have also expanded significantly in the postwar period, but the nature of the expansion has not been the same. Saudi Arabia's setting and demographic composition have been responsible for different emphases and direction. The Saudi military capabilities grew dramatically in the early 1970s; but their relative military inferiority vis-à-vis the expanding Iranian capabilities has continued. The Saudi economic power—both in terms of their potential resources and current oil revenues—has dramatically changed the Saudi regional and global policy perspective. However, in light of its economic success, Saudi Arabia faces new internal pressures of modernization and major absorption problems for its enormous oil revenues. Saudi Arabia has kept a watchful eye on developments in Iran.

In looking more closely at its relative military capability after World War II, certain points became apparent. First, Saudi Arabia has depended upon the United States for its defenses despite fluctuations in American-Saudi relations. Apart from external defense, Saudi Arabia in the 1940s and 1950s was primarily concerned with its internal stability and relied on the loyalties of tribal forces. After 1949 Israel was recognized as a potential threat, but Saudi Arabia did not see itself as a front-line state. In the early 1960s Saudi Arabia began to increase its defenses and military capabilities because of the new ideological threats in such neighboring countries as Yemen. Saudi Arabia then made a serious move to provide a new air-defense system.[63]

Although statistics for Saudi defense expenditures are unavailable for much of the early postwar period, there were no significant Saudi military buildups. However in the 1960s available statistics indicate that Saudi defense expenditures began to rise with its involvement in the Yemen civil war. Defense expenditures continued to rise throughout the decade and increased dramatically with the withdrawal of the British. In 1961 Saudi defense expenditures were placed at $54 million; in 1962 they rose to $71.6 million; and in 1963 they reached $92 million[64] (see Table 1). Expenditures reached $321 million in 1968, $383 million in 1971, $1.478 billion in 1973, $6.771 billion in 1975, $9.038 billion in 1976, and $13.170 billion in 1978.[65] These expenditures reflect the changing Saudi defense posture brought about by the withdrawal of the British, the increasing Iranian defense expenditures, the Iranian revolution, and, among other things, Saudi Arabia's own increasing oil revenues.

Saudi expenditures indicate a desire for sophisticated weapons; they acquired their first sophisticated aircraft as early as 1966.[66] Purchases of additional aircraft and missiles from Britain, France, and the United States indicate a continuing emphasis on sophisticated weaponry.

Saudi Arabia has had only a small navy. With the pending British withdrawal, Saudi Arabia began a program of naval expansion in 1969. It received three "Jaguar" fast patrol boats from France and West Germany in 1969. Additional patrol boats and hovercraft were acquired in the early 1970s.[67]

In light of the departure of the British in 1971 and developments in South Yemen and the Horn of Africa in the late 1970s, Saudi Arabia moved to provide more flexibility in its regional military posture. It is possible that with the cooperation of other Arab states in the gulf it will play a stabilizing role following the decline of Iran's regional role.

More significant than its military power is the Saudi economic power. Tied to oil revenues (*see* Table 3), Saudi Arabia's economic power mushroomed in the early 1970s, and its Gross National Product has risen accordingly. Although Saudi Arabia experienced financial problems in the late 1950s, it has expanded into a world economic power with soaring financial reserves (see Table 4). While these financial reserves are directly the result of oil revenues, Saudi Arabia also has a great deal of economic clout deriving from its untapped oil reserves. The oil embargo of 1973 ushered in a new era that has recognized Saudi Arabia as an economic superpower.

Apart from oil production (*see* Table 2), Saudi Arabia has no significant economic base. Accordingly it is actively seeking technological assistance in undertaking its ambitious program of industrial development. The first Saudi economic plan was approved in September 1970. The second five-year plan (see Table 6) was approved in May 1975.[68] In its attempt to develop, however, Saudi Arabia's major problem has been its human resources.[69]

Saudi Arabia is a sparsely populated state; its population was estimated to be only 7.73 million in 1978.[70] Because of its rural culture the population has faced severe problems in adapting to the

Table 6   SAUDI ARABIA'S FIRST AND SECOND PLANS
(*in millions of dollars*)

	First Plan	Second Plan
Economic Resource Development	1,714.0	26,174.7
Human Resource Development	2,897.4	22,762.8
Social Development	694.0	9,435.2
Physical Infrastructure Development	4,001.9	32,086.5
Administration	2,973.4	10,846.3
Defense	3,691.7	22,203.6
External Assistance, Emergency Funds, Food Subsidies, and General Reserve	—	18,033.6
Total Plan	15,972.4	141,542.7

SOURCE: Adapted from U.S., Department of Treasury, *Summary of Saudi Arabian Five Year Development Plan 1975-1980* (Washington, D.C.: Government Printing Office, 1975), p. 81.

needs of industrialization. One of the problems is that of adjusting to the demands for wage earners.[71] Moreover serious "shortages of experienced business, financial, and technological expertise" demand the influx of possibly as many as half a million foreign technicians to implement the new development plan.[72] It has been estimated that already 60 percent of the industrial work force is foreign, and 40 percent of that total is non-Arab.[73] The presence and continued influx of such large numbers of foreigners threaten the stability of the Saudi society and serve to amplify the internal pressures of modernization to a degree not previously encountered. Nevertheless Saudi Arabia is actively seeking to broaden its industrial base on an unprecedented scale, and increase its technological capacities in order to provide for that time in the future when oil revenues can no longer be relied on.

STRATEGIES

Strategies represent the course of action assumed by the participants "to manage base values for the achievement of policy objectives."[74] Strategies may be primarily categorized as diplomatic, economic, military, and public-relations oriented (ideological).[75] They can be further characterized by the general manner in which they are employed; strategies may be carried out unilaterally, bilaterally, and multilaterally.

Iran has generally relied on diplomacy as a strategy. Following World War II Iran's main concern was with the Soviet Union. It was successful in maneuvering diplomatically and eventually achieved its objective of the withdrawal of Soviet forces. Rouhollah Ramazani has noted that Iran has followed a policy of "equilibrium" that is "deep-rooted in Iranian foreign policy thinking."[76] The Iranian policy of equilibrium took the form of "negative equilibrium" under Mosaddeq. This was followed by the Shah's policy of "positive nationalism."[77] In the mid-1960s Iran assumed a "national independent policy," which sought to direct an independent course vis-à-vis the United States and the Soviet Union. While Iran maintained its good relations with the United States, in the early 1960s it was able to improve its relations with the Soviet Union considerably. This improvement enabled Iran to concentrate its attention on the growing importance of the Persian Gulf.

Iran has been active diplomatically and has moved to settle disputes with its neighbors in the Persian Gulf, especially after the announcement of the British withdrawal. Particularly important were the apparent settlement of the Bahrain question under the auspices of the United Nations,[78] the establishment of an offshore boundary between Iran and Saudi Arabia, and the settlement of the Shatt al-Arab dispute with Iraq.[79] Under the Shah, its advocacy of a Persian Gulf security pact caused Iran to push for a regional arrangement that would secure the oil lanes from possible disturbances and keep the Persian Gulf immune from superpower rivalries and intervention. Revolutionary Iran has voiced a similar concern for regional security cooperation within the gulf and the desire to exclude a superpower presence.

Economically Iran was first dependent upon the United States and others; it offered economic concessions to achieve its objectives. However the discontinuance of American economic aid (under the Foreign Assistance Act) on 30 November 1967 signaled the beginning of a new era for Iran. Oil revenues, which grew precipitously following the 1973 Arab oil embargo, have furthered Iran's economic strategies. The price rise in the year following the oil embargo raised Iranian oil revenues to over $18 billion—four times the projected $4.5 billion.[80] Iran, still a developing country, has used its oil revenues to encourage trade and development. It has extended large amounts of aid and loans to other developing states and even to advanced states.[81] In doing so, Iran has used its new economic power to complement its diplomatic strategies. For example, Iran moved to improve its relations with Arab states by such means as a "billion-dollar protocol signed with Egypt in May 1975; a $30 million loan extended to Morocco for agricultural and land reform projects; and an agreement in principle to provide Syria with $150 million worth of low-interest credits.[82]

Militarily Iran has chosen assertive as well as defensive strategies. In 1969 Iran declared the 1937 Irano-Iraqi Treaty on the Shatt al-Arab null and void and confronted Iraq with a show of force to back up its actions. Later, in 1971, Iran exercised its growing military strength by moving militarily to secure control of Abu Musa and the two Tumbs. Prior to the Iran-Iraq Accord of 1975, Iran provided military assistance and arms, in addition to humanitarian aid, to the Kurds in their struggle against Iraq. Iran also sent troops to Oman at the request of the Omani government to suppress the Dhofari rebels, who were endangering stability of the lower gulf. The Iran-Omani joint operations were reported successful in 1975. Each of these actions shows Iran's willingness and ability to use military force—unilaterally if necessary—in the achievement of Iranian objectives.[83]

In the 1970s, Iran moved forthrightly in the use of mass media to further its position and to counter negative propaganda. The Shah consented to numerous interviews for television and leading newspapers and magazines and traveled to many nations to promote good will, strengthen old ties, and establish new ties. Iran took full-page advertisements in leading newspapers to ensure that its positions would be presented without distortion.[84] Iran also chose to reply to certain negative editorials in leading newspapers.[85] Through its Ministry of Information Service Iran has disseminated government publications and information to various audiences abroad. Since the early 1970s, Iran under the Shah made a serious effort to promote its image abroad and to gain support for its policies. Similarly, opponents of the Shah used the mass median to undermine the Shah's legitimacy at home and abroad.

Saudi Arabia has maintained a conservative posture throughout the postwar period. Saudi policies have remained consistent, even under four kings.[86] In maintaining a conservative posture, Saudi Arabia has relied on diplomacy to achieve its objectives but has not refrained from employing economic pressure. It has eschewed the use of force and has actively pursued its objective through various international organizations, such as the League of Arab States,[87] the United Nations, and the Organization of Petroleum Exporting Countries (OPEC). While policy has been oriented toward moderation within the Arab world and in defense of Arab interests, Saudi Arabia has been very anti-Communist. Nevertheless, it sought to remain nonaligned in the Cold War, even though it depended on the United States for military equipment and protection. Saudi Arabia has found it difficult to align itself with the United States because of, *inter alia*, the American stance on the Arab-Israeli conflict and support for the Egyptian-Israeli treaty.

In the gulf area, especially after the British decision to withdraw, Saudi Arabia moved diplomatically to stabilize relations and resolve the lingering disputes with its neighbors. Following the offshore border agreement with Iran, Saudi relations with neighboring states have continued to improve. A Saudi-Abu Dhabi border agreement was announced on 29 July 1974, and a border agreement with Iraq was signed on 18 April 1975. However, in light of the professed intentions of Iran and Iraq and more recently Oman, to form a collective security system in the Gulf, Saudi Arabia has indicated its support, in principle, but has chosen to move cautiously.[88] Saudi Arabia appears to favor nonalignment in the gulf politics, just as it has in the Cold War.

Although usually relying on diplomacy, Saudi Arabia has employed its economic power to further its objectives. In the early postwar period, it obtained development assistance and military aid through the granting of oil concessions. As the importance of Saudi oil grew, Saudi Arabia used its oil resources and access to its oil to exert pressure to further its goals. Following the outbreak of the October War in 1973 Saudi Arabia initiated an oil embargo that rocked the industrial West.[89] Prior to the October War, Saudi Arabia warned that oil would be used as a political weapon.[90] The oil embargo served to boost oil prices and proved to be an economic boon for the oil exporters. Saudi Arabia and other Arab states have not only withheld oil from countries favoring Israel but also have blacklisted numerous companies and corporations.

In a different vein, Saudi Arabia has used its oil revenues and its newly realized economic power to improve its relations with other states. The Saudi strategies have been chosen primarily to benefit other Arab and Muslim states, but they have also been aimed at improving relations with developed states and promoting international concerns.[91] In order to improve ties with other developing and advanced states, Saudi Arabia has entered into joint ventures and has supported such undertakings as the Islamic Development Bank. Saudi Arabia has also used its oil money directly to influence policy and improve ties with such countries as the Yemen Arab Republic.[92]

While Saudi Arabia has often assumed an economic position that runs counter to that of the United States, it still relies on the United

States for much of its developmental technology. Saudi Arabia has used its oil as a bargaining tool to acquire not only political concessions but also developmental assistance.

Militarily Saudi Arabia has relied on the United States for its defense needs. It has maintained a defensive posture and has not undertaken assertive military actions. In some of the inter-Arab rivalries, such as the Yemen civil war, Saudi Arabia supported what might be termed a war of proxy, but has generally refrained from using its forces in direct combat. Saudi Arabia has sent token forces to fight in the Arab-Israeli war, but is better known as a major financial backer of the Arab cause.[93] It has been involved in some skirmishes with other states over borders but has not turned to its military to achieve its objectives. The current arms buildup by Saudi Arabia could add a new deterrent aspect on the Arabian side of the gulf, and might enable Saudi Arabia to assume a more active role in the maintenance of regional stability.

Saudi Arabia, like Iran, has turned to promoting its position throughout the world by improving its public relations. Since the Ministry of Information was formed in 1961, it has been active in bettering Saudi Arabia's image through various publications and advertising supplements in major newspapers, such as the *New York Times* and the *Washington Post*.[94] Saudi officials, such as Sheikh Zaki Yamani, have traveled, given speeches, granted interviews, and actively lobbied to promote Saudi policy. Moreover, King Khalid has made official visits and has granted interviews to enhance Saudi Arabia's position before the world public.[95]

Examining the process of interaction in the Persian Gulf with a view to Iran and Saudi Arabia, the complex and dynamic nature of the gulf system becomes apparent. A complicated mix of continuity and change prevails. On the one hand, tangible changes such as the withdrawal of the British, the unprecedented influx of sophisticated arms into the region, the fall of the Shah's government in Iran, and the growing importance of Persian Gulf oil have refocused the world's attention on the gulf. On the other hand, the underlying political rivalries continue. Iran and Saudi Arabia continue to revolve in their respective circles, both experiencing problems of developing states and simultaneously being partners and rivals. Both represent Islamic states but of a different kind. Both are pursuing their own national interests, but each seeks stability in the gulf. Both have realized a new international influence based upon their oil resources, and both have dared to confront United States policy on the subjects of oil and the Arab-Israeli conflict. Yet Saudi Arabia continues to rely on the United States and the industrialized West for arms and developmental technology. Revolutionary Iran also still looks to the United States as a balance against the Soviet Union.

NOTES

1. U. S., Department of State, Bureau of Intelligence and Research, *Sovereignty of the Sea*, Geographic Bulletin no. 3, rev. ed. (Washington, D. C.: Government Printing Office, 1969), pp. 18-27.

2. For a brief description of the geographical setting, *see* Richard Young, "The Law of the Sea in the Persian Gulf: Problems and Progress," in *New Directions in the Law of the Sea*, 10 vols., ed. Robin Churchill, K. R. Simmonds, and Jane Welch (Dobbs Ferry, N. Y.: Oceana, 1973), 3:231. For a more detailed description of the geographic and hydrographic setting, *see* U. S., Defense Mapping Agency, Hydrographic Center, *Sailing Directions for the Persian Gulf*, pub. 62, 5th ed. rev. (Washington, D. C.: U. S. Navy Hydrographic Office, 1975).

3. It should be noted that "the length of that part of the Strait of Hormuz having a breadth of 26 miles or less is 16-½ miles. The 12-mile arcs from the nearest points on opposite shores overlap over a distance of 13 miles." Navigation is possible on both sides of a median line through the strait and its approaches. *See* Commander R. H. Kennedy, "A Brief Geographical and Hydrographical Study of Straits which Constitute Routes for International Traffic," in U. N., *United Nations Conference on the Law of the Sea*, (A/CONF.13/37), 1:129-30.

4. In an area just off the Musandam Peninsula depths of about 146 meters have been reported. *See Sailing Directions for the Persian Gulf*, p. 3.

5. *Sovereignty of the Sea*, pp. 19-21.

6. Vattel's reference to the pearl fisheries of Bahrain is as follows: "Who can doubt that the pearl fisheries of Bahrain and Ceylon may be lawful objects of ownership?" Emerich de Vattel, *Le droit des gens, ou principles de la loi naturelle appliques à la conduit et aux affaires des nations et de souverains*, trans. Charles G. Fenwick in *The Classics of International Law*, ed. James Brown Scott (Washington, D. C.: Carnegie Institution of Washington, 1916) 3: 107.

7. For an examination of the early British role in the Persian Gulf, *see* Robert G. Landen, "The Modernization of the Persian Gulf: The Period of

British Dominance," in *Middle East Focus: The Persian Gulf*, Proceedings of the Twentieth Annual Near East Conference, ed. T. Cuyler Young (Princeton, N. J.: Princeton University Conference, 1969), pp. 1-24; and "Curzon's Analysis of British Policy and Interests in Persia and the Persian Gulf, 21 September 1899," in *Diplomacy in the Near and Middle East*, 3 vols., ed. J. C. Hurewitz (Princeton, N. J.: D. Van Nostrand, 1956), 1:219-49.

8. The British-Russian rivalry in Iran preceded the emergence of the Communist regime in the Soviet Union. *See* Rouhollah K. Ramazani, *The Foreign Policy of Iran, 1500-1941: A Developing Nation in World Affairs* (Charlottesville, Va.: University Press of Virginia, 1966).

9. Since the nature of the subsystem and its historical precedent are pertinent to international legal development, a brief overview of the Persian Gulf subsystem leading to the emergence (or reemergence) of the developing states of the region as actors in their own right is warranted.

10. For a breakdown of the Persian Gulf subsystem into the respective periods, *see* Rouhollah K. Ramazani, "The Settlement of the Bahrain Dispute," 12 *Indian Journal of International Law* 1 (1972). For discussions of the changing patterns of the Persian Gulf subsystem, *see* Center for Mediterranean Studies, *The Changing Balance of Power in the Persian Gulf*, ed. Elizabeth Monroe (New York: American Universities Field Staff, 1972).

11. For the text of the "General Treaty," *see* C. U. Aitchison, ed., *A Collection of Treaties, Engagements and Sanads Relating to India and Neighboring Countries Containing the Treaties, and etc., Relating to Aden and the South Western Coast of Arabia, the Arab Principalities in the Persian Gulf, Muscat (Oman), Baluchistan and the North-West Frontier Province*, 14 vols. (Delhi: Government of India, 1933). 11: 245-49.

12. *See* "Terms of a Maritime Truce for Ten Years agreed upon by the Chiefs of the Arabian Coasts, under the Mediation of the Resident in the Persian Gulf, dates 1st June 1843," ibid., pp. 250-51.

13. *See* "Treaty of Peace in Perpetuity agreed upon by the Chiefs of the Arabian Coast in Behalf of Themselves, their Heirs, and Successors, under the Mediation of the Resident in the Persian Gulf, 1853," ibid., pp. 252-54.

14. *See* Ramazani, *Foreign Policy of Iran 1500-1941*, pp. 171-257.

15. Ramazani, "The Bahrain Dispute," pp. 7-8.

16. Myres S. McDougal and Florentino P. Feliciano, *Law and Minimum World Public Order* (New Haven, Conn.: Yale University Press, 1961), p. 11, n. 25.

17. For the purposes of this study, the phases of "outcomes," "effects," and "conditions" are not included. For an explanation of phase analysis, *see* John Norton Moore, "Prolegomenon to the Jurisprudence of Myres

McDougal and Harold Lasswell," 54 *Virginia Law Review* 669 (1968); *see also* Myres S. McDougal and William T. Burke, *The Public Order of the Oceans* (New Haven, Conn.: Yale University Press, 1962), pp. 14-28.

18. Oman, while closely tied to Britain, and later to Iran, for protection, has been independent since 1650, except for a short period of Persian control. Its independent status was expressly recognized by Britain and France in a joint declaration in 1862. (For text, *see* Aitchison, *A Collection of Treaties,* pp. 304-5.) Britain reconfirmed its recognition of the Sultanate as a fully independent state in the Treaty of Friendship, Commerce and Navigation of 20 September 1951.

19. These gulf sheikhdoms had not been British protectorates, but were quasi-sovereign states that lacked control of their external relations. For a thorough examination of the international status of the Arabian Gulf Sheikhdoms, *see* Husain M. Albaharna, *The Legal Status of the Arabian Gulf States* (Dobbs Ferry, N. Y.: Oceana, 1968). *See also,* John Duke Anthony, *Arab States of the Lower Gulf: People, Politics, Petroleum,* James Terry Duce Memorial Series, vol. 3 (Washington, D. C.: Middle East Institute, 1975).

20. *See* Benjamin Shwadran, *The Middle East, Oil and the Great Powers* (New York: Wiley, 1974), pp. 89-156.

21. Ibid., pp. 315-85.

22. *See* "Cuba Moves to Widen Role in Middle East," *Middle East Monitor,* 15 April 1976, p. 2; and William Branigin, "Iran Says Guerrillas Trained in Cuba," *Washington Post,* 11 May 1976.

23. At least eight internal and external rivalries and conflicts are present. In analyzing policy formulation the interdependence of these underlying rivalries must be taken into consideration. As Ramazani points out: "Only analytically is the impact of the external and internal circumstances on foreign policy separable. In the world of reality they all interpenetrate." *See* Rouhollah K. Ramazani, "Iran's Changing Foreign Policy: A Preliminary Discussion," *Middle East Journal* 24 (Autumn 1970): 431.

24. *See* Rouhollah K. Ramazani, *The Persian Gulf: Iran's Role* (Charlottesville, Va.: University Press of Virginia, 1972), pp. 33-41.

25. The PFLOAG, formerly called the Dhofar Liberation Front and recently referred to as the Popular Front for the Liberation of Oman (PFLO), has openly called for the overthrow of all "traditional" governments in the Gulf. For an examination of the Iranian action in Oman against the Dhofari rebels, *see* "Iranian Troops Seal Insurgents' Doom," and "How Iranian Troops Dealt Defeat to Oman's Rebels," *Kayhan* (Tehran; Weekly International Edition), 1 February 1975.

26. The case of the United Arab Emirates with its various internal rival-

ries represents a special situation, inextricably involved with and representative of the inter-Arab complexity generated, *inter alia*, by unmarked borders.

27. For a discussion of the Iraqi claim to Kuwait *see* Albaharna, *The Legal Status of the Arabian Gulf States*, pp. 250-58.

28. For details of the Bahrain dispute, *see* Ramazani, "The Settlement of the Bahrain Dispute," pp. 1-13.

29. For discussions of boundary problems, *see* Sir Rupert Hay, "The Persian Gulf States and their Boundary Problems," *Geographical Journal*, 70 (December 1954): 433-45; Sir Rupert Hay, *Persian Gulf States* (Washington, D. C.: Middle East Institute, 1959); Shigeru Oda, "Boundary of the Continental Shelf," 12 *Japanese Annual of International Law* 264 (1968); and Albaharna, *The Legal Status of the Arabian Gulf States*, pp. 167-311.

30. For a table of the Gulf's current ruling families and their respective tribes, *see* Emile A. Nakhleh, *Arab-American Relations in the Persian Gulf* (Washington, D. C.: American Enterprise Institute, 1975), pp. 10-11.

31. For an account of ibn-Saud's consolidation of power in Arabia and his conflict with Sharif Husein, *see* H. St. John Philby, *Saudi Arabia* (New York: Praeger, 1955), pp. 265-385.

32. For selected quotations of statements made by the American President, Secretary of State, and Secretary of Defense regarding the use of American armed forces to deal with the oil embargo and price rise, *see* U. S. Congress, House, Committee on International Relations, *Oil Fields as Military Objectives: A Feasibility Study* (Washington, D. C.: Government Printing Office, 1975), pp. 77-82. *See also*, Robert W. Tucker, "Oil: The Issue of American Intervention," *Commentary* 59 (January 1975): 21-31.

33. In the case of Iranian goals, Ramazani examines the "crucial problem of priority" in his "Iran's White Revolution: A Study in Political Development," *International Journal of Middle Eastern Studies* 5 (April 1974): 124-39, where he indicates that "it was primarily the goal of national independence that most often received a higher priority over those of economic modernization and political participation from the dawn of the Constitutional Revolution to the early 1960s," but suggests that Iran's regional role in the gulf was accorded priority "at the expense of the current primary objective of socio-economic modernization."

34. Ramazani uses the terms *"winning* and *maintaining* freedom of decision-making in international politics." *See* Ramazani, "Iran's White Revolution," p. 125.

35. *See* "The Policy Statement of the Kingdom of Saudi Arabia," *Washington Post*, 15 April 1975.

36. In 1961 Saudi Arabia sent troops, along with other Arab League

states (the United Arab Republic, Jordan, and Sudan), to Kuwait to re-place British troops in face of Iraqi claims to Kuwait.

37. For accounts of Yemen, *see* A. I. Dawisha, "Intervention in the Yemen: An Analysis of Egyptian Perceptions and Policies," *Middle East Journal* 29 (Winter 1975): 47-63; Manfred Wenner, *Modern Yemen, 1918-1966* (Baltimore, Md.: Johns Hopkins University Press, 1967); and William Harold Ingrams, *The Yemen: Imams, Rulers, and Revolutionaries* (New York: Praeger, 1964).

38. *See* U. S., *Area Handbook for Saudi Arabia* (Washington, D. C.: Government Printing Office, 1971), p. 42.

39. *See* U. S., Department of the Treasury, *Summary of Saudi Arabian Five Year Development Plan (1975-1980)*, 23 October 1975. *See also,* "Saudi Development Plan May Total $150 Billion," *Middle East Monitor,* 15 May 1975, pp. 1-2; and "Saudi Arabia's Human Resources Strategy," *Middle East Monitor,* 15 July 1975, pp. 1-2.

40. A thorough examination of the development of Iran's military power in the gulf during the postwar period is not possible here. Instead, certain observations and generalizations will be made for the purpose of estab-lishing perspective.

41. Iran's defense expenditures rose from 1.5 billion rials in 1947 to 2.5 billion rials in the 1953-54 budget. *See The Middle East 1953,* 3rd ed. (Lon-don: Europa Publications, 1953), p. 254.

42. For details of Iran's efforts and frustrations *see* chapter 6, "Friendship in Frustration," in Rouhollah K. Ramazani, *Iran's Foreign Policy, 1941-1973: A Study of Foreign Policy in Modernizing Nations* (Charlottesville, Va.: University Press of Virginia, 1975), pp. 154-66.

43. Figure cited in Stockholm International Peace Research Institute (SIPRI), *The Arms Trade with the Third World* (Stockholm: Almqvist and Wiksell, 1971), p. 577.

44. Ibid.

45. These figures are approximate and based upon a fixed exchange rate, 1 rial = $.013. *See The Middle East 1955,* 4th ed. (London: Europa Pub-lications, 1955), p. 262; and *The Middle East and North Africa 1964-1965,* 11th ed. (London: Europa Publications Ltd., 1964), p. 192.

46. *See The Middle East and North Africa 1964-1965,* p. 192. *See also The Middle East and North Africa 1972-1973,* 19th ed. (London: Europa Publications, 1972), p. 314. (The dollar figures are based upon an exchange rate of 1 rial = $.013.)

47. For arms supplies to Iran, *see* SIPRI, *Arms Trade Registers: The Arms Trade with the Third World* (Stockholm: Almqvist and Wiksell, 1975), pp. 46-50.

48. Ibid.

49. The Shah's remarks were quoted in *Area Handbook for Iran* (Washington, D. C.: Government Printing Office, 1971), p. 582.

50. *See* International Institute for Strategic Studies, *The Military Balance 1970-1971* (London: Chatto & Windus, 1970), p. 70; and table 10, "Military Indicators," in Ramazani, *Iran's Foreign Policy, 1941-1973*, pp. 466-67.

51. *See* defense expenditures in *The Military Balance 1978-1979*, p. 88. *See also* Ray Cline, *World Power Assessment: A Calculus of Strategic Drift,* (Boulder, Colo.: Westview Press, 1975). Cline says Iran ranks seventeenth in the world in "military capability" (conventional forces). He ranked Saudi Arabia as twenty-ninth.

52. *See The Military Balance, 1978-79,* p. 88.

53. It was reported that Iran built the world's largest operational hovercraft fleet, and was receiving the advanced AH-1J helicopters even before the United States Army. *See* Dale R. Tahtinen, *Arms in the Persian Gulf* (Washington, D. C.: American Enterprise Institute, 1974), pp. 8-11. *See also* Arnaud de Borchgrave, "Colossus of the Oil Lanes," *Newsweek*, 21 May 1973, p. 40; and "Iran to Get Better Helicopters than U. S. Army," *Armed Forces Journal*, February 1973, p. 18.

54. SIPRI, *Arms Trade Registers*, p. 50.

55. De Borchgrave, "Colossus of the Oil Lanes," p. 41; and Tahtinen, *Arms in the Persian Gulf*, pp. 10, 15.

56. "Arms Build-Up Will Go On—Shahanshah," was the headline in *Kayhan* (Tehran: Weekly International Edition), 20 September 1975. The Shah, speaking at the graduation ceremonies of the Defense College, indicated that regional and even international responsibilities would be entrusted to Iran, and Iran had "no choice but to arm itself to the extent necessary for the preservation of its national interests, with the exclusion of atomic weapons."

57. For press reports, *see* Thomas O'Toole, "S. Africa Set to Sell Iran Uranium Ore," *Washington Post*, 12 October 1975.

58. *See* U. N., Department of Economic and Social Affairs, *World Energy Supplies 1950-1974* (New York: United Nations, 1976), p. 210 (ST / ESA / STAT/SER.J/19).

59. U. N., Department of Economic and Social Affairs, *Monthly Bulletin of Statistics*, 29 (June 1975): 230-31 (ST/ESA/STAT/SER.Q/30).

60. Iran's Fifth Development Plan (1973/74-1977/78) was originally approved in 1973. It was revised radically upward following the increased oil revenues that accompanied the price rise. The revised plan doubled the capital investment of the original to nearly $70 billion. *See* Jahangir Amuzegar, *Iran: An Economic Profile* (Washington, D. C.: Middle East Institute, 1977), p. 166.

61. *See The Military Balance, 1978-1979*, p. 37.

62. Developmental bottlenecks, such as ports, raise the question of whether even Iran with its larger population can effectively absorb the large oil revenues. *See* Lewis M. Simons, "Oil Wealth Overwhelms Two Nations: Costly Goods Clog Iran's Ports," *Washington Post*, 1 March 1976.

63. For an examination of the Saudi interest in acquiring an air defense system following the outbreak of the Yemen civil war, *see* SIPRI, *Arms Trade with the Thrid World*, pp. 562-65.

64. *See* table 17, "Defense Budget of Saudi Arabia, 1961-1965," in *Area Handbook for Saudi Arabia*, p. 327.

65. *The Military Balance 1975-1976*, p. 77; *The Military Balance 1978-79*, p. 89.

66. For a breakdown of arms supplies to Saudi Arabia, *see* SIPRI, *The Arms Trade Registers*, pp. 61-62.

67. SIPRI, *The Arms Trade Registers*, p. 62.

68. *See Summary of Saudi Arabian Five Year Development Plan (1975-1980)*.

69. About one-fourth of the first development plan was aimed at the development of Saudi Arabia's human resources. *See Area Handbook for Saudi Arabia*, p. xxxiv.

70. *The Military Balance, 1978-1979*, p. 41. (It should be noted that reported population figures vary greatly for Saudi Arabia.)

71. For a discussion of some of the labor problems found in Saudi Arabia, *see Area Handbook for Saudi Arabia*, p. 259.

72. *See* "Saudi Arabia's Human Resources Strategy," *Middle East Monitor*, 15 July 1975, pp. 1-2.

73. *See* "Saudi Development Plan May Total $150 Billion," *Middle East Monitor*, 15 May 1975, pp. 1-2.

74. McDougal and Feliciano, *Law and Minimum World Public Order*, p. 309.

75. For a discussion of strategies, *see* ibid., pp. 309-33.

76. Ramazani maintains that the doctrine of equilibrium was introduced in the late nineteenth century by Mirza Taqi Khan Amir Kabir simply as *movazeneh*. Ramazani, "Iran's Changing Foreign Policy," p. 433.

77. For an explanation of positive nationalism, *see* His Imperial Majesty Mohammed Reza Shah Pahlavi, Shahanshah of Iran, *Mission for My Country* (New York: McGraw-Hill, 1961), pp. 125, 297.

78. *See* Ramazani, "The Settlement of the Bahrain Dispute."

79. For the Iran-Saudi agreement, *see* Richard Young, "Equitable Solutions for Offshore Boundaries: The 1968 Saudi-Iran Agreement," 64 *American Journal of International Law* 152 (1972). For the Iran-Iraq settlement, see "Iran-Iraq Joint Communiqué Settling Shatt Al-Arab Dispute," *Middle East Monitor*, 15 March 1975, pp. 4-5; "Final Iraq-Iran Settlement

Hailed," *Middle East Monitor*, 1 June 1975, p. 4; and "Frontier Dispute Formally Ended," *Kayhan* (Tehran: Weekly International Edition), 26 June 1976.

80. *See* "A Second Look at Budget Priorities," *Kayhan* (Tehran: Weekly International Edition), 12 April 1975.

81. Iran's vice-minister of industry indicated that Iran had given $7.7 billion in loans, aid, and grants to other nations in the first eleven months of 1974. Forty percent went to developed countries. *See* "Asians told of Iran Aid Worth $7.7b," *Kayhan* (Tehran: Weekly International Edition), 7 December 1974.

82. *See* "Iranian Money to Arab States," *Middle East Monitor*, 15 June 1974, pp. 2-3.

83. The Shah repeatedly indicated that "you have first of all to count on yourself." *See* "We Must Count on Ourselves," *Kayhan* (Tehran: Weekly International Edition), 26 October 1974.

84. For example, *see* "The Shahanshah's Proposal for a New Oil Pricing System," *Washington Post*, 11 November 1974.

85. *See* Ardeshir Zahedi's letter to the editor, " 'Imperial Iran': A Reply from the Ambassador," *Washington Post*, 7 January 1975.

86. In a policy statement of King Khalid of Saudi Arabia, made soon after he became king, he repeatedly referred to the wishes and policies of the late king, King Faisal. *See* "Policy Statement of King Khalid of Saudi Arabia—March 31, 1975," *Middle East Monitor*, 15 April 1975, pp. 4-6.

87. *See* Bakor Omar Kashmeeri, "The Role of Saudi Arabia in the Arab League" (unpublished thesis, University of Virginia, 1971).

88. The *Washington Post* reported that King Khalid, in his first extended interview, expressed concern over the moves by Iran and Iraq to establish a gulf-wide security arrangement. He indicated that "cooperation in all fields among gulf countries can be achieved without the existence of alliances." *See* Jim Hoagland, "Saudi Leader Admits Israeli Right to Exist," *Washington Post*, 25 May 1975.

89. Saudi Arabia had also embargoed oil during the 1956 Suez crisis, but the effects were not as evident because of the availability of alternative sources. Since the 1973 oil embargo coincided with declining American oil supplies and rising world demand, its effects were multiplied.

90. *See* Prince Saud's comments on the use of the "oil weapon" in "Saudi Arabia's 'Oil Weapon' Explained," *Middle East Monitor*, 1 October 1973, pp. 5-6.

91. For example, in July 1975, on the same day that the United States announced its $6 million contribution to UNRWA, Saudi Arabia announced an $11.2 million contribution. *See* "U. S., Saudi Arabia Increase Aid to Ailing UNRWA," *Middle East Monitor*, 1 August 1975, p. 3. *See also* "Arabs

Replacing U. S. as UNESCO Bankroller," *Washington Post,* 20 September 1975.

92. *See* "Yemen Turns to Oil Money," *Middle East Monitor,* 1 September 1975, p. 2.

93. *See* Jonathan C. Randal, "Arabs Set Up 'Front-Line' War Chest," *Washington Post,* 30 October 1974.

94. *See* "Policy Statement of the Kingdom of Saudi Arabia," *Washington Post,* 15 April 1975.

95. *See* Jim Hoagland, "Saudi Leader Admits Israeli Right to Exist," *Washington Post,* 25 May 1975.

CHAPTER 2

The Basic Community Interests in the Persian Gulf

The primary concern of this chapter is to determine the nature of the community interests in the Persian Gulf and the general nature of the legal principles that serve these interests. This chapter provides a general survey of what is at stake in the development of the law of the sea in the Persian Gulf.

Generally speaking, the uses of the sea or marine activities that are of major importance to the international community are "uses of ocean space" and "exploitation of marine resources."[1] The uses of ocean space can be examined in terms of transport, offshore structures, generation of energy, and other uses, for example, recreation, land reclamation, waste disposal, and marine research. The exploitation of marine resources can be viewed in terms of living resources and mineral resources. In addition to the direct community interest in marine activities, there are corresponding interests in coastal state security, preservation of the environment, and maintenance of minimum public order.

The importance of the sea usage in the Persian Gulf is primarily reflected by the interests in transport and the exploitation of marine resources.[2] Also of concern in the gulf are the security interests of the coastal states, the problem of pollution, and the propensity of the sea to be an arena of conflict. The basic community interests in the area can be approached in terms of an avenue for trade and transportation, the exploitation of offshore resources, coastal state security, preservation of the marine environment, and minimum public order.

AN AVENUE OF TRADE AND TRANSPORTATION

The Persian Gulf is most important to the international community for its use as a pathway for trade and transportation, especially the transportation of oil. Oil is carried by tanker from the gulf to the major oil-consuming nations of Western Europe and to Japan. The supply of Persian Gulf oil is vital to Japan and Europe and is becoming increasingly important to the United States. At one time the Persian Gulf supplied over half of Western Europe's oil needs and over 90 percent of Japan's needs; estimates indicate that the gulf may supply as much as 50 percent of the United States' imports by the 1980s. A former Iranian ambassador to the United States characterized the Persian Gulf as "an economic lifeline vital to the whole world, not only to the region."[3] Approximately twenty million barrels of oil currently pass through the Persian Gulf each day.

The tanker has proved to be the most efficient mode of oil transport by far. This is especially apparent in the Persian Gulf, where the volume of tanker traffic has tripled in the last ten years and still continues to rise. An oil tanker passes through the Strait of Hormuz about every fifteen minutes. The increasing reliance on tankers for the movement of oil is based not only on monetary concerns but also reflects the political problems often associated with pipelines.[4] Because of increasing tanker traffic, the employment of the water of the Persian Gulf as an avenue of oil transport is of utmost importance.

The movement of oil from the Persian Gulf to most of the major oil-consuming nations is a vital interest for those nations and for the economy of the international community as a whole; it is equally vital for the Persian Gulf states, which depend on the large oil revenues to finance ambitious economic-development plans and large defense-procurement programs. Any interruption of the free movement of oil through the gulf would threaten the foundation of their governmental budgets and, subsequently, their entire economies.

Directly related to the outflow of oil from the gulf and the resulting accumulation of expanding oil revenues are increasing imports for the unprecedented development plans. For example, Iran's Fifth Development Plan provided for the import of $80 billion worth of machinery and goods.[5] The Shah remarked at a news conference in 1975 that "in less than 10 years, [Iran] will be a $40,000-million-a-year import market and most of this will come through our southern ports."[6] Although the Iranian revolution has limited the volume of imported goods, the development plans of other gulf states also call for extensive imports, which must enter through the gulf. For example, the proposed Saudi development plan has been placed at over $141 billion, with the most prestigious sector being industrialization. It has been reported that the handling capacity at Saudi ports will increase 153 percent between 1977 and 1981.[7]

Moreover, the general prosperity generated by oil income has engendered large increases in imports that are derived from the broad-based development spending. This expansion of imports further increases the importance of the gulf for maritime trade and non-oil shipping. In other words, as well as being a vital oil artery for the international community, the gulf is rapidly becoming a trade lifeline for gulf states.

The gulf's importance as an oil artery and an avenue of non-oil trade has been recognized by the international community, as well as by the littoral states. In the Persian Gulf community and national interests appear to coincide in a mutual desire for freedom of navigation. This desire is reflected throughout traditional and contemporary international law.

In traditional international law, as Grotius points out, "by the Law of Nations navigation is free to all persons whatsoever," and "every nation is free to travel to every other nation, and to trade with it."[8] It was traditionally assumed that the use of the high seas for navigation and fishing was inexhaustible. In the words of Vattel in the eighteenth century,

one who sails on the high seas or who fishes therein injures no one, and the sea in both these respects can satisfy the needs of all men. . . . Hence no Nation has the right to take possession of the high seas, or claim the sole right to use them to the exclusion of others.[9]

This freedom of the high seas has continued to reflect the interest of the international community in contemporary international law. In 1958 the Convention on the High Seas recognized that the high seas were "open to all nations," and that no nation could "validly purport to subject any part of them to its sovereignty."[10] The Revised Informal Composite Negotiating Text (ICNT/Rev. 1) of the Third

United Nations Conference on the Law of the Sea reiterates that "the high seas shall be open to all States," and indicates that such freedom comprises freedom of navigation, freedom of overflight, freedom of fishing, freedom of scientific research, and freedom to lay cables and pipelines and to construct artificial islands.[11]

Although there is a consensus on the need for freedom of navigation on the high seas, there is a question as to what comprises the high seas. The Persian Gulf, including the Strait of Hormuz, was traditionally considered to be the same as open sea or high seas.[12] In recent times, however, with the claims to expanded national jurisdiction, the Strait of Hormuz has been claimed for the territorial sea jurisdiction of Oman and Iran, the bordering coastal states. This has given rise to a conflict of the exclusive interests of the coastal states with the inclusive interest of the international community over the passage through straits.

In traditional international law the right of passage through straits was clearly acknowledged as long as it did not endanger the strait states. For example, Vattel points out:

It must be specifically noted with regard to straits that when they connect two seas the navigation of which is common to all or to several Nations, the owner of the strait cannot refuse passage to the other Nations, provided such passage be innocent and without danger to the owner.[13]

In contemporary international law a similar right of passage through straits has been recognized. For example, in the Convention on the Territorial Sea and the Contiguous Zone, signed in 1958, it was recognized that

there shall be no suspension of the innocent passage of foreign ships through straits which are used for international navigation between one part of the high seas and another part of the high seas or the territorial sea of a foreign state.[14]

Considerable disagreement has arisen, however, over the determination of "innocent passage." Transit through straits has become a highly controversial issue with the inclusive interests of the international community conflicting with the exclusive interests of the strait states.[15]

What is at stake in the controversy over freedom of navigation within the Persian Gulf and through the Strait of Hormuz is, *inter alia*, the transport of oil and the gulf's growing non-oil trade. In other words, the very use of the Persian Gulf as an avenue of trade and transportation is at stake in the ongoing development of the law of the sea in the Persian Gulf.

THE EXPLOITATION OF OFFSHORE RESOURCES

The second broad area of community concern in the Persian Gulf involves the exploitation of marine resources, which consist of mineral and living resources. Mineral resources include deposits in bedrock (for example, oil, gas) and surface and placer deposits (for example, sand, gravel, manganese nodules).[16] Mineral resources also include such activities as the extraction of dissolved chemicals and desalination. Marine activities involving living resources are fisheries, aquaculture, and drug extraction.[17]

In the Persian Gulf offshore oil and gas deposits and fisheries are currently most important to the coastal states and international community. Previously the Persian Gulf was known for its pearling, but commercial pearling in the gulf is now regarded as defunct.[18]

Since the world's demand for oil has been rising and the technology for offshore oil production has been improving, the offshore deposits in the Persian Gulf have become exceedingly important both to the coastal states in terms of needed oil revenues and to the international community in terms of needed oil supplies. Little needs to be said about the importance of oil to the international community, especially after the major energy crises following the Arab oil embargo of 1973-74 and the revolution in Iran in 1978-79.

The statistics for offshore oil production in the gulf indicate its crucial significance. Of the 6.5552 billion barrels of oil produced by the gulf states in 1972, 1.351 billion barrels were produced from offshore fields.[19] Offshore production has proved to be significant for most of the gulf states, with the exception of Iraq and Bahrain. In 1973 the proved recoverable offshore reserves for Iran and Saudi Arabia were placed at 62.338 billion barrels, with the world offshore reserves put at only 93.1156 billion barrels.[20] In other words, as of 1973, about 70 percent of the world's proved offshore recoverable reserves were located in the Persian Gulf. Despite the realization of large offshore discoveries off Mexico, the Persian Gulf remains the world's oil heartland.

Although the gulf contains the world's largest known offshore reserves, offshore production is a post-World War II phenomenon. The first major offshore concession in the Persian Gulf was the Saudi concession to Aramco on 10 October 1948. Iran did not begin to exploit its offshore oil until its Petroleum Act of 1957 was passed.[21] Since the offshore production of oil represented a new phenomenon in the gulf, its inception and development have been controversial and have raised a number of international legal questions.[22]

In addition to the gulf's offshore mineral resources, there are its living resources—its fisheries. Fishing, although important to the coastal areas since early times, did not advance beyond traditional methods until the postwar period for two reasons. First, fishing was limited to the needs of the coastal inhabitants, because transportation and refrigeration were not adequate to transport fish inland to the more populated areas. Second, the inland populations did not have a taste for the species of fish from the gulf. Certain religious mores also inhibit the eating of some gulf species. In the postwar period the growing demand for food by the international community, as well as the improvement of fish-processing methods and storage facilities, have brought an increased community interest in the Persian Gulf fishery resources. Similarly, the gulf states have expressed an increased interest in the gulf fisheries not just for food but also for the commercial value that can contribute to their development plans.

This increased interest in the Persian Gulf fisheries has resulted in a clash between the interests of the international community and the interests of the coastal states. For example, when distant-water fishing boats, such as those of Japan, began to exploit the gulf's fishery resources, the coastal states became concerned about the depletion of those resources.[23] Because they are not as technologically advanced as the distant-water fishing states, the gulf states contend that the benefits of the fishery resources should be reserved to further the development of the coastal states within the gulf. Also relevant has been a growing food deficit in some of the gulf states. It has been estimated, perhaps optimistically, that Iran will be importing as much as 20 percent of its food needs by 1990.[24] In such a case, coastal states like Iran will have a special interest in developing their offshore fishing capabilities despite previous consumption patterns.

The fishery potential in the Persian Gulf appears to be quite large. Although a few observers seem to believe that fishery resources will be as valuable as oil resources, as Ramazani points out, this probably is an exaggeration.[25] Nevertheless, reputable estimates place the annual potential as high as 600,000 tons.[26] The annual catch in the Persian Gulf has been estimated to be 75,000 tons.[27] The possibility exists that fishery production in the gulf could increase eightfold, which would represent a significant increase in revenues, especially in light of increases in the price of fish. For instance, in 1973 alone world fisheries experienced an upswing in prices that, in some cases, was as much as 25 percent.[28] Because of the rising demand for, and value of, fishery resources, and since such a potential for expansion in the Persian Gulf exists, these fishery resources represent a considerable value to the gulf states and to the international community.

The interests of the international community in exploiting offshore resources (living and mineral) have been reflected in traditional international legal principles. Some of these principles were based on assumptions that are not valid today, while others remain surprisingly appropriate. In the case of the use of the sea near the coasts, Vattel once wrote:

The various uses to which the sea near the coasts can be put render it a natural object of ownership. Fish, shells, pearls, amber, etc., may be obtained from it. Now, with respect to all these things, the resources of coast[al] seas are not inexhaustible, so that the Nation to which the shore belongs may claim itself an advantage thus within its reach and may make use of it, just as it has taken possession of the lands which people inhabit.[29]

According to traditional international law, the offshore resources that "are not inexhaustible" are subject to appropriation, and their ownership can be claimed by coastal states. That is, exclusive interests of coastal states are recognized for exhaustible resources. While this principle could pertain to offshore oil, in the case of fishery resources there is some question. Grotius maintains that "the same principle which applies to navigation applies also to fishing, namely, that it remains free and open to all."[30] Vattel expanded upon Grotius with the assumption that "the use of the high seas for the purposes of navigation and fishing is innocent in character and inexhaustible," and "nature does not give men the right to appropriate things the use of which is innocent and the supply inexhaustible and sufficient for all."[31] In other words, there was an assumption that the supply of fish was virtually inexhaustible.

Grotius, however, recognized the possibility of "fencing off with stakes an inlet of the sea (to) make a fish pond for himself, and so establish a private preserve." Grotius did not think that "the expanse of sea which is visible from the shore" should be regarded in the same way as "the outer sea, the ocean."[32]

An additional qualification for appropriation of fish near the coast is provided by Vattel:

Although the supply of fish is less easily exhausted, yet if a Nation has specially profitable fisheries along its coasts, of which it can take possession, are we not to allow it to appropriate that gift of nature as being connected with the territory it occupies, and to keep to itself the great commercial advantage which it may enjoy, should there be fish enough to supply neighboring Nations? But if, instead of taking possession of its coastal waters, it should once recognize the common right of the Nations to fish therein, it may no longer exclude them, having left those fisheries in their primitive condition of common property, at least with respect to those who have been making use of them.[33]

In light of this special consideration for "fisheries along coasts," it would appear that the question of the boundary of the high seas was not taken as fixed, but would vary in accord with the state's ability and desire to maintain its offshore possessions effectively. In other words, in traditional international law a state could claim and appropriate offshore resources "within its reach," but if the state failed to take possession, the offshore resources were recognized as common property.

In contemporary international law two concepts have developed that provide for the exploitation and conservation of offshore resources. These concepts—the continental shelf and the fishery conservation zone (exclusive fishing zone)—were devised to provide for the utilization and conservation of offshore resources in a changing world of technological advancement.

The continental shelf concept provides for the exploration and exploitation of the mineral and other nonliving resources of the seabed and its subsoil, together with the living resources belonging to the sedentary species. The continental shelf doctrine, as promulgated in the Truman Proclamation of 1945,[34] received widespread attention and acceptance. However the "shelf" concept, which pertained to a geological formation, quickly assumed a more generalized definition based on the criterion of "exploitability." This became apparent in the initial consideration of the continental shelf doctrine by the International Law Commission, which noted that there was no "continental shelf" in the Persian Gulf.[35] The 1958 Geneva Convention on the Continental Shelf further incorporated the concept of "exploitablility" as the limiting factor of a state's claim. Currently the nature and bounds of the continental shelf are under consideration at the Third United Nations Conference on the Law of the Sea. In the ICNT/Rev. 1 the continental shelf is considered to extend "to the outer edge of the continental margin, or to a distance of 200 nautical miles . . . where the outer edge of the continental margin does not extend up to that distance."[36] In other words, a fixed limit is now being considered for the control of fixed offshore resources.

While the continental shelf concept has provided for the exploitation of mineral resources and certain "sedentary" living resources, it has not provided for fisheries. At the time of the Truman Proclamation on the Continental Shelf, an accompanying "Fisheries" Proclamation was made that provided for the creation of "conservation zones for the protection of fisheries in certain areas of the high seas contiguous to the United States."[37]

This concept of a fisheries conservation zone developed in response to the realization that traditional assumptions of "inexhaustible" fishery resources were invalid. The concept was later incorporated into the 1958 Geneva Convention on Fishing and Conservation of the Living Resources of the High Seas. Article 7 of the convention included the provision that

any coastal State may, with a view to the maintainance of the productivity of the living resources of the sea, adopt unilateral measures of conservation appropriate to any stock of fish or other marine resources in any area of the high seas adjacent to its territorial sea, provided that negotiations to that effect with other States concerned have not led to an agreement within six months.[38]

However, despite the apparent community acceptance of the fishery conservation zone concept, new problems have arisen with the promulgation of "exclusive fishing zones." These exclusive fishing zones have varied in breadth and have sometimes been associated with continental shelf delimitations.

An additional proposal providing for the appropriation and control of both mineral and living resources is the "exclusive economic zone."[39] This zone, which received broad support at the Third United Nations Conference on the Law of the Sea, allows a coastal state to assume responsibility for offshore resources up to 200 nautical miles. The economic zone has been accepted in principle, but some questions remain. The primary problem is the failure of the international community to arrive at an acceptable balance between inclusive community interest and an assortment of exclusive national interests. The problems of the establishment of offshore resource boundaries and fishery zones are yet to be resolved.

Because of the uncertainty in the law of the sea and the continuing conflicts of interest in the law of the sea negotiations, no single comprehensive set of accepted principles exists. Instead there are various claims and counterclaims found throughout the various oceans and seas. At stake in the continuing controversy over the law of the sea are, *inter alia,* the laws pertaining to the exploitation of offshore resources, such as the offshore oil fields and the fishery resources of the Persian Gulf. Thus the enjoyment of the gulf resources is at stake.

COASTAL STATE SECURITY

As has been seen, states recognize in the law of the sea that certain offshore areas can come under the exclusive control of coastal states for purposes of exploiting offshore resources that benefit the international community as well as coastal states. In addition, coastal states also assume exclusive control of certain offshore areas and activities for the purposes of ensuring their "security and welfare." The international community, while having certain inclusive interests, also recognizes that there are exclusive interests that all coastal states share. Because of the possibility of hostile attacks by sea, the international community recognizes the necessity of some form of regulation or control by the coastal state of its sea approaches. Also to be considered, apart from hostile attacks, are those offshore actions and activities that could harm the good order of the coastal state.

In traditional international law the general principle of coastal state security was explicit. In the words of Vattel:

A Nation may appropriate such things as would be hurtful or dangerous to it if open to free and common use. . . . It is a matter of concern to their security and their welfare that there should not be a general liberty to approach so near their possessions, especially with ships of war, as to hinder the passage of trading vessels and disturb navigation.[40]

However the precise determination of the extent of a state's jurisdiction based on a general consent of nations was difficult to prove. Vattel indicates that

the most reasonable rule that can be laid down is that in general the sovereignty of a State over its marginal waters extends as far as is necessary for its safety and as far as it can effectively be maintained.[41]

State practice resulted in what became known as the cannon-shot rule; state control over its marginal seas generally was agreed to be three nautical miles—the distance a cannonball could be shot from shore.

Such considerations as "necessary for its safety" and "can effectively be maintained" were not controversial in a less complicated world of limited technology when cannons could reach three miles. Today however, additional concerns have arisen that make some traditional principles inapplicable. Currently in the Persian Gulf there remains the possibility of attacks from the sea by states and also by terrorist groups. The gulf areas most susceptible to invasion have been discussed by Robert Tucker in his work considering the feasibility of invading certain gulf oil-producing states.[42] However, in addition to the traditional coastal state security concerns, technological development has created new threats to the coastal states. These involve certain types of vessels the very presence of which might be considered a danger. Such vessels include supertankers, nuclear-powered vessels, nuclear-armed vessels, and other vessels carrying dangerous cargoes. The presence of such vessels has come to be considered a threat to the coastal state, especially if the effect of a terrorist attack on such vessels or other disabling action could effectively close a vital shipping lane upon which the coastal state's defense and economy depend. In such case, the threat would be to the vital interests of the coastal state and would transcend the purely environmental concerns.

In the Persian Gulf the concern for coastal state security has intensified as the gulf states have benefited from their oil riches, which depend on the freedom of transit and navigation through the gulf and the Strait of Hormuz. Any threat to navigation is a direct threat to coastal state security in the gulf. One of the major considerations of the gulf states is the possibility of a terrorist attack on supertankers. The Shah pointed out the example of the Palestinian guerrilla attack on an Israeli tanker in the Strait of Bab el Mandeb as a very serious precedent. He indicated that such an attack in the Strait of Hormuz could close the straits and be disastrous for the gulf states.[43] Thus, the danger of the presence of unseaworthy ships as well as the danger of offshore terrorist attacks, including the possibility of offshore mining, add a new dimension to the security needs of the coastal states of the Persian Gulf.

Along with the vital interest of the coastal states in free and un-impeded navigation, there are corresponding vital interests of the oil-consuming states that depend on the continuing supply of Persian Gulf oil. As previously noted, any cessation of shipping from the gulf could destabilize the economies of the oil-importing states of Europe, Japan, and the United States. Such an action would, in effect, threaten the entire international community.

To what extent can the international community recognize the vital interests of coastal states when broader community interests may be affected? Can the international community entrust vital interests to the authority of coastal states? In what way might the perceived vital interests of the coastal states be compatible with broader community interests in unimpeded transit? Questions such as these represent the importance of the developing law of the sea in the Persian Gulf and emphasize the vital interests at stake both in terms of coastal state security and the international community's desire for free and unimpeded transit and the right to guarantee such transit.

PRESERVATION OF THE MARINE ENVIRONMENT

Another focus of international legal concern is environmental protection. Environmental dangers resulting from, and accompanying, technological advancement contribute new threats to coastal states and potential threats to the international community. The threats to coastal states are often more immediate, while the threats to the international community are usually perceived as abstract or peripheral. The disparate responses to these perceived environmental dangers have heightened tensions in the law of the sea; serious problems have developed over such unilateral actions as the establishment of pollution control zones.

In the Persian Gulf the foremost environmental problem is oil pollution because of the heavy tanker traffic and intensive offshore activity, but others are likely to develop as the coastal states continue to push their industrialization programs.[44] The problems associated with seepage from offshore wells, transfer problems, and oil spills in general are especially acute in the gulf because it is semi-enclosed and small in terms of its volume of water and absorption capacity. Furthermore the gulf's currents are slow, and there is only a gradual exchange of water. The special pollution danger in the gulf was recognized in the 1973 International Convention for the Prevention of Pollution from Ships; the Persian Gulf and the Sea of Oman were together defined as a "special zone requiring additional precautions for the protection of the marine environment."[45]

Despite the recognition of pollution problems in the gulf, international legal regulations have proved to be insufficient. Much of the trouble lies in the general failure of the traditional principle of "flag-state responsibility," that is, the responsibility of the state in which the ship is registered. Often pollution problems and other environmental dangers do not directly threaten the flag states; there has not been sufficient motivation for them to act. In light of such inaction and perceived continuing danger, coastal states have sometimes responded with unilateral claims to special pollution control zones. These claims have been challenged as contradicting broader community policies, such as free and unimpeded navigation. In other words, what is at stake in the Persian Gulf is not only the condition of the environment, but also broader community principles, such as freedom of navigation. The vital interests of coastal states are becoming dangerously entangled with the vital interests of the international community at large because of the uncertainties of the law of the sea.

MINIMUM PUBLIC ORDER

Underlying the other community concerns in the Persian Gulf is the maintenance of a minimum public order. Minimum public order, "understood as freedom from expectations of severe deprivations by unauthorized coercion and violence,"[46] is at stake as threats of conflict accompany the changing perceptions of states' interests in the sea. Four underlying threats to minimum public order that emanate from the developing law of the sea are present in the Persian Gulf. Such threats to minimum public order include the threat of hostilities over conflicting claims to exclusive control of offshore areas and resources, the threat of conflict resulting from a destabilization of both regional and global equilibrium brought about by the limiting of international access and an altering of tactical and strategic military balances, the threat of conflict from the vulnerability of straits and other arteries through which vital strategic resources must pass, and the threat of conflict resulting from the detention of, or interference with, ships on the high seas for the purpose of exercising a functional authority over such areas as pollution control zones and fishery conservation zones.

Whether unauthorized violence and coercion will become manifest in the Persian Gulf because of these threats to minimum public order remains to be seen. What is at stake in the development of the law of the sea in the gulf is not only the freedom of transit and navigation, the enjoyment of mineral and living resources, and the gulf's environment but also the security interests of the coastal states and the security of the international community. The future direction of the law of the sea in the Persian Gulf will be determined primarily by the actions of the gulf states—developing states—as they interact with each other and with the international community. In the balance will be minimum public order in the gulf, and possibly world minimum public order, that is, world peace.

NOTES

1. The marine activities delineated here are identified in a report prepared by the Secretariat of the Third United Nations Conference on the Law of the Sea. *See* U. N., Secretariat of the Third United Nations Conference on the Law of the Sea, *Problems of Acquisition and Transfer of Marine Technology* (A/CONF.62/C.3/L.3), 25 July 1974, p. 7 (mimeographed).

2. Other uses of ocean space within the gulf, such as marine research, have generated considerable interest, but are not of major importance to the international community.

3. For a report of Ambassador Zahedi's remarks *see* "Iranian Aims a Guarantee to Stability," *Kayhan* (Tehran: Weekly International Edition), 26 April 1975.

4. The experience of the Trans-Arabian Pipeline (Tapline) illustrates such political problems. For example, the oil flow throught the Tapline was cut off on 9 February 1975; on 11 April 1975 it was announced that operations would be closed down altogether, because "it is cheaper for tankers to transport oil directly from the Gulf" and because of disagreements with Lebanon over the price of oil. The Tapline later resumed pumping "to avert an energy shortage in Lebanon," even though the use of tankers "could save as much as $2 per barrel over oil pumped through the pipeline." *See* "Tapline Closed," *Middle East Monitor*, 15 April 1975, p. 4; and "Saudi Arabia Orders Tapline to Resume Pumping," *Middle East Monitor*, 15 May 1975, p. 6.

5. *See* "Persian Gulf Pact Gaining Favor," editorial, *Kayhan* (Tehran: Weekly International Edition), 24 May 1975.

6. For a report of the news conference at Blair House, *see* "Oil Price Rise in September Likely—Monarch," *Kayhan* (Tehran: Weekly International Edition), 24 May 1975.

7. *See* "Saudi Development Plan May Total $150 Billion," *Middle East Monitor*, 15 May 1975, p. 1. For report by Saudi Port Authority *see Middle East Economic Survey* (Beirut) 22 (January 15, 1979): 9.

8. Hugo Grotius, *The Freedom of the Seas* (1608; reprint ed., New York: Arno Press, 1972), p. 7.

9. Emerich de Vattel, *Le droit des gens, ou principes de la loi naturelle appliques à la conduite et aux affaires des nations et de souverains*, trans. Charles G. Fenwick in *The Classics of International Law*, ed. James Brown

Scott (Washington, D. C.: Carnegie Institution of Washington, 1916), 3:106.

10. *See* article 2 of the Convention on the High Seas (U. N. Doc. A/CONF. .13/L.53).

11. *See* ICNT/Rev. 1, article 87.

12. A Special Committee of Jurists at the Conference for the Supervision of the International Trade in Arms and Ammunition and in Implements of War in 1925 determined that

The status of the Persian Gulf from the point of view of international law is the same as that of the open sea. The same applies to the Strait of Ormuz [Hormuz] and the Gulf of Oman.

It should be noted that the Persian delegate to the conference strongly protested the inclusion of the Persian Gulf and the Sea of Oman in a "Special Maritime Zone" because such would infringe upon the Persians' right of free navigation. *See* League of Nations, *Proceeding of the Conference for the Supervision of the International Trade in Arms and Ammunition and in Implements of War* (Geneva, 4 May-17 June 1925), A.13.1925.IX, pp. 375-81, and Appendix 14, pp. 770-71.

13. Vattel, *Le droit de gens*, p. 109.

14. *See* article 16 (4) of the Convention on the Territorial Sea and the Contiguous Zone (U. N. Doc. A/CONF.13/L.52).

15. *See* "Straits used for International Navigation," articles 34-44, part 3, ICNT/Rev. 1.

16. U. N., *Problems of Marine Technology*, p. 7.

17. Ibid.

18. *See* Richard Young, "The Law of the Sea in the Persian Gulf: Problems and Progress," in *New Directions in the Law of the Sea*, 10 vols., ed. Robin Churchill, K. R. Simmonds, and Jane Welch (Dobbs Ferry, N. Y.: Oceana, 1973), 3:235. For Persian Gulf pearling, *see* Richard LeBaron Bowen, Jr., "The Pearl Fisheries of the Persian Gulf," *Middle East Journal* 5 (Spring 1951): 161-80; and George Frederick Kunz and Charles Hugh Stevenson, *The Book of the Pearl* (New York: Century Co., 1908), pp. 85-99.

19. U. S., Department of Interior, *Summary of 1972 Oil and Gas Statistics for Onshore and Offshore Areas of 151 Countries*, by Sherwood E. Frezon, Geological Survey Professional Paper no. 885 (Washington, D. C.: Government Printing Office, 1974), p. 159. (It should be noted that although statistics are often broken down into onshore and offshore production, some fields are partly onshore and partly offshore.)

20. U. S., *Summary of 1972 Statistics for Onshore and Offshore Areas*, p. 159.

21. For a table of offshore oil fields in the Gulf and their respective discovery dates, *see International Petroleum Encyclopedia 1975* (Tulsa, Okla.: Petroleum Publishing Co., 1975), pp. 290-92.

22. For a discussion of the Gulf's offshore oil concessions and the ensuing disputes over overlapping concessions *see* Shigeru Oda, "Boundary of the Continental Shelf," 12 *Japanese Annual of International Law* 265 (1968).

23. *See* Amir Taheri, "The South—5: The Fish Myth," *Kayhan International* (Tehran), 17 May 1970.

24. *See* Eric Pace, "Iran Fighting Rising Food Deficit," *New York Times*, 21 May 1975; and "Rouhani's Dual Goal in Agricultural Strategy," *Kayhan* (Tehran: Weekly International Edition), 17 May 1975.

25. *See* Rouhollah K. Ramazani, *The Persian Gulf: Iran's Role* (Charlottesville, Va.: University Press of Virginia, 1972), p. 87, citing Ziy'e ed-din Sadrzadeh, *Sadirat-i Iran as Didgah-i Rushd-i Iqtisadi: Tajziyeh va Naqd, Mushgelat va Rah-hay-i Behboody* (Tehran, 1346 [1967 / 1968]), p. 169.

26. *See* Food and Agricultural Organization, *The Fish Resources of the Ocean*, ed. J. A. Gulland (Surrey, England: Fishing News Ltd., 1971), p. 103. It should be noted that there is a problem of determining fishing statistics for the Persian Gulf because coastal states often fish in the Gulf of Oman, the Arabian Sea, and the Indian Ocean. The same is true for the statistics of external fishing states. The Persian Gulf is often included for statistical purposes as part of the Indian Ocean. *See* Food and Agricultural Organization, *Yearbook of Fishery Statistics, 1973*, 34:15 (FAO 1/F52/34).

27. *See* table 19, "Persian Gulf," in Lewis M. Alexander, "Regionalism and the Law of the Sea: The Case of Semi-enclosed Seas," 2 *Ocean Development and International Law* 180 (1974).

28. Food and Agricultural Organization, *F.A.O. Commodity Review and Outlook 1973-1974* (Rome: Food and Agricultural Organization, 1974), p. 213 (FAO 1/C73/973-74).

29. Vattel, *Le droit de gens*, p. 107.

30. Grotius, *Freedom of the Seas*, p. 32.

31. Vattel, *Le droit de gens*, p. 105.

32. Grotius, *Freedom of the Seas*, p. 32.

33. Vattel, *Le droit de gens*, p. 107.

34. For text and history of the Truman Proclamation on the Continental Shelf, *see* Marjorie M. Whiteman, *Digest of International Law*, 15 vols. (Washington, D. C.: Government Printing Office, 1965), 4:752-64.

35. Judge Manley O. Hudson was quick to point out the "practical problem" of the offshore oil drilling in the Persian Gulf—where there is no "continental shelf." *See* U. N., *Yearbook of the International Law Commission 1950*, 1:214, 218 (A/CN.4/SER.A/1950/9Apr1957). *See also* the dis-

cussion in McDougal and Burke, *Public Order of the Oceans*, pp. 669-87.

36. *See* ICNT/Rev. 1, part II, article 62.

37. For text and history of the Truman "Fisheries" Proclamation, *see* Whiteman, *Digest*, 4:945-62.

38. *See* Convention on Fishing and Conservation of the Living Resources of the High Seas (U. N. Doc. A/CONF.13/L.54).

39. *See* ICNT/Rev. 1, part V, articles 55-75.

40. Vattel, *Le droit de gens*, pp. 107-8.

41. Ibid., p. 108.

42. *See* Robert W. Tucker, "Oil: The Issue of American Intervention," *Commentary* 59 (January 1975): 21-31. *See also* U. S., House, Committee on International Relations, *Oil Fields as Military Objectives: A Feasibility Study* (Washington, D. C.: Government Printing Office, 1975).

43. *See* "Shah's Press Interview, January 1972," in Ramazani, *The Persian Gulf: Iran's Role*, appendix E, pp. 143-48.

44. The possibility of thermal pollution and other potential problems, such as radiation leaks, could accompany the creation of nuclear power plants on the shores of the gulf.

45. *See* "International Convention for the Prevention of Pollution from Ships, 1973," 12 *International Legal Materials* 1319 (1973).

46. Myres S. McDougal and Florentino P. Feliciano, *Law and Minimum World Public Order* (New Haven, Conn.: Yale University Press, 1961), p. 261.

CHAPTER **3**

Claims to Authority
Over Offshore Areas

The purpose of the law of the sea in the Persian Gulf, as elsewhere, is to serve the interests of the international community in the use of the seas and the enjoyment of maritime resources. The interests of the international community are composed of both inclusive (community) interests that pertain to a shared usage, and exclusive (national) interests that pertain to a nonshared usage.[1] Since the international community consists of states, the inclusive interests are those of the states that realize the advantage of sharing authority over certain areas, activities, and resources with other states. On the other hand, a state may see that it is in its interest to maintain an exclusive control over certain areas, activities, and resources, rather than share control with other states. The law of the sea develops as states within the community balance their interests with those of other states, thereby establishing exclusive control for certain areas, activities, and resources and recognizing an inclusive interest for others. The changes in, or progressive development of, the law of the sea reflects the changes in community interests and expectations concerning the mix of inclusive and exclusive interests.

FACTUAL BACKGROUND

Coastal state authority over offshore areas traditionally has varied from a zone of total sovereignty in the area immediately adjacent to shore to a relative lack of authority on the high seas.[2]

Claims to exclusive coastal state authority have been recognized in international law for the zone "which washes the coast," but the precise limits and the means of determining such a zone have remained a subject of controversy. Coastal state claims to authority over offshore areas have been countered by the opposing claims of other states to be free of such coastal state authority or to assert their own authority. The development of the law of the sea and the establishment of authority over offshore areas have been the result of this ongoing process of claim and counterclaim.[3] In other words, the development of law in the international community is the result of the eventual acceptance or denial of given national claims. The process of claim and counterclaim relating to authority over offshore areas, resources, and access represents the changing law of the sea.

Iran defined its initial claim to authority over an offshore area in the Persian Gulf in July 1934.[4] In the Act relating to the Breadth of the Territorial Waters and Zone of Supervision, 19 July 1934,[5] it was declared that "the waters adjoining the Persian coast to a distance of six nautical miles from and parallel to shore" were "Persian territorial waters" and formed "part of the national property."[6] Iran, "with a view to ensuring the operation of certain law and conventions concerning the security and protection of the country and its interests for the safety of navigation," established a second zone known as the "zone of marine supervision" that extended to a distance of twelve nautical miles from shore.[7] Iran recognized the right of innocent passage in the Persian territorial waters for foreign vessels of war, including submarines navigating on the surface, "except in the case they belong to countries in a state of war, in which other regulations as pertain to neutrality would come into effect."[8] Iran also reserved the right to prohibit, for reasons of national defense or other vital interests, foreign ships from entering certain parts of their territorial waters. In such case, the prohibited areas would be called "closed zones."[9]

Saudi Arabia's decree defining Saudi authority over its immediate offshore areas was the second major legal development in the gulf. On 28 May 1949, King ibn-Saud promulgated Decree No. 6/4/5/3711,[10] which defined the Saudi territorial waters as "embracing both the inland waters and the coastal sea."[11] The Saudi territorial waters were claimed to be under the "sovereignty of the Kingdom" but "subject to the provisions of international law as to innocent passage of vessels of other nations through the coastal sea."[12] In article 5 of the decree Saudi Arabia defined its coastal sea as extending six nautical miles beyond its inland waters. In article 9 it claimed the right to exercise "maritime surveillance" relating to security, navigation, and fiscal matters in a contiguous zone extending six miles beyond the coastal sea.

In 1957, following the realization of an Israeli presence in the Gulf of Aqaba, Saudi Arabia presented an additional claim. In a four-page letter to the Secretary General of the United Nations it registered a claim to its "legal and historical rights in the Straits of Tiran and the Gulf of Aqaba."[13] In the letter Saudi Arabia claimed that the islands Tiran and Sanafir, located at the gulf entrance, were Saudi Arabian and the straits separating them "were and still are closed straits, under the sovereignty and jurisdiction of the Kingdom of Saudi Arabia."[14] Saudi Arabia, basing its claim upon the provisions of the Treaty of Constantinople of 1888, maintained that the waters of the Gulf of Aqaba, its entrance, and the straits were territorial. Since the width of the gulf entrance did not exceed nine miles, Saudi Arabia claimed that "it could not be considered an international waterway."[15]

Later in 1957 in a speech to the United Nations General Assembly the Saudi representative again spoke on the question of the Gulf of Aqaba, but with a different emphasis.[16] He referred to the Gulf of Aqaba as "as national inland waterway" and not as "territorial waters." He claimed that the Gulf of Aqaba was a "historic gulf" that fell "outside the sphere of international law."[17] He claimed further that it was "the historical route for fourteen centuries to the Holy Places in Mecca," was "an exclusively Arab route under Arab sovereignty," and was not open for international navigation.[18]

In February 1958 the king promulgated a new decree that redefined and expanded the Saudi territorial waters.[19] Decree No. 33 repealed the previous Decree No. 6/4/5/3711 of 28 May 1949. In the new decree Saudi Arabia chose to discontinue its use of the concept "territorial waters" and adopted in its place the concept "territorial sea."[20] It also claimed that its territorial sea extended seaward to a breadth of twelve nautical miles.[21] Saudi Arabia extended its contiguous zone seaward six additional miles as well. In the contiguous zone it added an additional special jurisdiction over sanitary matters to the previously claimed jurisdictions over security, navigation, and fiscal matters. Thus eight days prior to the start of the 1958 United Nations Conference on the Law of the Sea Saudi Arabia claimed a territorial sea of twelve miles and expanded its contiguous zone to eighteen miles.

Saudi Arabia and Iran both participated in the United Nations Conference on the Law of the Sea held from 24 February to 27 April 1958, but their policies remained mostly unchanged. Four conventions and an optional protocol were prepared at the conference and later came into force, but Saudi Arabia did not sign and has not acceded to any of them. Iran did sign the four conventions on 28 May 1958 but only with a number of reservations. Iran did not sign the optional protocol and did not ratify any of the four conventions.

In April 1959 Iran amended its earlier act of July 1934 and redefined its authority over its "territorial sea." Just as Saudi Arabia had done in February 1958, Iran referred to "the belt of the sea adjacent to its coast" as the "territorial sea," and not, as previously, Persian territorial waters.[22] Iran also replaced the phrase "part of national property" with the concept of "sovereignty."[23] The major change, however, was the extension of the Iranian territorial sea to twelve miles.[24]

A Second United Nations Conference on the Law of the Sea was held from 17 March to 26 May 1960 to reconsider the questions concerning the breadth of the territorial sea and fishery limits. Iran and Saudi Arabia both participated. There was no agreement at the conference on the breadth of the territorial sea nor on fishery limits. The conference had little effect on the law of the sea in the Persian Gulf.

The Third United Nations Conference on the Law of the Sea, which commenced on 3 December 1973, marked the beginning of a major transition in the law of the sea. Unlike the previous conferences, the third conference undertook to establish a comprehensive law of the sea treaty by codifying, revising, and creating acceptable rules and regulations on the law of the sea. At the time of this writing, the work of the third conference is continuing, and the policy positions on the various questions are being negotiated.

INTERNATIONAL LEGAL PERSPECTIVE

Discussion often focuses on the breadth of a state's territorial sea and contiguous zone, but from a legal perspective the degree of authority claimed and the method of determining the boundaries to such authority are also significant and must be considered. In the development of the law of the sea persisting disagreements are as important as rules and principles resulting from a clear community consensus. In this section the claims of Iran and Saudi Arabia will be examined in depth; their specific content will be determined, as well as their relationship to suggested community standards.

THE JURIDICAL STATUS OF THE TERRITORIAL SEA

Of major importance in examining the claims relating to the juridical status of the territorial sea is the controversy involving the terminology used and the degree of authority claimed. The terminology in question are the terms "territorial waters" and "territorial sea." The degree of authority in question involves the type, subject, and possible limitations on such authority.

Iran's 1934 claim was to "Persian territorial waters" parallel to shore that formed a "part of the national property together with the sea bed and subsoil thereunder and the air above."[25] Iran did recognize the right of innocent passage in these territorial waters for foreign vessels of war, including submarines navigating on the surface, unless they belonged to belligerents, in which case neutrality laws would come into effect.[26] Iran claimed the right to prohibit foreign ships from certain areas of its territorial waters called "closed zones."[27]

Similarly, Saudi Arabia defined its territorial waters and the "air space above and the soil and subsoil beneath them" as "under the sovereignty of the Kingdom, subject to the provisions of international law as to the innocent passage through the coastal sea."[28] Saudi Arabia allowed no special provisions for warships.

When Saudi Arabia redefined its claim in 1958, it adopted the use of the term "territorial sea" to replace "territorial waters." It also changed the wording of its claim by recognizing that the sovereignty over the territorial sea was "subject to the established rules of international law,"[29] rather than the previous "subject to the provisions of international law as to the innocent passage of vessels of other nations through the coastal sea."[30] Saudi Arabia omitted the provision for "innocent passage."

Iran amended its initial claim on 12 April 1959. In the new Iranian act relating to the breadth of the territorial sea, Iran replaced the phrase "part of national property" with the use of the concept "sovereignty."[31] Iran also replaced its previous use of "territorial waters" with the concept "territorial sea."[32]

The basic community policies relating to the juridical status of the territorial sea can be envisioned from the records of international conferences on the law of the sea, from conventions, and from the work of the International Law Commission and the International Court of Justice. However, in many instances there are no recognized standards, only proposed standards. Since the standards of the international community have varied with the changing circumstances, there is often no single applicable standard with universal acceptance, as illustrated by the lack of agreement at the various international conferences.

Nevertheless, these proposed standards provide a background against which the claims of states can be analyzed. What then is the relationship of Saudi and Iranian claims to recognized or proposed community standards? First, on the question of terminology, at the 1930 Hague Conference for the Codification of International Law, the Committee on Territorial Waters (Second Committee) preferred the concept "territorial sea" to "territorial waters" because of the confusion sometimes attributed to the various meanings of "territorial waters."[33] The territorial sea concept was similarly preferred by the International Law Commission and was used in the 1958 Convention on the Territorial Sea and Contiguous Zone. Thus the selection of the "territorial sea" concept by both Saudi Arabia[34] and Iran was in accord with preferred community usage.

The claim of sovereignty over the territorial sea made by Saudi Arabia and the similar claim made by Iran after an initial reference to national property coincide with the usage proposed in the Draft Convention of the 1930 Hague Conference, the work of the International Law Commission, and the 1958 Convention on the Territorial Sea and Contiguous Zone.[35] Concerning the extent of authority, the claims extending coastal state sovereignty to the air space above and the soil and subsoil beneath the territorial sea, as asserted by both Iran and Saudi Arabia, coincide with the provisions of the Second Committee's final text at the 1930 Hague Conference.[36] Similarly article 2 of the 1958 Convention on the Territorial Sea and Contiguous Zone provides that "The sovereignty of a coastal State extends to the air space over the territorial sea as well as to its bed and subsoil."

Concerning limitations on sovereignty in the territorial sea, Saudi Arabia's initial recognition of "the innocent passage of vessels of other nations through the coastal sea" paralleled the agreement on the general principle of innocent passage at the 1930 Hague Conference.[37] The Saudi position, changed later to recognize only that its sovereignty was "subject to the established rules of international law," did not preclude a recognition of the principle of innocent passage, and generally followed the trends of the 1930 Hague Conference and the 1958 Convention on the Territorial Sea and Contiguous Zone.[38] The claims of Iran and Saudi Arabia relating to the juridical status of the territorial sea were in accord, in principle, with previously proposed community standards.

THE BREADTH OF THE TERRITORIAL SEA

Community agreement on the breadth of the territorial sea has proved to be far more elusive than agreement on the juridical status of the territorial sea. A related subject of controversy has been the determination of the points from which the breadth of the territorial sea is to be measured.

The initial claim of Iran in 1934 to a breadth of six nautical miles for its territorial waters represented a dramatic departure from the three-mile limit recognized by the British, the predominant power in the gulf at the time. The initial claim of Saudi Arabia in 1949 was also to six nautical miles. In 1958, however, Saudi Arabia claimed a twelve-mile territorial sea, as did Iran in 1959.

There has been no single, universally accepted limit for the breadth of a territorial sea.[39] For the most part the three-mile limit was traditionally accepted in international law, with a number of historically based exceptions. At the 1930 Hague Conference an attempt to reach a consensus on the three-mile limit proved futile. In 1956 the final draft on the "Breadth of the Territorial Sea," as drawn up by the International Law Commission, noted that "international practice was not uniform as regards the traditional limitation of the territorial sea to three miles."[40] However, the commission did state "that international law did not justify an extension of the territorial sea beyond twelve miles."[41] At the 1958 and 1960 United Nations conferences on the law of the sea the participants were unable to reach agreement on the breadth of the territorial sea. Thus Saudi Arabia and Iran, in extending the breadth of their territorial seas to twelve miles, did not contradict any universally accepted rule. Rather they asserted their claim in an area of international law in which a community consensus had not formed.

Closely related to the question of the breadth of the territorial sea is the method by which the breadth is to be measured. Iran, in 1934, specified that its territorial waters would extend "to a distance of six nautical miles from and parallel to shore at the low-water mark."[42] It also used this method of measurement to determine the territorial seas of its islands.[43] Saudi Arabia in 1949 similarly claimed that for the area "where the shore of the mainland or an island is fully exposed to the open sea" the baseline from which the coastal sea is measured would be "the lowest low-water mark on the shore."[44] For areas having islands and shoals Saudi Arabia claimed the use of straight base lines.[45] In 1958 Decree No. 33 redefined the territorial waters, but the provisions establishing baselines remained unchanged. Iran, on the other hand, in 1959 omitted its previous reference to the low-water mark as a baseline. Instead Iran claimed that "the baseline will be determined by the Iranian Government in accordance with the established rules of International Law."[46]

There has been a general community consensus, in principle, on the use of the low-water mark as the baseline from which to measure the breadth of the territorial sea,[47] although special exceptions to the rule have been recognized. The bases of discussion drawn up for the 1930 Hague Conference recognized that "the low-water line along the entire coast was the appropriate baseline except where particular configurations required deviations from the main coastline."[48] In 1951 the International Court of Justice in the Anglo-Norwegian Fisheries Case recognized the use of straight baselines in special circumstances. In 1956 the International Law Commission found that "according to the international law in force, the extent of the territorial sea is measured either from the low-water line along the coast,. . . from straight baselines independent of the low-water mark."[49] Article 3 of the 1958 Convention on the Territorial Sea and Contiguous Zone provides that "the normal baseline along the coast is marked on large-scale charts officially recognized by the coastal state."[50]

nized by the coastal state."[50]

The use of the low-water mark by Iran and Saudi Arabia has thus been in general agreement with the usage accepted by the international community, including provisions for exceptions that were also recognized. Although Iran did replace its preference for the low-water mark, it did so with a broad generality that did not in itself contradict any established community standard.[51]

THE BOUNDARY BETWEEN INTERNAL WATERS AND THE TERRITORIAL SEA

The exceptions to the use of the low-water mark generally pertain to straight baselines.[52] Straight baselines are used to delimit the boundary between internal waters and the territorial sea for such irregular coastal features as bays, ports, islands, and archipelagoes. The geographical features of the Persian Gulf are such that Iran and Saudi Arabia have each made specific claims to the use of straight baselines. The general use of straight baselines has been a subject of controversy, and special problems have arisen concerning islands and island groups.

First, on the use of straight baselines with bays, in 1934 Iran claimed that

the breadth of [its] territorial waters outside a bay shall be measured from a straight line drawn across the opening of the bay; where the opening of a bay exceeds ten miles, such line shall be drawn across the bay, in the part nearest to the entrance, at the first point where the opening does not exceed ten miles.[53]

Saudi Arabia in 1949 claimed that "where a bay confronts the open sea, lines drawn from the headland to headland across the mouth of the bay" would be the baselines.[54] In the 1958 decree it did not change the previous claim. Nor, in 1959, did Iran amend its previous reference to straight baselines for bays.

The international community's approach to the use of straight baselines for bays has changed through time, as have the claims to the breadth of the territorial sea. At the 1930 Hague Conference Subcommittee II formulated the following rule for bays:

In the case of bays the coasts of which belong to a single state, the belt of territorial waters shall be measured from a straight line drawn across the opening of the bay. If the opening of the bay is more than ten miles wide, the line shall be drawn at the nearest point to the entrance at which the opening does not exceed ten miles.[55]

This was essentially the same rule included in the 1934 Iranian act. The Saudi claim was more general and did not specify a maximum length for a straight baseline to be used for a bay.

In the 1958 Convention on the Territorial Sea and Contiguous Zone the maximum length of a bay's opening for the purpose of drawing a straight baseline was extended to twenty-four miles. The general provisions of the 1959 Iranian act provided only that the baseline be determined "in accordance with the established rules of International Law." Iran's 1959 act provides for the changing community consensus on the acceptable size of bays, as did Saudi Arabia's general claim. Thus Iran and Saudi Arabia were both in agreement with the previous and changed community standards pertaining to the use of straight baselines for bays.

Concerning ports, in 1934 Iran claimed that "outside a port the territorial waters shall be measured from a line drawn between the fixed installations of the port furthest to seaward."[56] Saudi Arabia similarly claimed in 1949, and reiterated in 1958, that "where a port or harbor confronts the open sea," the baselines would be "the lines drawn along the seaward side of the outermost works of the port or harbor and between such works."[57] These positions coincided with the Report of the Second Committee of the 1930 Hague Conference, which provided that "in determining the breadth of the territorial sea, in front of ports the outermost permanent harbour works shall be regarded as forming part of the coast."[58] This same provision was included in article 8 of the 1958 Convention on the Territorial Sea and Contiguous Zone, which regarded the outermost permanent harbor works as forming part of the coast.

The question of the use of straight baselines to delimit the boundary between the internal waters and the territorial sea for islands and archipelagoes has proved to be much more complex and controversial. The controversy generally involves questions pertaining to island territorial seas, the status of shoals, the use of straight baselines to link islands with the coast and into groups, and the status of the areas of water enclosed within the straight baselines between the islands. In the Persian Gulf, Iran and Saudi Arabia have each claimed the use of straight baselines for islands and island groups. Saudi Arabia has also made specific claims pertaining to shoals. In the initial Iranian claim the use of straight baselines was implicit. Iran claimed that each island had its own territorial waters and that "islands comprising an archipelago shall be deemed to form a single island," with the "breadth of the territorial waters measured from the islands remotest from the center of the archipelago."[59]

The initial Saudi claim, on the other hand, was explicit and detailed. In article 6 of Decree No. 6/4/5/3711 Saudi Arabia claimed the following as the baselines from which its territorial sea was to be measured:

(e) where an island is not more than twelve nautical miles from the mainland, lines drawn from the mainland and along the outer shores of the islands;

(f) where there is an island group which may be connected by lines not more than twelve nautical miles long, of which the island nearest to the mainland is not more than twelve nautical miles from the mainland, lines drawn from the mainland and along the outer shores of all the islands of the group if the islands form a chain, or along the outer shores of the outermost islands of the group if the islands do not form a chain;

(g) where there is an island group which may be connected by lines not more than twelve nautical miles long, of which the island nearest to the mainland is more than twelve nautical miles from the mainland, lines drawn along the outer shores of all the islands of the group if the islands form a chain, or along the outer shores of the outermost islands of the group if the islands do not form a chain.[60]

In 1958 Saudi Arabia repeated its previous claim pertaining to the use of straight baselines with islands even though it had expanded its territorial sea claim to twelve miles.[61] In 1959 Iran modified the wording of its earlier claim by asserting that

every island belonging to Iran, whether it is within or beyond the Iranian territorial sea, has its own territorial sea according to this law. Islands separated from each other by the distance of less than twelve maritime miles are considered as one single island and the baselines of its territorial sea measure from the islands which are farthest from the center of the archipelago.[62]

In so doing, Iran did recognize a limit of twelve miles for individual straight baselines between islands.

On the question of the status of the water within the baselines, Saudi Arabia defined as inland waters

the waters between the mainland and a Saudi Arabian island not more than twelve nautical miles from the mainland, and the waters between Saudi Arabian islands not farther apart than twelve nautical miles.[63]

Saudi Arabia also claimed that "any area of high sea wholly surrounded by the territorial sea and extending not more than twelve nautical miles in any direction" formed "part of the territorial sea."[64] Any "pronounced pocket of high sea" that could be wholly enclosed by drawing a single straight line not more than twelve nautical miles long would also be considered a part of the territorial sea.[65]

Compared to the Saudi claim, Iran's 1959 claim is more general, and does not provide for the existence of a status of "territorial sea" for any enclosed area. Iran's claim is as follows:

The waters between the Iranian coast and the baseline, as well as the waters between islands belonging to Iran, whose distance from each other does not exceed twelve maritime miles, are considered as internal water of the country.[66]

The international community's approach to the status of offshore areas adjacent to islands and island groups is not clearly defined.

It is generally accepted that each island has its own territorial sea, but the use of straight baselines to connect islands into groups and with points on shore remains open to question. The Report of the Second Committee at the 1930 Hague Conference recognized that "every island has its own territorial sea."[67] That an island has its own territorial sea was also recognized in article 10 of the 1958 Convention on the Territorial Sea and Contiguous Zone. However, controversy over the breadth of such territorial seas has remained and has affected the status of island groups and the status of offshore areas within such groups. The preparatory committee for the 1930 Hague Conference suggested that

in the case of a group of islands which belong to a single State and at the circumference of the group are not separated from one another by more than twice the breadth of territorial waters, the belt of territorial waters shall be measured from the outermost islands of the group. Waters included within the group shall also be territorial waters.

The same rule shall apply as regards islands which lie at a distance from the mainland not greater than twice the breadth of the territorial waters.[68]

Despite the recommendation of the preparatory committee, agreement on the question of archipelagoes was not reached at the conference. The International Law Commission in 1956 was also unable to arrive at any consensus on archipelagoes because of the disagreement over the breadth of island territorial seas and the lack of technical data on the various island groups.[69]

Among the problems associated with archipelagoes are the questions of the length of baselines and the status of enclosed waters. Proposals were initiated at the 1930 Hague Conference to limit the length of baselines that could be used to connect islands into groups and with points on shore, but such proposals did not receive general acceptance. There has also been considerable disagreement over whether enclosed waters can be considered territorial or inland. Many have favored the prescription of territorial because of the potential threat to international navigation in channels between islands arising from the claim to inland waters. These points in question were all previously subjects of consideration at the 1930 Hague Conference. As Sir Humphrey Waldock pointed out,

Unquestionably, there was a marked tendency in 1930 to favor the intro-
duction of a special rule for archipelagoes, whether coastal or ocean, but
subject to a limit of width (10 miles) between the islands and with a strong
reservation by some states against waters being treated as *inland waters*.[70]

Thus it appears that the claims of Iran and Saudi Arabia to the
use of straight baselines to delimit island groups and connect islands
with points on shore are not without precedent. However, these
claims are in a highly controversial area of law in which no clearly
defined community standard has emerged.[71]

On the question of shoals, it is generally recognized that "shoals
which are wholly or partly within the territorial sea, as measured
from the mainland or an island, may be taken as points of departure
for measuring the extension of the territorial sea."[72] This provision
was included in article 11 of the 1958 Convention on the Territorial
Sea and is in accord with the previous Saudi claim pertaining to
shoals.

THE BOUNDARY BETWEEN PROXIMATE STATES

Associated with the delimitation of the territorial seas are claims
to delimit the boundary between adjacent and opposite states. The
claims to delimit such boundaries usually are general and vulnerable
to the problems of interpretation and application. The Saudi and
Iranian claims are both general but vary slightly in substance.

Saudi Arabia in article 8 of its Decree No. 6/4/5/3711 provided
that if its inland waters or coastal sea "should be overlapped by the
waters of another State, boundaries will be determined by Saudi
Arabia in agreement with the State concerned in accordance with
equitable principles." It reiterated the claim in Decree No. 33 in
1958, only with the use of "territorial sea" in the place of "coastal
sea."[73]

Iran, on the other hand, after including no specific provision for
overlapping waters in its 1934 claim, in 1959 called for the use of
the median line to determine the boundary between the Iranian
territorial sea and that of the adjacent or opposite states, except
where there was an agreement to the contrary. Article 4 of the Iranian

act of 12 April 1959 provides the following:

Where Iranian coasts are adjacent or opposite to the coast of another State, in the absence of agreement to the contrary, the boundary of the Iranian territorial sea and that State is the median line, every point of which is equidistant from the nearest points on the baselines of the other State.

While Saudi Arabia maintains that the boundary line must be the result of an agreement that is in accord with equitable principles, Iran maintains that if there is no agreement, the boundary line will be the median line. Saudi Arabia's claim to determine the boundary in accordance with equitable principles does not exclude a median line but does offer the possibility for other considerations in order to reach a political accomodation. Iran, on the other hand, does not eschew the possibility of such an agreement but specifies that the median line would be the boundary in the absence of any special agreement. The drawing of a median line itself would have to be the subject of agreement because of the possible baselines from which median lines could be demarcated. Given the controversy over the width of territorial seas and the choice of baselines, the drawing of a median line to delimit the boundary between proximate states is no simple task.

The international community has generally recognized a rule of equidistance and the drawing of median lines for delimiting the territorial seas of proximate states but has also recognized the existence of special circumstances.[74] Article 12 of the Convention on the Territorial Sea and Contiguous Zone provides the following:

Where the coasts of two States are opposite or adjacent to each other, neither of the two States is entitled, failing agreement between them to the contrary, to extend its territorial sea beyond the median line every point of which is equidistant from the nearest point on the baselines.

These provisions remained intact in article 15 of the ICNT/Rev. 1.

In light of the technical difficulties associated with determining the median line of the territorial sea, the claims of Iran and Saudi Arabia are not in conflict with the broad provisions proposed by the international community. Moreover, both the claims of Iran and Saudi Arabia provide for the possibility of negotiation.

SPECIAL JURISDICTION IN OCEAN AREAS ADJACENT TO THE TERRI-
TORIAL SEA

While the territorial sea has been the primary area of coastal
state jurisdiction, jurisdictional claims to areas beyond the territorial
sea have been a subject of legal concern. Coastal states have traditionally exercised a limited or functional authority in the area contiguous to the territorial sea.

In 1934 Iran claimed the establishment of a "zone of marine
supervision" extending twelve nautical miles from the shore in which
Iran would exercise a right of supervision "with a view to ensuring
the operation of certain laws and conventions concerning the security
and protection of the country and its interests, or the safety of navigation."[75] Saudi Arabia in article 9 of Decree No. 6/4/5/3711 claimed
the following:

With a view to securing compliance with the laws of the Kingdom relating
to security, navigation, and fiscal matters, maritime surveillance may be
exercised in a contiguous zone outside the coastal sea, extending for a distance of six nautical miles and measured from the baselines of the coastal
sea, provided however that nothing in this Article shall be deemed to apply
to the rights of the Kingdom with respect to fishing.

In 1958 Saudi Arabia restated its contiguous zone claim and included "sanitary matters" as subject to its jurisdiction.[76] In restating
the claim it retained the provision that the contiguous zone extended
beyond the territorial sea "a further distance of six nautical miles."
This, with the extension of the territorial sea to twelve miles, had
the effect of extending the contiguous zone to eighteen miles.[77] The
1959 Iranian act did not amend the previous provisions for its "zone
of marine supervision."

The international community has generally recognized the existence
of contiguous zones, but the breadth of such zones and the types of
jurisdiction exercised within such zones have been subjects of controversy. It was proposed in the Bases of Discussion of the 1930
Hague Conference that

on the high seas, adjacent to its territorial waters, the coastal State may exercise the control necessary to prevent, within its territory or territorial waters, the infringement of its customs or sanitary regulations or interference with its security by foreign ships.[78]

A limit of twelve miles was proposed in the bases of discussion for the exercise of such control.[79] However, the second committee was unable to reach agreement on the contiguous zone at the conference.[80]

In 1958 a slightly different proposal for contiguous zones was accepted. Article 24 of the Convention on the Territorial Sea and Contiguous Zone provided the following:

1. In a zone of the high seas contiguous to its territorial sea, a coastal State may exercise the control necessary to:
    a. Prevent infringement of its customs, fiscal, immigration or sanitary regulations within its territory or territorial sea;
    b. Punish infringement of the above regulations committed within its territory or territorial sea.
2. The contiguous zone may not extend beyond twelve miles from the baseline from which the breadth of the territorial sea is measured.

In 1958, as in the earlier 1956 draft text of the International Law Commission, there was no provision for the exercise of control for security interests. The commentary for the International Law Commission's draft text in 1956 indicated that special security rights were not recognized because of the vagueness of the term "security" and because security interests could be dealt with according to "the general principles of international law and the Charter of the United Nations."[81] While diverging from the proposal of the Preparatory Committee of the 1930 Hague Conference on the question of security, the 1958 convention included the previously proposed limitation of twelve miles for the contiguous zone.

Iran and Saudi Arabia both included navigation interests in their claims to jurisdiction in the areas adjacent to their territorial seas. These were not specifically mentioned in the proposals of the international community. However, the provisions of Iran and Saudi Arabia for "security" were previously put forth at the 1930 Hague Conference. While Saudi Arabia added a provision for the inclusion of "sanitary matters" under its contiguous zone supervision in 1958, Iran did not amend its previous claim. Iran's 1934 claim could be interpreted broadly because it provided for a "right of supervision" for matters involving "its interests."[82] On the question of breadth, Iran's claim to a zone of marine supervision extending to a distance of twelve nautical miles and the initial Saudi claim both were in accord with the twelve-mile limit proposed at the 1930 Hague Conference. However, the 1958 Saudi claim to "six miles beyond its territorial sea" exceeded the twelve-mile limit generally accepted by the international community, and is representative of the interrelated problem of the breadth of the territorial sea.

PERSIAN GULF CONTEXT

While a legal analysis of given national claims is concerned with the relationship of the claims to the prevailing community standards, a contextual analysis provides a broader perspective in which to view the individual claims. A legal analysis often does not provide an insight into the timing of national claims, the determinants of national policies in areas for which no community consensus exists, or the reasons that some national claims do not coincide with accepted community policies. By examining specific claims according to the context in which they are made, the underlying interests and principles upon which they are based can be generally determined, and an insight into the general nature of legal development can be achieved.[83]

IRAN: ACT OF 19 JULY 1934, RELATING TO THE BREADTH OF THE TERRITORIAL WATERS AND ZONE OF SUPERVISION

The Iranian act of 19 July 1934 represented Iran's first claim to authority over offshore areas under modern international law. When this Iranian claim is placed in the Persian Gulf context, certain provisions can be explained in terms of Iranian national interests and motivations. First, present throughout Iran's initial claim is an interest in security; as reflected in the claim to six-mile Persian territorial waters, a twelve-mile zone of maritime supervision, and the right to establish "closed zones" in which foreign warships would be prohibited. This 1934 claim reflects Iran's special concern for maintaining neutrality and its desire to avoid becoming entangled in foreign rivalries. The act responded to the ongoing rivalry of Britain, the Soviet Union, and Germany at the time.

Second, in terms of the physical characteristics of the Persian Gulf, two particular Iranian concerns stand out: the concern over islands and archipelagoes and the concern over navigation in the zone of maritime supervision. Iran's archipelago claims and its use of straight baselines reflect its interests in the islands that make up the irregular configuration of Iran's coastline. Similarly, Iran's claim to a right of supervision in the zone of maritime supervision reflects its interest in ensuring navigational freedom in vital shipping lanes.

Third, when viewed in historical perspective, the Iranian claim also illustrates a broader nationalistic concern. Under Reza Shah, Iran, playing on the fact that the British government favored a strong Iranian state in the Persian Gulf at the time,[84] consciously pursued a policy that asserted Iran's independence. Thus Iran's claim to a six-mile breadth for its territorial waters not only fit Iran's concern for neutrality but also its assertion of nationalism in its relationship with Britain.

Moreover, Iran was very aware of its position vis-à-vis the European powers during the interwar period and was especially displeased with the condescending treatment it received at the 1925 Conference for the Supervision of the International Trade in Arms and Ammunition and in Implements of War. The inclusion of the Persian Gulf and the Sea of Oman in a "Special Maritime Zone," in which Persian vessels could be stopped and searched, was totally unacceptable to Iran. Iran's 1934 claim to a twelve-mile zone of marine supervision in the Persian Gulf reflects not only the language of the 1925 arms-traffic conference, but also the assertion of Iranian nationalism and national interests in response to the positions assumed at the conference.[85]

The relative timing of the 1934 Iranian claim can be interpreted, in part, as a reaction to the 1925 conference, as a reflection of an Iranian move toward autonomy in the early 1930s, and as a definition of Iran's law of the sea claims following the failure of the 1930 Hague Conference to reach an agreement on the law of the sea.

SAUDI ARABIA: DECREE NO. 6 / 4 / 5 / 3711 DEFINING THE TERRITORIAL
WATERS OF THE KINGDOM, 28 MAY 1949

A number of insights can be drawn from the context in which
the initial Saudi claim was made. These contribute not only to the
identification of the interests and principles upon which the claim
was based but also the the understanding of relative timing of the
claim and of the nature of legal development.

It is important to note that the Saudi claim was prepared by Judge
Manley O. Hudson and Richard Young, American international
legal experts from Harvard Law School, acting in a private capacity.[86]
Following Aramco's offshore concession of 10 October 1948, the
company wished to proceed with its offshore oil exploration and
exploitation. The company requested from the Saudi government
the nature of the limits of their jurisdiction. Since the limits had not
been defined, Saudi Arabia sought the assistance of Judge Hudson
at the recommendation of Aramco. Saudi Arabia was primarily
interested in establishing a claim to the submerged lands off its
coast for the purpose of oil exploitation, but Hudson and Young
advised the government to clarify its offshore legal situation and
proposed a definition of the territorial waters, a claim to the seabed
and subsoil beyond the territorial waters, and claims to certain
offshore islands.[87]

The nature of the Persian Gulf context is evident in the provisions
adopted by Saudi Arabia as recommended by Hudson and Young.
First, Saudi Arabia's claim to a six-mile coastal sea and an additional six-mile contiguous zone was directed toward a general
Saudi interest in security. However, such a claim was the result
of legal advice rather than a response to a specific security concern.
As Young indicated,[88] the six-mile limit was recommended for
Saudi Arabia because of regional practice. He pointed to the action
of the Sublime Porte of the Ottoman Empire in 1914 and to the
Iranian claim to a six-mile limit in 1934 as the guiding factors for
such a regional claim of six miles.[89]

The Saudi provisions for the use of straight baselines to delimit
its coastal sea off its islands, archipelagoes, and shoals reflect the
geographic irregularities of the Saudi coastline. The straight baseline method of delimitation, similar to that previously established
by Iran, represented a means of delimitation applicable to the physical

irregularities of the Persian Gulf.[90] The straight baseline method of delimitation in the 1949 Saudi claim preceded the findings of the International Court of Justice in the Anglo-Norwegian Fisheries Case, which did provide that straight baselines would be acceptable under certain conditions. However, the Saudi straight baseline method of delimitation was, in fact, based on Norwegian legislation establishing straight baselines.[91]

The relative timing of the Saudi Decree No. 6/4/5/3711 must be viewed in relation to both the proposals by Hudson and Young and the desire of Saudi Arabia to define its claim to the seabed and subsoil adjacent to its coast—a claim embodied in the Royal Pronouncement concerning the Policy of the Kingdom of Saudi Arabia with Respect to the Subsoil and Sea Bed of Areas in the Persian Gulf contiguous to the coasts of the Kingdom of Saudi Arabia.[92] In fact, the decree represented a prerequisite for the delimitation of national jurisdiction over the seabed and subsoil of areas beyond the territorial waters. Saudi Arabia acted to define its claim to offshore jurisdiction in order for the offshore drilling to proceed in a sound legal environment. Thus the Saudi 1949 claim defining its territorial waters was not the result of immediate security interests but was indirectly brought about by economic motivations and a desire to provide for offshore oil exploitation.

SAUDI ARABIA: DECREE NO. 33 DEFINING THE TERRITORIAL WATERS OF THE KINGDOM, 16 FEBRUARY 1958

While the initial Saudi offshore claim defined the nature and limits of Saudi territorial waters, Decree No. 33 of 16 February 1958 redefined the claim with two significant changes. First was the extension of its territorial sea to twelve miles and the resulting extension of its contiguous zone to eighteen miles. Second was the omission of the specific reference to "innocent passage."

Both changes were closely related to the realization of an Israeli presence in the Gulf of Aqaba in 1957 and the relative position of Saudi Arabia in the Arab-Israeli conflict. Saudi Arabia moved to clarify its offshore claims in the Strait of Tiran and the Gulf of Aqaba in a letter to the Secretary of the United Nations in 1957 in which it protested to the Security Council that Israeli warships were violating its territorial waters in the Gulf of Aqaba and that the presence of those warships represented a grave threat to Saudi security.[93]

One contentious point was the question of the "right of innocent passage" through territorial waters. A problem of conflicting legal interpretation emerged because of the Saudi provision for the "innocent passage of vessels of other nations" and the question of the nature of the state of belligerency between the Arabs and the Israelis.

In October 1957 the Saudi position shifted; it claimed that the Gulf of Aqaba was a "national inland waterway," a historic gulf that was an exclusively Arab pilgrimage route under Arab sovereignty and not open to international navigation.[94] Saudi Arabia maintained that "the matter could not be decided exclusively on judicial grounds" since it was "of the highest order pertaining to pilgrimage and other national political considerations."[95] Accordingly King Saud, as Keeper of the Holy Places, was "not prepared to expose to question any matter touching upon the Holy shrines and the free passage of pilgrims to Mecca."[96]

Subsequently, because of the Israeli presence in the Gulf of Aqaba, Saudi Arabia moved to redefine its claim to offshore authority in the interest of increasing its security. It therefore extended its territorial sea to twelve miles and omitted the troublesome provision permitting innocent passage through its territorial waters.

The timing of Decree No. 33 was also significant in that it took place eight days prior to the start of the 1958 United Nations Conference on the Law of the Sea.[97] The timing enabled Saudi Arabia to pursue a negotiating position at the conference based on the expanded limit.

One additional security consideration of Saudi Arabia related to the Saudi expansion of its territorial sea was the desire to avoid involvement in a possible East-West conflict. Although Saudi Arabia was anti-Communist, it eschewed alliances and pursued a nonaligned foreign policy. It was thought that an extension of a territorial sea to twelve miles would contribute to noninvolvement in the East-West rivalry. This position was posited at the 1960 United Nations Conference on the Law of the Sea. Thus the Saudi Decree No. 33 was closely tied to Saudi offshore security interests in the Persian

Gulf and in the Gulf of Aqaba as influenced by, *inter alia*, the Arab-Israeli conflict and the East-West rivalry.

IRAN: ACT OF 12 APRIL 1959 AMENDING ACT RELATING TO THE
BREADTH OF THE TERRITORIAL SEA AND CONTIGUOUS ZONE OF IRAN
DATED 19 JULY 1934

The Iranian act of 12 April 1959 amended rather than repealed its previous claim to authority in offshore areas. The major change in the new Iranian claim, apart from its legal terminology, was the extension of the Iranian territorial sea to twelve miles. The Iranian national interests leading to this expanded claim can be derived from the underlying political rivalries present in the Persian Gulf.

Following the 1958 Iraqi coup, Iran became extremely concerned with the potential threat of a radical Iraq on its border. Iraq, at the beginning of 1959, came to represent not only a hostile Arab state and a state with which Iran had numerous disputes but also an ideological challenge and an opening for the Soviet Union. Ramazani has indicated that "the single most important event in the 1950s that focused Iran's attention on the Persian Gulf was the Iraqi revolution of 1958."[98] Iran's growing concern with the implications of the 1958 Iraqi revolution was sharpened by the presence of Soviet ships in the Persian Gulf.[99] Moreover, in remarks at a news conference in early 1959 concerning the disputed Shatt al-Arab, Iraq's President Qasim suggested that a disputed strip of five kilometers of the Shatt al-Arab that had been previously granted to Iran should be restored "to our [Iraqi] motherland."[100] The Iranian foreign minister responded to the Iraqi claim in a statement to the Majlis and cited the "unfriendly actions against Iran."[101] Two days after his remarks appeared in *Ittila'a Hava'i* (10 April 1959) Iran extended its territorial sea to twelve nautical miles in its act of 12 April 1959. The new Iranian claim, made for obvious security reasons, presaged the forthcoming Shatt al-Arab crisis.

The Iranian claim to a twelve-mile territorial sea followed the Saudi twelve-mile claim of 16 February 1958 and the failure of the 1958 United Nations Conference on the Law of the Sea to agree to a limit for territorial seas. Nevertheless, it was closely tied to the Persian Gulf context and the national interests of Iran.

CONCLUSIONS

From the foregoing examination of the trends in the development of the law of the sea in the Persian Gulf, as represented by the claims to authority over offshore areas, the following observations may be made.

First, the two Persian Gulf states, Iran and Saudi Arabia, generally based their claims on previously established international law. Their claims were made in accord with accepted international practices and principles as expressed in various international forums, such as the 1930 Hague Conference, the International Law Commission, and the United Nations Conference on the Law of the Sea. In this way Iran and Saudi Arabia have viewed the established international law as given—a restraint on what actions or claims could be made. As the law of the sea became more sophisticated and as accepted usages for general terms crystallized, Iran and Saudi Arabia each amended their claims to reflect the community preference. This is clearly illustrated by the adoption of the term "territorial sea" in the place of the previously used "territorial waters" and "coastal sea."

Second, in areas of the law of the sea in which there was no clear community consensus, Iran and Saudi Arabia based their respective claims on the international legal principles and rules suggested in international forums that best satisfied their national interests in the Persian Gulf context. In other words, they each used international law as an instrument through which they could assert their own national interests as determined by the Persian Gulf context with its political rivalries and geographic peculiarities. For example, the lack of community agreement on the limit for the territorial sea led to the definition of the Iranian and Saudi territorial seas at six nautical miles and then to their extension to twelve miles. The lack of community consensus on the status of offshore islands and archipelagoes led to the claims of Iran and Saudi Arabia to use the straight baseline method of delimitation.

In the claims of Iran and Saudi Arabia provisions were also made to deal with potential conflicts deriving from interpretation and application and to establish a basis for accommodation based on "equitable principles" and "general principles of international law."

In this way, the law of the sea claims represent both an instrument and a restraint.

NOTES

1. For a detailed explanation of "inclusive and "exclusive" claims to the uses of the seas, *see* Myres S. McDougal and William T. Burke, *The Public Order of the Oceans* (New Haven, Conn.: Yale University Press, 1963) pp. 1-2; n. 1.

2. This chapter is basically concerned with claims to authority over the territorial sea and contiguous zone. Claims to authority over offshore areas for the purposes of resource jurisdiction and environmental control will be examined as claims to authority over offshore resources and claims to regulate international access, respectively, in chapters four and five.

3. *See* McDougal and Burke, *The Public Order of the Oceans,* p.29.

4. The Sublime Porte of the Ottoman Empire had earlier defined its territorial waters in the Persian Gulf as extending to a distance of six miles. *See* "Circulaire Note Verbale of 1er Octobre 1914," in G. FR. de Martens, *Nouveau Recueil General des traites et autres actes retatifs aux rapports de droit international,* 47 vols., ed. Heinrich Triepel (Leipzig: Librairie Theodor Weicher, 1920) 10:701-2.

5. For text, *see* U. N., *Law and Regulations on the Regime of the Territorial Sea,* United Nations Legislative Series (ST/LEG/SER.B/6), pp. 24-25. Although this first Iranian claim to offshore jurisdiction preceded World War II, it is included because it remained in effect after the war, and set the stage for the postwar claims.

6. *See* article 1 of the act of 19 July 1934, relating to the Breadth of the Territorial Waters and Zone of Supervision.

7. Ibid.

8. Ibid., article 4.

9. Ibid., article 6.

10. For text, *see* 43 *Supplement to the American Journal of International Law* 154 (1949).

11. Decree No. 6/4/5/3711, article 3.

12. Decree No. 6/4/5/3711, article 2.

13. U. N., *Letter dated April 12, 1957, from the Permanent Representative of Saudi Arabia to the United Nations, addressed to the Secretary General,* A/3575.

14. Ibid.

15. Ibid.

16. *See* U. N. General Assembly, 9th Session, 2 October 1957, *Official Records*, p. 233 (A/PV 697).

17. Ibid.

18. Ibid.

19. *See* Decree No. 33 defining the Territorial Waters of the Kingdom, 16 February 1958, in *Supplement to Laws and Regulations on the Regime of the High Seas and Concerning the Nationality of Ships*, United Nations Legislative Series (ST/LEG/SER.B/Suppl.), pp. 29-30.

20. "Territorial waters" traditionally included both inland waters and the coastal sea. "Territorial sea" assumed the meaning of "coastal sea."

21. Decree No. 33, article 4.

22. *See* Act of 12 April 1959, Amending Act relating to the Breadth of the Territorial Sea and Contiguous Zone of Iran dated 19 July 1934, in U. N., *Second United Nations Conference on the Law of the Sea* (A/CONF. 19/5), p. 15.

23. Ibid.

24. Iran also amended its earlier claim concerning the "method of measurement" of the territorial sea and the use of "straight baselines."

25. Act of 19 July 1934, article 1.

26. Ibid., article 4.

27. Ibid., article 6.

28. *See* Decree No. 6/4/5/3711, article 2.

29. *See* Decree No. 33, article 2.

30. *See* Decree No. 6/4/5/3711, article 2.

31. *See* Act of 12 April 1959, article 1.

32. Ibid.

33. *See* League of Nations, *Final Act, Conference for the Codification of International Law, The Hague, March-April 1930*, p. 183. *See also* the discussion of the juridical status of the territorial sea in Marjorie M. Whiteman, *Digest of International Law*, 15 vols. (Washington, D. C.: Government Printing Office, 1965), 4:1-13.

34. The Saudi representative to the 1958 United Nations Conference on the Law of the Sea suggested that the adoption of the territorial sea concept "would not only remove confusion, but also prevent abuses such as had arisen in complaints lodged with the Security Council, in which the term 'territorial waters' was used as meaning exclusively inland waters." *See* U. N., *United Nations Conference on the Law of the Sea* (A/CONF.13/39), 3: 35.

35. *See* Whiteman, *Digest*, 4:1-3.

36. For a discussion of air space, seabed, and subsoil, *see* ibid., pp. 7-13.

37. Although there was no convention agreed upon at the 1930 Hague Conference, Whiteman notes that "no disagreement was voiced concerning

the recognition of the general principles of the right of innocent passage." Ibid., p. 348.

38. For example, article 1, paragraph 2 of the Convention on the Territorial Sea and Contiguous Zone states: "This sovereignty is exercised subject to the provisions of these articles and to other rules of international law."

39. For a review of the territorial sea and its theoretical and historical foundations, *see* Sayre A. Swarztrauber, *The Three-Mile Limit of the Territorial Sea* (Annapolis, Md.: Naval Institue Press, 1972).

40. U. N., *Yearbook of the International Law Commission* 1956, 2: 265-66 (A/CN.4/SER.A/1956/Add.1).

41. Ibid.

42. *See* Act of 19 July 1934, relating to the Breadth of the Territorial Waters and Zone of Supervision, article 1.

43. Ibid., article 3.

44. *See* Decree No. 6/4/5/3711, article 6 (a).

45. Ibid., article 6 (e-g).

46. Act of 12 April 1959, article 3.

47. For a discussion of the low-water mark and its use, *see* McDougal and Burke, *The Public Order of the Oceans*, pp. 319-27.

48. Ibid., p. 323.

49. *See* Whiteman, *Digest*, 4:140.

50. While there is agreement, in principle, on the use of the low-water mark, the technical applications of such a principle are often difficult. For example, the low-water mark might be considered to be "the mean low-water spring tide," "the line of low tide at spring tide," or "the line of low water," or "the lowest water mark." For a discussion of such technical aspects, *see* Whiteman, *Digest*, 4:141.

51. On the related question of the delimitation of the continental shelf, Iran in its reservation to article 6 of the Convention on the Continental Shelf maintained that "one method of determining the boundary line in special circumstances would be that of measurement from the high-water mark."

52. The distinction between normal baselines and straight baselines, as pointed out by Whiteman, is "the former are land baselines and the latter are water baselines." *See* Whiteman, *Digest*, 4:139.

53. *See* Act of 19 July 1934, relating to the Breadth of the Territorial Waters and Zone of Supervision, article 2.

54. Decree No. 6/4/5/3711, article 6 (b).

55. *See* Whiteman, *Digest*, 4:219.

56. *See* Act of 19 July 1934, relating to the Breadth of the Territorial Waters and Zone of Supervision, article 1.

57. *See* Decree 6/4/5/3711, article 6 (d); and Decree No. 33, article 5 (d).

58. For discussion *see* Whiteman, *Digest*, 4:261-63.

59. *See* Act of 19 July 1934, relating to the Breadth of the Territorial Waters and Zone of Supervision, article 3.

60. Decree No. 6/4/5/3711, article 6 (e-g).

61. *See* Decree No. 33, article 5 (e-g).

62. Act of 12 April 1959, article 5.

63. *See* Decree No. 6/4/5/3711, article 4 (c-d); and Decree No. 33, article 3 (c-d).

64. *See* Decree No. 6/4/5/3711, article 7; and Decree No. 33, article 6.

65. Ibid.

66. *See* Act of 12 April 1959, article 6.

67. *See* discussion in Whiteman, *Digest*, 4:293-94.

68. League of Nations, *Bases of Discussion, No. 13*, C.74.M39.1929.V., p. 51. *See also,* Whiteman, *Digest*, 4:289-90.

69. *See* Whiteman, *Digest*, 4:295, 299-303.

70. Sir Humphrey Waldock, "The Anglo-Norwegian Fisheries Case," 28 *British Yearbook of International Law* 144 (1951).

71. The use of straight baselines was recognized by the International Court of Justice for special circumstances in their findings in the Anglo-Norwegian Fisheries Case, but the application of such a principle to disparate island groups near shore remains problematic.

72. Whiteman, *Digest*, 4:304-7.

73. *See* Decree No. 33, article 7.

74. The two most common exceptions to the rule of equidistance are navigable channels located predominately on one side of the median and "historical waters." For a discussion of delimitation between adjacent and opposite states, *see* Whiteman, *Digest*, 4:323-36.

75. Act of 19 July 1934, relating to the Breadth of the Territorial Waters and Zone of Supervision, article 1.

76. *See* Decree No. 33, article 8.

77. Ibid.

78. League of Nations, *Bases of Discussion, No. 5,* C.351(b).M.145 (b).130.V., p. 179.

79. Ibid.

80. Concerning the type of jurisdiction exercised in the contiguous zone, "fiscal" matters were included under "customs" at the conference. *See* Whiteman, *Digest*, 4:487.

81. Ibid., 483.

82. Act of 19 July 1934, relating to the Breadth of the Territorial Waters and Zone of Supervision, article 1.

83. While the relationship of any claim or national action to its context can be taken to the extreme, what is sought here is to demonstrate the nature of the relationship of context to legal development in order to shed light upon the approaches of developing states to the changing law of the sea.

84. For Iran's foreign policy concerns as they relate to Britain during this period, *see* Rouhollah K. Ramazani, *The Foreign Policy of Iran: 1500-1941: A Developing Nation in World Affairs* (Charlottesville, Va.: University Press of Virginia, 1966), pp. 242-57.

85. Iran (Persia) abruptly withdrew from the conference prior to its adjournment. For the text of the Convention on Supervision of International Trade in Arms and Ammunition and in Implements of War signed at Geneva on 17 June 1925, *see* Manley O. Hudson, ed., *International Legislation*, 9 vols. (Washington, D. C.: Carnegie Endowment for International Peace, 1931), 3: 1634-38.

86. Richard Young indicated that each of them had to register in the United States as foreign agents because they were, in their professional capacity, working for Saudi Arabia. Richard Young, private interview, Washington, D. C., 23 April 1976.

87. Ibid.

88. Ibid.

89. Ibid.

90. The United States reacted to the Saudi decree in a note to the Saudi Government on 19 December 1949, in which it protested the extension of the coastal sea to six miles and the use of straight baselines. For the text of the note, *see* Charles B. Selak, Jr., "Recent Developments in the High Seas Fisheries Jurisdiction under the Presidential Proclamation of 1945," 44 *American Journal of International Law* 675 (1950).

91. Young indicated that he and Hudson had been closely following the developments of the Anglo-Norwegian Fisheries Case, and had used the Norwegian legislation as a model for the Saudi provisions on straight baselines. Richard Young, private interview, Washington, D. C., 23 April 1976.

92. For text, *see* 43 *Supplement to the American Journal of International Law* 156 (1949).

93. For the Saudi protests, *see* U. N., *Letters from the Representative of Saudi Arabia to the President of the Security Council, dated May 7 and 27; June 5, 19, and 24; July 2 and 10, 1957* (S/3825, S/3833, S/3841, S/3843, S/3846, and S/3849.) For an Israeli denial of the allegations, *see* U. N., *Letter dated June 10, 1957 from the Representative of Israel to the President of the Security Council* (S/3838).

94. U. N. General Assembly, 9th Session, 2 October 1957, *Official Records*, p. 233 (A/PV 697).

95. Ibid.

96. Ibid.

97. For an in-depth examination of the Saudi role at the 1958 and 1960 United Nations conferences on the law of the sea and the relationship of the Arab-Israeli question to the Saudi approach to the law of the sea *see* chapter six.

98. Rouhollah K. Ramazani, *Iran's Foreign Policy, 1941-1973: A Study of Foreign Policy in Modernizing Nations* (Charlottesville: University Press of Virginia, 1975), p. 399.

99. For a discussion of Iran's focusing on the gulf after the Iraqi revolution, *see* ibid., pp. 399-427.

100. *See* translation of remarks quoted in *Ittila'at Hava'i*, 10 April 1959, in Ramazani, *Iran's Foreign Policy*, p. 402.

101. Ibid.

CHAPTER 4

Claims to Authority
Over Offshore Resources

The claims to authority over offshore resources are examined in this chapter as they concern those areas in the Persian Gulf extending beyond the territorial sea.[1] Legal development pertaining to resource control generally consists of those national actions defining a state's claim to authority over the resources of the seabed and subsoil, on the one hand, and to authority over fishery resources on the other. In so far as claims to authority over offshore resources are often countered by conflicting claims of other states, the process of claim and counterclaim prevails, a process that includes acts manifesting acquiescence, objection, and compromise. In addition to the national claims to authority over offshore resources there are treaties and agreements that demarcate resource boundaries, namely, the boundaries of the continental shelf. These treaties and agreements, together with the national claims, make up a significant part of the developing law of the sea.

FACTUAL BACKGROUND

Iran and Saudi Arabia have each defined claims to offshore resources by specific national actions. These claims have been clarified by continental shelf treaties,[2] which have served to delimit areas of the Persian Gulf according to resource jurisdiction.

The initial claim to authority over offshore resources in the Persian Gulf was made by Saudi Arabia on 28 May 1949 in the form of the

Royal Pronouncement claimed that "the subsoil and sea bed of those Saudi Arabia with Respect to the Subsoil and the Sea Bed of Areas in the Persian Gulf contiguous to the Coasts of the Kingdom of Saudi Arabia.[3] On 19 May 1949 Iran had submitted to the Majlis a bill defining its claim to Persian Gulf subsea resources but did not enact its continental shelf claim into law until 1955.[4] The Saudi royal pronouncement claimed that "the subsoil and sea bed of those areas of the Persian Gulf seaward from the coastal sea" but contiguous to its coasts "appertain to the Kingdom of Saudi Arabia" and are "subject to its jurisdiction and control." Saudi Arabia provided that the "character as high seas" of such offshore areas would remain unchanged and that submarine boundaries would be based upon "equitable principles."

On 19 June 1955 Iran claimed that "the areas and natural resources of the seabed and subsoil" extending from the Iranian coast and the Iranian islands to the limits of the continental shelf "belong to" and "are under the sovereignty of the Government of Iran."[5] It provided that the law would "in no way affect the regime of the waters of the continental shelf with respect to the right of freedom of navigation" and that the borders of the Iranian continental shelf with those of adjoining states would be determined "in conformity with the rules of equity."[6] In its 1955 claim Iran defined its continental shelf in the Persian Gulf and the Gulf of Oman, but the 1949 Saudi claim was limited to the Persian Gulf.

The first delimitation of submarine boundaries between two states in the Persian Gulf was set forth in the Saudi Arabia-Bahrain Continental Shelf Boundary Agreement of 22 February 1958.[7] This agreement represented the first of many bilateral treaties demarcating continental shelf areas in the oil-rich Persian Gulf. Saudi Arabia signed an "Agreement on Marine Boundaries" with Qatar on 27 June 1965,[8] and a similar agreement concerning sovereignty over Al-Arabiyah and Farsi islands and the delimitation of boundary line separating submarine areas with Iran on 24 October 1968.[9] On 7 July 1965 Saudi Arabia signed an agreement with Kuwait on the partition of the Neutral Zone that included provisions relating to offshore resources.[10]

Just prior to the agreement establishing the submarine boundary between Iran and Saudi Arabia, Saudi Arabia defined its claim to submerged lands in the Red Sea. In Royal Decree No. M-27 of 7 September 1968, it claimed ownership of "all Hydrocarbon materials and minerals existing in the strata of the seabed" in the "zone extending in the Red Sea bed adjacent to the Saudi continental shelf."[11] Saudi Arabia recognized "similar rights" for neighboring governments and suggested the possibility of "sharing" with the neighboring governments resources in "common zones."[12] It indicated that the application of such regulations relating to the ownership of Red Sea resources would not affect "the description of the high seas or obstruct navigation therein."[13]

Following the Iran-Saudi Arabia submarine boundary agreement, Iran moved to demarcate its continental shelf boundaries with other proximate states. It signed a continental shelf boundary agreement with Qatar on 20 September 1969,[14] with Bahrain on 17 June 1971,[15] and with Oman on 25 July 1974.[16] Iran signed a continental shelf boundary agreement with Dubai on 31 August 1974, but some question remains about the status of the agreement in the United Arab Emirates.[17] Earlier, on 7 September 1971, Iran had initialed an agreement on the continental shelf with Abu Dhabi, but the agreement did not enter into force.[18] Shortly thereafter, in November 1971, special arrangements that included provisions on offshore resources were made between Iran and Sharjah in a "Memorandum of Understanding" on the status of Abu Musa.[19] This memorandum was subsequently challenged by Sharjah; its application and interpretation are disputed. Iran had also reached an agreement with Kuwait on the delimitation of the continental shelf on 13 January 1968, but the agreement was never finalized because of a worsening of relations between the two countries.[20]

Thus Saudi Arabia and Iran have each delineated continental shelf boundaries with most of their neighbors in the Persian Gulf.[21] However, submarine boundaries for several areas remain disputed and undemarcated.

Closely associated with the continental shelf claims and the continental shelf boundary agreements are the nascent claims to exclusive fishing zones in the Persian Gulf. In the Proclamation of 30 October 1973 Iran claimed an exclusive fishery zone in the waters superjacent to its continental shelf in the Persian Gulf and extending to a distance of fifty nautical miles in the Sea of Oman.[22] Saudi Arabia made a similar proclamation on 30 April 1974.[23]

INTERNATIONAL LEGAL PERSPECTIVE

Resource claims and treaties are commonly associated with the limits and boundaries of resource jurisdiction, but from a legal perspective it is also necessary to distinguish between the nature of the authority claimed and the principles upon which the claims and treaties are based. Here the resource claims of Iran and Saudi Arabia, as well as their respective treaties relating to resource jurisdictions, are examined with a view to determining their legal content and their relationship to the standards and practices of the international community.

THE JURIDICAL STATUS OF THE SEABED AND SUBSOIL

The pattern of controversy associated with claims to the seabed and subsoil generally involves the theory of jurisdiction upon which a claim is based, the terminology used, and the degree of authority claimed. The theory of jurisdiction and the terminology in question are primarily concerned with the developing legal status of the continental shelf.

In its initial claim, the Royal Pronouncement of 28 May 1949, Saudi Arabia did not make any reference to the continental shelf concept. Instead, Saudi Arabia, "aware of the need for the greater utilization of the world's natural resources" and of "the desirability of giving encouragement to the efforts to discover and make available such resources," "appreciating that recognized jurisdiction over such resources is required in the interest of their conservation and prudent utilization," and "deeming that the exercise of jurisdiction over such resources by the contiguous nation is reasonable and just," declared that

the subsoil and sea bed of those areas of the Persian Gulf seaward from the coastal sea of Saudi Arabia but contiguous to its coasts . . . appertain to the Kingdom of Saudi Arabia . . . [and are] subject to its jurisdiction and control.[24]

Since the Persian Gulf has no continental shelf, technically speaking, but is a relatively shallow basin with an average depth of about 40 meters and a maximum depth of about 100 meters, Saudi Arabia based its claim on the principle of contiguity. Although not precisely defined, this principle is clearly expressed in the premise that "the exercise of jurisdiction over such resources by the contiguous nation is reasonable and just."[25] Saudi Arabia indicated that the jurisdiction exercised by "various other nations" over "the subsoil and sea bed in areas contiguous to their coasts" was a consideration but did not use "continental shelf" as other states did in their claims.

In its subsequent claim to "resources" in the Red Sea, Saudi Arabia claimed ownership for resources "in the strata of the seabed in the zone extending in the Red Sea bed adjacent to the Saudi continental shelf."[26] Here Saudi Arabia used the concept of contiguity in the form "adjacent to the shelf."[27]

Unlike Saudi Arabia, Iran based its claim to the resources of the seabed and subsoil on the continental shelf concept. In the 1949 bill relating to subsea resources—which was approved by the Council of Ministers but not by the Majlis—Iran claimed that "the natural resources existing at the bottom of the sea and under the bottom of the sea up to the limits of the continental shelf on the Iranian coasts in the Persian Gulf and Oman Sea belong to [the] Iranian Government."[28] In the law of 19 June 1955 Iran claimed that

the area and the natural resources of the seabed and the subsoil thereof to the limits of the continental shelf . . . in the Persian Gulf and the Gulf of Oman, belong to the Iranian Government and are under the sovereignty of the Government of Iran.[29]

In this 1955 claim Iran provided that the term *"falat gharreh"* would have the same meaning as the English term "continental shelf" and the French term *"plateau continental."*[30]

The Iranian claim clearly is based upon the continental shelf concept. Since the 1949 bill indicated in its opening paragraph that the Iranian claim was prepared "in view of international regulations passed recently on the subject of natural resources," Iran apparently adopted its use of the continental shelf concept from the earlier claims of other states.

It appears that the claims of Iran and Saudi Arabia to the resources of the seabed and subsoil in the Persian Gulf were both based on prior claims of other states. Iran, however, chose to employ the concept of "continental shelf"; Saudi Arabia avoided the use of the term and emphasized the concept of "contiguity." In order to determine the relationship of these Persian Gulf claims to international community standards, it is necessary to consider the earlier claims upon which the gulf claims were based and the prevailing community standards.

At the end of World War II the international community had not yet seriously considered questions relating to subsea resources.[31] Therefore, the Truman Proclamation on the Continental Shelf of 28 September 1945[32] represented not only a significant legal precedent, but also a landmark in the development of international law relating to the enjoyment of the resources of the subsoil and seabed of the continental shelf.[33] In the Truman Proclamation the United States said that it was aware of "the long-range worldwide need for new sources of petroleum and other minerals" and the need to encourage "efforts to discover and make available new supplies of these resources." It further recognized that "jurisdiction over these resources is required in the interest of their conservation and prudent utilization" and that "the exercise of jurisdiction over the the natural resources of the subsoil and sea bed of the continental shelf by the contiguous nation is reasonable and just." On these grounds, the United States proclaimed that

the Government of the United States regards the natural resources of the subsoil and seabed of the continental shelf beneath the high seas but contiguous to the coasts of the United States as appertaining to the United States, subject to its jurisdiction and control.[34]

Accompanying the Truman proclamation was a White House press release that defined the continental shelf. The press release indicated that the "generally, submerged land which is contiguous to the continent and which is covered by no more than 100 fathoms (600 feet) of water is considered as the continental shelf."[35]

By comparing the provisions of the Truman Proclamation on the Continental Shelf with those of the Saudi Royal Pronouncement of

28 May 1949, it is clear that the Saudi claim was based on the Truman Proclamation and in many instances even used the precise wording.[36] However, a most obvious difference between the two claims does exist in the Saudi avoidance of the use of the term "continental shelf,"[37] which reflects the adaptation of the United States claim to the Persian Gulf situation.[38] The fact that Saudi Arabia emphasized the concept of "contiguity" instead of "continental shelf" did not represent a contravention of an international standard but rather affected the actual community approach toward the continental shelf concept. This can be seen in the International Law Commission's consideration of the doctrine of the continental shelf.

In the commission's initial consideration of the continental shelf concept, special attention was given to the Persian Gulf. Manley O. Hudson was quick to remark that the matter of the continental shelf "was one of great importance," and that "the continental shelf was not only a legal or juridical concept but was also of economic and social significance."[39] Hudson "felt that lawyers had no right to prevent the exploitation of those resources (as exist in the subsoil of the Persian Gulf) for the benefit of mankind."[40] Noting the non-existence of a shelf in the Persian Gulf and the social considerations involved, Hudson suggested that the commission "should consider in what way it could adapt the rules of international law to the requirements of humanity."[41] When the International Law Commission considered the first question of the report on the high seas[42] that pertained to the continental shelf—"Should recognition of special rights as regards the working of the marine subsoil and the protection of marine resources be limited with the presence of the continental shelf?"—Hudson immediately brought up the "practical problem" of the Persian Gulf.[43] In light of this "practical consideration," the commission adopted the criterion of "exploitability," rather than that of a strict physical configuration, in its consideration of the continental shelf as a legal concept. The concept was thus broadened to include such areas as the Persian Gulf. In its report to the General Assembly in July 1950 the commission indicated that

a littoral State could exercise control and jurisdiction over the sea-bed and subsoil of the submarine areas situated outside its territorial waters with a view to exploring and exploiting the natural resources there. The area over which such a right of control and jurisdiction might be exercised should be limited; but, where the depth of the waters permitted exploitation, it should not necessarily depend on the existence of a continental shelf. The commission considered that it would be unjust to countries having no continental shelf if the granting of the right in question were made dependent on the existence of such a shelf.[44]

The initial interpretation of the International Law Commission was apparent in the 1958 Convention on the Continental Shelf.[45] In article 1 of the Convention the term "continental shelf" was used to refer

(a) to the seabed and subsoil of the submarine areas adjacent to the coast but outside the area of the territorial sea, to a depth of 200 meters or, beyond that limit, to where the depth of the superjacent water admits of the exploitation of the natural resources of the said areas;
(b) to the seabed and subsoil of similar submarine areas adjacent to the coasts of islands.

The use of the term "continental shelf" in the 1949 Iranian bill had been subject to criticism even though based on the Truman Proclamation. When the Law of 19 June 1955 came into existence, however, the term "continental shelf" had already assumed a broader meaning and was clearly applicable to the Persian Gulf. Iran's 1955 claim was, therefore, in accord with prevailing community standards.

In addition to the theory of jurisdiction upon which the Iranian and Saudi claims were based there is the question of the degree of authority claimed. In its Royal Pronouncement of 28 May 1949 Saudi Arabia claimed jurisdiction and control over those "areas" of the subsoil and seabed contiguous to its coasts rather than over the "resources" of such areas (as was claimed in the Truman Proclamation).[46] However, this appears to be a question of semantics and is not especially significant in itself because of the clearly stated premises relating to "the exercise of jurisdiction over such resources."[47] Moreover, as was pointed out by Barry B. L. Auguste, the United States practice has been to recognize American jurisdiction over the shelf as well as over its resources.[48] Also to be noted is the Saudi provision that indicated the following:

The character as high seas of the waters of such areas, the right to the free and unimpeded navigation of such waters and the air space above those waters, fishing rights in such waters, and the traditional freedom of pearling by the peoples of the Gulf, are in no way affected.[49]

This resembled, in part, a similar disclaimer in the Truman Proclamation that "the character of the high seas of the waters above the continental shelf and the right to free and unimpeded navigation are in no way affected." Saudi Arabia likewise indicated in its Red Sea claim that the application of the regulations relating to its ownership of Red Sea resources "shall not affect the description of the high seas or obstruct navigation therein."[50]

In its Law of 19 June 1955, Iran claimed that "the area and the natural resources of the seabed and subsoil . . . belong to Iran."[51] This claim generally followed the precedent set by the United States and Saudi Arabia. Iran also provides that the 1955 law "shall in no way affect the regime of waters of the continental shelf with respect to the right of freedom of navigation and arrangements concerning submarine cables."[52]

The practice of the international community generally followed the precedent set by the Truman Proclamation. When a community consensus on the continental shelf eventually emerged in the form of the 1958 Convention on the Continental Shelf, the provisions pertaining to the degree of authority exercised by the coastal state were in general agreement with the previous claims of Saudi Arabia and Iran.[53] For example, article 2 of the convention provides that "the coastal state exercises over the continental shelf sovereign rights for the purpose of exploring it and exploiting its natural resources."Article 3 also provides that "the rights of the coastal state over the continental shelf do not affect the legal status of the superjacent waters as high seas, or that of the airspace above those waters."

THE DELIMITATION OF RESOURCE BOUNDARIES

Perhaps the most significant feature of claims to authority over offshore resources is the provision that concerns the delimitation of boundaries. The delimitation of resource boundaries and the allocation of offshore resources represent a focal point for defining offshore claims and for resolving conflicting claims. Of importance from a legal perspective are the principles upon which delimitations are based and the specific applications of such principles leading to demarcated submarine boundaries and fixed resource allocations.

Because of the presence of offshore petroleum deposits in the Persian Gulf, the delimitation of offshore resource boundaries has been extremely important to Saudi Arabia and Iran. Saudi Arabia, in its Royal Pronouncment of 28 May 1949, provided that the boundaries of the subsoil and seabed contiguous to its coasts would be "determined in accordance with equitable principles" by the Saudi Government "in agreement with other States having jurisdiction and control over the subsoil and sea bed of adjoining areas."[54] In its Red Sea claim Saudi Arabia did not specify provisions for the delimitation of offshore boundaries but did anticipate a "sharing with neighboring governments" of resources in "common zones."[55]

Iran, in its bill of 19 May 1949, proposed that

should the continental shelf of Iran extend to the coasts of another country or be common with another adjacent country, the limits of the interested countries will be fixed equitably between the interested governments with respect to the natural resources of the continental shelf.[56]

In its Law of 19 June 1955, Iran similarly indicated that

where the continental shelf . . . extends to the coast of another or coincides with that of a neighboring country, and if disputes arise concerning the limits of Iran's continental shelf, such disputes shall be settled in conformity with the rules of equity.[57]

Iran went on to call for "the settlement of any [such] dispute through diplomatic channels."[58] Iran's claim was similar to that of Saudi Arabia in that each was sufficiently general[59] in its respective provisions that the boundaries in question would be established on the bases of the rules of equity and in accordance with equitable principles. Both also indicated that the boundaries would be determined through agreements. Saudi Arabia explicitly indicated that boundaries would be determined "by Saudi Arabia in agreement with other States."[60] Iran was more implicit in suggesting that Iran would "take the necessary steps for the settlement of any [continental shelf] disputes through diplomatic channels."[61] Thus, although neither state limited its negotiating position, both recognized the importance of pursuing an *equitable* agreement.

Although the Saudi and Iranian claims containing provisions relating to the delimitation of resource boundaries were made in the absence of any clearly defined community standard, they were preceded by the widely accepted Truman Proclamation. In that proclamation the United States provided for the resource boundaries by claiming that

in cases where the continental shelf extends to the shores of another State, or is shared with an adjacent State, the boundary shall be determined by the United States and the State concerned in accordance with equitable principles.

Although the Truman Proclamation provided for boundaries to be determined on the basis of "equitable principles," this did not indicate a specific method of delimitation, since "equitable principles" represent general principles of law that might be applied in a number of different ways. Nevertheless, the wording used in the Truman Proclamation represented a clear precedent for the Saudi and Iranian claims, however different the application of such general principles might be.

In 1953 the International Law Commission failed to adopt this provision for "equitable principles" in general and emphasized the more specific concept of "equidistance" and the use of a "median line."[62] However, it did note the possibility of an agreement, and that "special circumstances" could justify a boundary line other than a median line or a line determined by the "application of the principle of equidistance." Since the International Law Commission's 1953 "Draft Articles on the Continental Shelf" preceded the 1955 Iranian claim, it is significant that the Iranian claim did not adopt the Commission's recommendations but rather emphasized the importance of the "rules of equity."

The agreements relating to the delimitation of resource boundaries not only represent an application of the principles set forth in national claims but also provide a clarification of the principles. An important part of the international legal development in the Persian Gulf has been the result of these agreements delimiting offshore resource boundaries—continental shelf boundaries. Especially important from a legal perspective is the use of "equitable principles" in these agreements.[63]

Saudi Arabia-Bahrain Agreement of 22 February 1958

The Saudi Arabia-Bahrain Agreement of 22 February 1958[64] was the first delimitation of submarine areas between two states in the Persian Gulf (see Map 3). The agreement provided for the establishment of a central boundary line to delimit the submarine areas of the two countries and also delimited a hexagonal area to be under Saudi jurisdiction, with revenue received from the exploitation of petroleum resources in the area to be shared equally by Saudi Arabia and Bahrain.

The first article of the agreement provided for a "boundary line between the Kingdom of Saudi Arabia and the Government of Bahrain to be established on the basis of the median line."[65] However, the boundary line only approximated a median line in that it was based on "predetermined landmarks" and did not strictly follow the configuration of the coast nor give consideration to certain small islands.[66] In particular, the agreement did not provide for territorial seas for the islands of Lubaynah al-Saghirah and Lubaynah al-Kabirah, which represented points on the boundary line.

The Fasht Bu Saafa Hexagon was demarcated in the second article, where it was recognized that

the oil resources in the area mentioned and delimited above in the part belonging to the Kingdom of Saudi Arabia [Fasht bu Saafa Hexagon] shall be developed in the manner which His Majesty [King of Saudi Arabia]

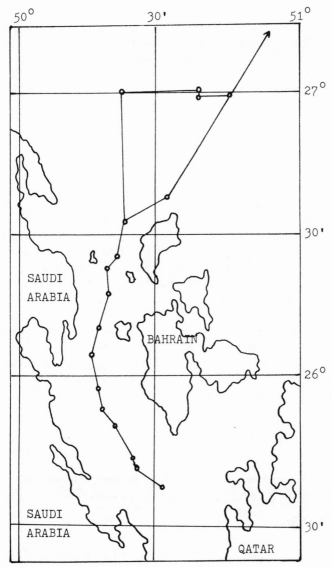

Map 3. Saudi Arabia-Bahrain offshore boundary. *Adapted by Mrs. G. H. MacDonald from* Limits in the Seas, no. 12 (Department of State).

may choose, on condition that he give the Government of Bahrain half of
that which pertains to the Saudi Arabian Government of the net income
derived from this development. It is understood that this shall not impair
the right of sovereignty and administration of the Saudi-Arabian Government in the above-mentioned area.

Thus the Saudi Arabian-Bahrain Agreement was based, in part, on
a median line and the principle of equidistance but was also based
on a sharing of the revenues arising from the exploitation of oil
resources of a specified area.

Saudi Arabia-Kuwait Agreement of 7 July 1965

The Saudi Arabia-Kuwait Agreement of 7 July 1965 was made
for the purpose of partitioning the Neutral Zone but included provisions on offshore resources. The agreement provided for each
state to annex an equal part of the Neutral Zone but with joint
ownership of the mineral rights for the entire zone remaining un-
affected. Concerning the delimitation of offshore areas, article 7
provided for each state to consider the waters adjoining the part
of the Partitioned Zone annexed to its territory to be its territorial
waters, except that "for the purposes of exploiting the natural resources in the Partitioned Zone, not more than six marine miles of
the sea-bed and subsoil adjoining the Partitioned Zone shall be
annexed to the mainland of the Partitioned Zone." Furthermore, in
article 8 it is provided that

the two Contracting Parties shall exercise their equal rights in the submerged area beyond the aforesaid six-mile limit mentioned in the preceding
article by means of joint exploitation, unless the two Parties agree otherwise.

Thus between Saudi Arabia and Kuwait "equitable principles" provided for the joint exploitation of the given area.

Saudi Arabia-Iran Agreement of 24 October 1968

Perhaps the most significant agreement regarding boundaries
in the Persian Gulf, which also established the longest such boundary
in the Persian Gulf, is the Saudi Arabia-Iran Agreement of 24 October
1968 (*see* Map 4). This "Agreement concerning the Sovereignty over
Al-Arabiyah and Farsi Islands and Delimitation of Boundary Line
separating Submarine Areas between the Kingdom of Saudi Arabia
and Iran," which followed years of negotiation, not only established

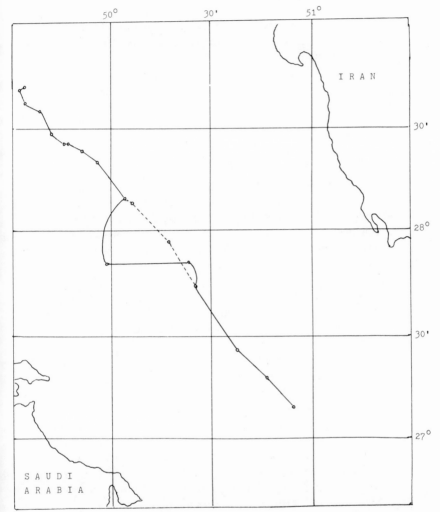

Map 4. Saudi Arabia-Iran offshore boundary. *Adapted by Mrs. G. H. MacDonald from* Limits in the Seas, *no. 24 (Department of State).*

a submarine boundary between Saudi Arabia and Iran,[67] but also resolved conflicting claims to al-Arabiyah and Farsi islands and conflicting offshore oil concessions.

The final boundary, as decided upon in the agreement, is divided into three main segments. The first, the southern segment, extends from the Saudi-Bahrain offshore boundary[68] and consists essentially of a median line between the opposite coasts. The central segment of the boundary involves the islands of al-Arabiyah and Farsi. Saudi sovereignty is recognized over al-Arabiyah, Iranian sovereignty over Farsi. A twelve-mile territorial sea is recognized for both. Where the respective territorial seas overlap, an equidistant boundary line is drawn. Thus the boundary extends upward from the southern segment until it meets the boundary of the territorial sea of al-Arabiyah and follows it until it meets the median line drawn between the two islands. The boundary continues on this median line until it reaches the boundary of the territorial sea of Farsi; it then follows that boundary clockwise until it reaches a point approximately equidistant from the two mainlands again.[69] The northern segment of the boundary continues slightly irregularly until it intersects the de facto offshore boundary between Saudi Arabia and the Neutral Zone.

The northern segment of the boundary was the most difficult to delimit. Its delimitation represents an excellent example of the extent to which "equitable principles" could be carried and reflects the multiplicity of factors involved. The first problem involved the presence of Kharg Island. Saudi Arabia wanted a median line established between the two mainlands. Iran wanted a median line measured from Kharg Island. A compromise was reached in 1965 by establishing a boundary line equidistant from the two proposed medians, thus giving half-effect to Kharg Island. However, the compromise fell through when Iran learned that the oil discovered by the Iranian concessionaire was mostly on the Saudi side of the boundary.[70] When a final agreement was eventually reached, it was based on an adjustment of the boundary line in the northern segment to divide the known deposits equitably.

The Saudi Arabia-Iran Agreement of 24 October 1968 not only represented a broad application of "equitable principles" with the boundary line being based in part, on the principle of equidistance and the median line but also stressed the importance of what is at stake in such submarine boundary agreements: the natural resources. In order to determine offshore resource boundaries on the basis of "equitable principles," these resources must be taken into consideration.[71]

Iran-Qatar Agreement of 20 September 1969

Following Iran's agreement with Saudi Arabia on a submarine boundary, Iran moved to delimit its offshore resource boundaries with other Persian Gulf states (*see* Map 5). These Iranian boundaries, unlike the Iran-Saudi boundary, are termed "continental shelf boundaries."

The first such boundary agreement following the Saudi Arabia-Iran Agreement was the Iran-Qatar Agreement of 20 September 1969. In this the continental shelf is demarcated "in accordance with international law and the law of sovereignty in a just, equitable, and exact manner."[72] The boundary is generally based on the principle of equidistance. But, a number of small islands are disregarded,[73] and the northern terminal point is not demarcated. (It remains indefinite, pending the delimitation of the Qatar-Bahrain offshore boundary.)

Iran-Bahrain Agreement of 17 June 1971

The Iran-Bahrain Agreement of 17 June 1971 recognized a desire to establish "in a just, equitable, and precise manner" the continental shelf boundary between the two states.[74] The boundary, so established, consists of straight lines connecting four points (*see* Map 6). The two end points were determined from other agreements; the two middle points are based on the principle of equidistance. In the agreement it appears that full effect is given to the islands of Nakhilu and Jabrin on the Iranian side but not to the island of Muharraq on the Bahraini side,[75] which apparently was not considered a part of the mainland for delimitation purposes. Although the agreement is generally based on the principle of equidistance, its application remains subject to interpretation.

Iran-Sharjah "Memorandum of Understanding" of November 1971

The "Memorandum of Understanding," which recognizes that

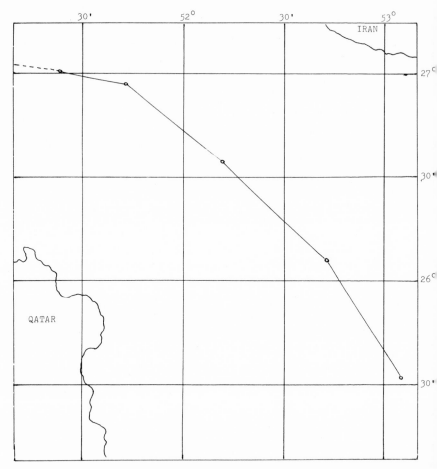

Map 5. Iran-Qatar offshore boundary. *Adapted by Mrs. G. H. MacDonald from* Limits in the Seas, *no. 25 (Department of State).*

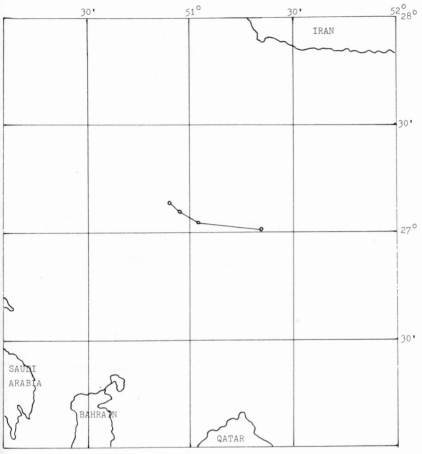

Map 6. Iran-Bahrain offshore boundary. *Adapted by Mrs. G. H. MacDonald from* Limits in the Seas, *no. 58 (Department of State).*

"neither Iran nor Sharjah will give up its claim to Abu Musa nor recognize the other's claim," provides for Iranian "full jurisdiction" in given areas of Abu Musa and "full jurisdiction" for Sharjah in others, but it also provides for a "joint sharing" of revenues arising from the exploitation of Abu Musa's resources. Article 4 indicates the following:

Exploitation of petroleum resources of Abu Musa and of the seabed and subsoil beneath its territorial sea will be conducted by Buttes Gas and Oil Company under the existing agreement which must be acceptable to Iran. Half of the government oil revenues hereafter attributable to the said exploitation shall be paid directly by the Company to Iran and half to Sharjah.[76]

The memorandum provides for a single company, the Buttes Gas and Oil Company, to exploit the resources, with the revenues arising therefrom to be divided equally between the two states.

Iran-Oman Agreement of 25 July 1974

The Iran-Oman Agreement of 25 July 1974 was based on the desire of Iran and Oman to establish "in a just, equitable, and precise manner the boundary line between respective areas of the continental shelf"[77] (see Map 7). As in earlier arrangements the two terminal points are not delimited, pending the delimitation of other offshore boundaries. In this case, the boundaries to be delimited are the boundaries between Oman and Ras al-Khaimah, and Oman and Sharjah. The Iran-Oman boundary, for the most part, is determined by points that are equidistant from each coast, except that some turning points are not equidistant.[78]

Iran-Dubai Agreement of 31 August 1974

The Iran-Dubai Agreement of 31 August 1974 was based on the desire for the continental shelf boundary to be established "in a just, equitable and precise manner," as were earlier agreements[79] (see Map 8). The boundary, as delimited, consists of straight lines connecting five fixed points, showing that boundaries can be delimited through agreement even in geographically irregular and politically disputed areas. Although the application of the principle of equidistance cannot be readily determined because of questions relating to the effect given to the various offshore islands, especially to such

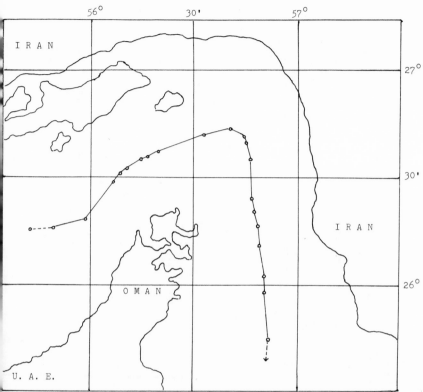

Map 7. Iran-Oman offshore boundary. *Adapted by Mrs. G. H. MacDonald from* Limits in the Seas, *no. 67 (Department of State).*

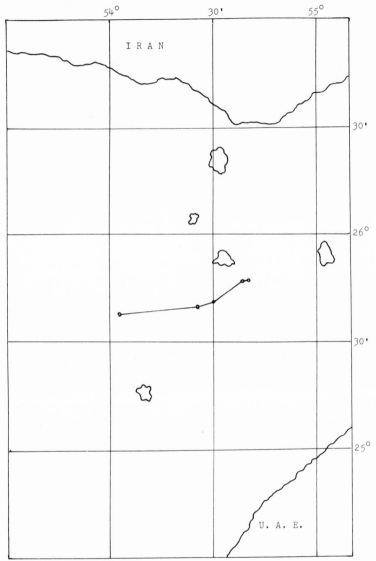

Map 8. Iran-Dubai offshore boundary. *Adapted by Mrs. G. H. MacDonald from* Limits in the Seas, *no. 63 (Department of State).*

disputed islands as Abu Musa, the importance of negotiation and decision is dramatically underlined.[80]

When these various continental shelf boundary agreements of the Persian Gulf are considered as they relate to the application of "equitable principles," it is apparent that the principle of equidistance and median lines were important considerations. However, also of major importance were the equitable distributions of the resources of the submarine areas. Such equitable distributions were accomplished by joint exploitation of given resource areas, by joint sharing of the revenues arising from the exploitation of resources in given areas, and by adjusting the boundary line to divide equally known resources in place. "Equitable principles" also were applied in a climate of compromise to the geographic irregularities, thus granting partial effect to certain islands.

Whereas the numerous continental shelf boundary agreements in the Persian Gulf represent the growth of conventional international law and a clarification of the "equitable principles" upon which they were based, it is important to determine their relationship to the prevailing community standards pertaining to continental shelf delimitation. In this regard, two developments are especially important. First is the 1958 Convention on the Continental Shelf; second is the judgment of the International Court of Justice in the North Sea Continental Shelf Cases.

Article 6 of the 1958 Convention on the Continental Shelf gives the following provisions pertaining to the delimitation of continental shelf boundaries:

1. Where the same continental shelf is adjacent to the territories of two or more States whose coasts are opposite each other, the boundary of the continental shelf appertaining to such States shall be determined by agreement between them. In the absence of agreement, and unless another boundary line is justified by special circumstances, the boundary is the median line, every point of which is equidistant from the nearest points of the baselines from which the breadth of the territorial sea of each State is measured.
2. Where the same continental shelf is adjacent to the territories of two adjacent States, the boundary of the continental shelf shall be determined by agreement between them. In the absence of agreement, and unless another boundary line is justified by special circumstances, the boundary shall be determined by application of the principle of equidistance from the

nearest points of the baselines from which the breadth of the territorial sea of each State is measured.

The way in which the article is written emphasizes the use of the median line and the principle of equidistance: the "special circumstances" remaining vague. This generally followed the International Law Commission's preference in its consideration of marine boundaries.[81]

The general practice in the Persian Gulf would be in accord with a broad interpretation of the provisions of article 6, with special circumstances pertaining to the existence of subsea resources and the irregular geographic configuration of the gulf. However, it would not be in accord with a narrow interpretation of article 6, which emphasized a strict adherence to the principle of equidistance and the use of the median line as a "general rule."[82] Just such a question of usage was treated by the International Court of Justice in 1969.

In a major decision on 20 February 1969, the International Court of Justice in the North Sea Continental Shelf Cases further clarified the principles applicable to the delimitation of continental shelf boundaries.[83] Concerning the principle of equidistance, the Court indicated that although no other method of delimitation might have such a "practical convenience and certainty of application" as the equidistance method, such

factors do not suffice of themselves to convert what is a method into a rule of law, making the acceptance of the results of using that method obligatory in all cases in which the parties do agree otherwise, or in which 'special circumstances' cannot be shown to exist.[84]

In its judgment the Court found, *inter alia*, that the principles and rules of international law applicable to the delimitation as between the parties of areas of the continental shelf are as follows:

(1) Delimitation is to be effected by agreement in accordance with equitable principles, and taking account of all the relevant circumstances, in such a way as to leave as much as possible to each Party all those parts of the continental shelf that constitute a natural prolongation of its land territory into and under the sea, without encroachment on the natural prolongation of the land territory of the other;

(2) If, in the application of the preceding sub-paragraph, the delimitation leaves to the Parties areas that overlap, these are to be divided between them in agreed proportions or, failing agreement, equally, unless they decide on a regime of joint jurisdiction, uses, or exploitation for the zones of overlap or any part of them.[85]

The Court went on to identify three factors to be considered in negotiations: the general configuration of the coasts, the structure and natural resources of the continental shelf areas involved, and a reasonable degree of proportionality.[86]

In these findings the International Court of Justice reduced the emphasis given to the principle of equidistance and effectively broadened the concept of "equitable principles" in stressing that "all relevant circumstances" be taken into account in the delimitation of continental shelf boundaries. The judgment is in general agreement with the practice of Iran and Saudi Arabia in the Persian Gulf.

The practice of Iran and Saudi Arabia was further supported in the decision of 30 June 1977 of the Court of Arbitration on the delimitation of the continental shelf between Britain and France.[87] The presence of a number of islands was among the difficulties hindering attempts to delimit the continental shelf between the two states. In delimiting the boundaries the Court granted full effect to some islands, including the Eddystone, half-effect to the Scilly Islands, and a special twelve-mile enclave boundary for the Channel Islands. The Court noted that in a large proportion of delimitations the equidistance principle was applied but modified according to the particular geographic features. The Court sought such a "method modifying or varying the equidistance method" in its solution.[88] In paragraph 251 of the decision the Court indicated the following:

A number of examples are to be found in State practice of delimitation in which only partial effect has been given to offshore islands situated outside the territorial sea of the mainland. The method adopted has varied in response to the varying geographic and other circumstances of the particular cases; but in one instance, at least, the method employed was to give half, instead of full, effect to the offshore island in delimiting the equidistant line. The method of giving half-effect consists in delimiting the line equidistant between the two coasts, first, without the use of the offshore island as a base-point and, secondly, with its use as a base-point; a boundary giving half-effect to the island is then the line drawn mid-way between those two equidistance lines. This method appears to the Court to be an appropriate and practical method of abating the disproportion and inequity which otherwise results from giving full effect to the Scilly Isles as a base-point for determining the course of the boundary.

Here the Court clearly followed the precedent of Iran and Saudi Arabia in giving Kharg Island half-effect.

The provisions in the delimitation of the continental shelf in the ICNT/Rev. 1 emphasize the importance of "agreement in accordance with equitable principles" and the "taking account of all the relevant circumstances."[89] Article 83, paragraph 1 of the ICNT/Rev. 1 provides the following:

1. The delimitation of the continental shelf between adjacent or opposite States shall be effected by agreement in accordance with equitable principles, employing, where appropriate, the median or equidistance line, and taking account of all the relevant circumstances.

The Saudi and Iranian boundaries were clearly based on "equitable principles," agreements, and other "relevant circumstances."

AUTHORITY OVER LIVING RESOURCES

The fishery potential in the Persian Gulf appears to be quite large. In the past, with an apparent abundance of fishing resources, there was little concern for the regulation of the Persian Gulf fisheries, except that pearling was limited to the local inhabitants. More recently a growing concern has been registered in the form of claims to exclusive fishing zones. Iran's Proclamation of 30 October 1973 and the Saudi Fishing Zone Communiqué of 30 April 1974 are obvious examples.

Iran, "aware of the danger of the exhaustion or even extermination of certain species in its coastal waters," established an exclusive fishery zone in the Persian Gulf and in the Gulf of Oman "in order to protect its fishing industry."[90] Iran based its claim on "the historical rights of the inhabitants of the coasts of Iran" and on "the importance of the natural resources of the sea for the economic and social development of the country."[91] The limits of the exclusive fishery zone were put at fifty nautical miles in the Gulf of Oman; in the Persian Gulf the limits correspond to "the outer limits of the continental shelf" as established in agreements.[92] For areas in the Persian Gulf where agreements do not exist, the exclusive fishery zone is delimited by the median line equidistant from the baselines used to measure the extent of the territorial sea of the states concerned.[93] If a situation should arise in which Iran were not able to exploit the fishery resources up to the scientifically justifiable catch, Iran indicated that it would "permit others to exploit the surplus" on Iranian terms.[94]

Saudi Arabia similarly established exclusive fishing zones in "those areas lying contiguous to the coastline of the Kingdom and the coastline of its islands, which extend from the coastal sea of the Kingdom to the open sea but are contiguous to its coastlines."[95] The following considerations were given as bases of the Saudi claim: "fishes are considered a staple food for the people of the Kingdom of Saudi Arabia"; "fishing resources are an essential factor for furthering its [Saudi Arabia's] socio-economic development"; "recognized jurisdiction over such fishing resources is required in the interest of their conservation and prudent utilization"; and "other states have currently affirmed their exclusive jurisdiction over fishing resources in areas contiguous to their territorial sea."[96] In the case that Saudi zones overlap with those of other states, it is provided that "the boundaries shall be drawn on the median line every point of which is equidistant from the baseline from which measurement of the territorial sea begins."[97] Non-Saudis are prohibited from any type of fishing operations in the exclusive fishing zones, unless they have received prior permission from the Saudi government.[98] Also included is the disclaimer that the application of the fishing communiqué "shall not affect the character of the fishing zones as part of the high seas."[99]

From the standpoint of the international community, standards relating to authority over fishery resources are not clearly established. Although the claims to authority have varied widely in the postwar period, there have been significant developments. The Truman "Fisheries" Proclamation of 22 September 1945,[100] even though not followed up by the United States, set an important precedent that has been adapted to suit the national interests of numerous states.[101]

In that proclamation the United States, recognized that "fishery resources have a special importance to coastal communities as a source of livelihood and to the nation as a food and industrial resource," that "the progressive development of new methods and techniques contributes to intensified fishing over wide sea areas and in certain cases seriously threatens fisheries with depletion," and that "there is an urgent need to protect coastal fishery resources from destructive exploitation." It therefore proclaimed the following:

In view of the pressing need for conservation and protection of fishery resources, the Government of the United States regards it as proper to establish conservation zones in those areas of the high seas contiguous to the coasts of the United States wherein fishing activities have been or in the future may be developed and maintained on a substantial scale.[102]

In addition to the Truman "Fisheries" Proclamation and the subsequent state practice, the findings of the International Court of Justice, as in the Anglo-Norwegian Fisheries Case, further contributed to the development of international law pertaining to fisheries. Among other things, the Court identified certain criteria, "which though not entirely precise," could be taken into consideration on questions involving the delimitation of coastal state jurisdiction in offshore areas. Although the Court was considering the use of straight baselines in the delimitation of territorial seas, such considerations as whether given sea areas are "sufficiently closely linked" to the land domain and "the economic interests peculiar to the region" are pertinent to other state claims to jurisdiction in the offshore areas.[103]

In 1958 international community preferences were indicated in the Convention on Fishing and the Conservation of Living Resources of the High Seas.[104] Of special importance was article 7, which provided the following:

Having regard to the provisions of paragraph 1 of Article 6 [A coastal state has a special interest in the maintenance of the productivity of the living resources in any area of the high seas adjacent to its territorial sea.], any coastal State may, with a view to the maintenance of the productivity of living resources of the sea, adopt unilateral measures of conservation appropriate to any stock of fish or other marine resources in any area of the high seas adjacent to its territorial sea.

These three legal developments indicate certain trends. First is the recognition of a need for conservation and prudent utilization of fishery resources. Second is a recognition of a special land-sea relationship of the coastal state with its adjoining offshore areas, a relationship based upon economic interests and historic use. Third is the growing propensity of coastal states to establish exclusive fishery zones. The claims to such exclusive national zones are a reflection of the first two trends; they are made in response to a danger of fishing stocks being depleted and for special economic interests of the inhabitants of coastal areas.

These trends have continued. In 1974 in the Fisheries Jurisdiction Case (Britain v. Iceland) the International Court of Justice recognized that

two concepts have crystallized as customary international law in recent years . . . The first is the concept of the fishery zone, the area in which a State may claim exclusive fishery jurisdiction independently of its territorial sea . . . The second is the concept of preferential rights of fishing in adjacent waters in favor of the coastal State in a situation of special dependence on its coastal fisheries.[105]

The United States claimed a 200-mile exclusive fishing conservation and managment zone.[106] This represented a culmination of the three trends and reinforced the more modest Iranian and Saudi claims. Furthermore, the movement for an exclusive economic zone at the Third U. N. Conference on the Law of the Sea envelops the Iranian and Saudi fishery claims. The ICNT/Rev. 1 provides that the coastal state has "sovereign rights" over its living resources in the exclusive economic zone.[107]

The provisions of the Iranian and Saudi claims indicate an adherence to the trends and a recogniton of the principles set forth in such precedents as the Truman "Fisheries" Proclamation, the findings of the International Court of Justice, and the preferences negotiated at international conferences. The American claim and the potential establishment of an exclusive economic zone further endorse the provisions of the Persian Gulf claims as being in general accord with the evolving international community preferences.

PERSIAN GULF CONTEXT

When the claims to authority over offshore resources are examined in terms of the Persian Gulf context, various considerations peculiar to the area and to the respective national interests of Saudi Arabia and Iran can be discerned. Such considerations affect not only the substance of the claims but also the timing. They similarly affect the substance and timing of the various agreements based upon such claims. The contextual considerations are reflected in specific provisions of the claims and agreements and determine the broader climate of conflict or compromise in which the agreements are negotiated. These contextual considerations, while not legal considerations as such, offer a useful insight into the respective approaches of Saudi Arabia and Iran to international law and an insight into legal development in general.

SAUDI ARABIA: ROYAL PRONOUNCEMENT, 28 MAY 1949

The Royal Pronouncement of 28 May 1949 was the first claim to jurisdiction over the subsoil and seabed of the area contiguous to the coast in the Persian Gulf. When viewed in terms of the Persian Gulf context, the general purpose of the claim, as well as the specific provisions, can be explained. First, Saudi motivations in making such a claim were based upon economic interests, as suggested by the physical characteristics of the Persian Gulf. The geological structure of the seabed and subsoil of offshore areas indicated that it would yield large quantities of petroleum. Second, also based on the Persian Gulf's physical characteristics, was the Saudi decision not to employ the term "continental shelf" in its claim. Instead, Saudi Arabia emphasized the concept of contiguity.

Moreover, the Saudi claim was influenced by the presence and interests of the American oil companies in Saudi Arabia. Since the oil companies were interested in establishing a firm legal basis for their offshore exploration and oil exploitation, American lawyers played no small part in the definition of the Saudi claim, which closely followed the precedent set by the Truman Proclamation. The relative timing of the claim was dictated by the need to define the Saudi claim to jurisdiction over adjacent submarine areas following the offshore concession granted to Aramco on 10 October 1948. Also of importance was the Iranian bill in the Majlis as of 19 May 1949, which claimed Persian Gulf subsea resources for Iran.

IRAN: LAW OF 19 JUNE 1955

Although the initial Iranian bill relating to subsea resources had preceded the Saudi claim, the Iranian claim did not become law until 19 June 1955. The delay in the enactment of the claim stemmed, in part, from Iran's domestic situation and its preoccupation with the dispute over its land-based petroleum resources (the Anglo-Iranian oil dispute). Of special importance in this regard were the results of the Qatar Case of 1950 and the Abu Dhabi Case of 1951, which indicated that prior concessions did not include the seabed and subsoil of those areas contiguous to the territorial waters of the states involved.[108] In light of its oil controversy, Iran put off defining its claim to such offshore areas until later. When eventually passed, the Law of 19 June 1955 did reflect Iran's economic interests in its potential offshore petroleum resources. At that time oil was already being exploited by other states in the Persian Gulf. Iran's claim, however, did precede that of its neighbor, Iraq.

On the question of the use of the term "continental shelf," as has been noted, Iran did have a continental shelf in the physical sense in the Sea of Oman. At the time of its application to the Persian Gulf, its legal meaning had been sufficiently broadened by the International Law Commission.[109]

SAUDI ARABIA: ROYAL DECREE NO. M-27, 7 SEPTEMBER 1968

The Royal Decree No. M-27, pertaining to areas in the Red Sea, contains certain provisions that can be clarified according to the context. While the Red Sea claim was clearly based on Saudi economic interests in the "hydrocarbon materials and minerals," it was made in respect to the zone extending in the Red Sea adjacent to the Saudi continental shelf. This has raised some questions because the claim was to the "area beyond the Saudi continental shelf." However, this can be explained in terms of the physical characteristics of the

Red Sea, where a narrow shelf gives way to extreme volcanic depths. In certain areas "the value of the gold, silver, copper, and zinc in the upper 30—of a possible 300—feet of sediments alone has been estimated at more than two billion dollars."[110] Thus the Saudi Red Sea claim is based on economic interests in resources other than petroleum resources and has been phrased to take into account the physical characteristics of the Red Sea.

IRAN: PROCLAMATION OF 30 OCTOBER 1973

When seen in the Persian Gulf context, Iran's Proclamation of 30 October 1973 represents two specific Iranian concerns. First is the concern for Iran's economic interests in Persian Gulf fishery resources. When Iran announced the extension of its exclusive fishing zone, Foreign Minister Kalatbari indicated to the Majlis that Iran's action was in response to the practices of certain "developed" countries.[111] Other governmental sources indicated that the Iranian claim was to curb the fishing of such nations as Japan.[112] The second Iranian concern, apart from conserving fishery resources for its inhabitants, pertains to Iranian security interests. The Proclamation of 30 October 1973 enabled Iran to regulate foreign fishing in areas contiguous to its territorial sea. This could give Iran a control over foreign vessels that might be ostensibly designed for fishing but in fact utilized for the transport of subversives and terrorists and for other foreign-intelligence purposes.[113]

SAUDI ARABIA: COMMUNIQUÉ ON FISHING ZONES, 30 APRIL 1974

The Saudi fishing zone regulations serve several Saudi national interests in the Persian Gulf context. Politically, the Saudi claim represents a preventive action aimed at protecting the rights of Saudi citizens to Persian Gulf fisheries by prohibiting foreign fishing vessels and factory ships from fishing in areas adjacent to the Saudi territorial sea. It also serves to clarify the Saudi fishery jurisdiction in light of claims to exclusive jurisdiction promulgated by other littoral states. Economically, it reserves the fishing resources off the Saudi coast for the Saudis, with the benefits contributing to the economic and social development of the Kingdom. Indirectly, it also serves the Saudi security interests by establishing a control over foreign vessels in given offshore areas. Such a control could provide for the identification of potentially dangerous vessels engaged in activities other than fishing. Since Saudi Arabia did follow Iran's lead in establishing exclusive fishing zones, the Saudi action could also be aimed at improving relations in the Persian Gulf as well as clarifying its legal situation.

SAUDI ARABIA AND IRAN: AGREEMENTS DELIMITING OFFSHORE RESOURCE BOUNDARIES

When the various Iranian and Saudi agreements regarding the delimitation of offshore resource boundaries are viewed in the Persian Gulf context, four general observations are evident. First, such agreements are fundamentally influenced by complex physical features. Second, long-standing territorial and island disputes complicate the delimitations and broaden the scope of the agreements. Third, immediate tangible national interests are reflected in each agreement. Fourth, broader national interests that are often affected by the changing political relationships can be discerned.

The physical features of the Persian Gulf that most often influence agreements delimiting offshore resource boundaries are islands and known fields of petroleum. All Persian Gulf boundary agreements have had to deal with the presence of islands, but practice is not uniform. In the Saudi Arabia-Iran agreement Kharg Island was given "half-effect." In the Iran-Bahrain agreement the islands of Nakhilu and Jabrin on the Iranian side were given full effect, but the island of Muharraq on the Bahraini side was not. Sometimes the islands appear to have been disregarded altogether. Another way islands are considered concerns the recognition of their territorial seas in the delimitations of the respective boundaries. In the Saudi Arabia-Bahrain agreement, the territorial seas of the islands of Lubaynah al-Kabirah and Lubaynah al-Saghirah were not recognized in the boundary. In the Iran-Saudi Arabia agreement the boundary line in the central segment was dramatically adjusted to follow the arcs of the territorial seas of the islands of al-Arabiyah and Farsi. In the Iran-Dubai agreement the boundary line was similarly adjusted to follow the arc of the territorial sea of the island of Sirri.[114]

In addition to islands, known fields of offshore oil have had a major effect on the agreements delimiting offshore resource boundaries. Various provisions have been adopted to deal with those areas known to contain petroleum resources. For example, the Saudi Arabia-Bahrain agreement provided for the hexagonal area known as the Fasht Bu Saafa to be under the jurisdiction of Saudi Arabia, but the revenue arising from the oil exploitation in the area is to be divided equally between Saudi Arabia and Bahrain. The problem posed by the discovery of petroleum resources by an Iranian concessionaire was resolved in a different manner: the boundary line in the area was adjusted to divide the petroleum resources in place. The Saudi Arabia-Kuwait agreement of 1965 on the Neutral Zone and the "Memorandum of Understanding" between Iran and Sharjah also provided for equitable allocations of offshore resources in given areas. In the Saudi Arabia-Kuwait agreement joint exploitation was provided.[115] The "Memorandum of Understanding" provided for the revenues arising from the oil exploitation to be divided equally.[116]

A second major influence on agreements delimiting offshore resource boundaries is the problem of island disputes and other territorial disputes. The very presence of islands creates problems for delimitation, but such problems are further complicated if the islands themselves are disputed. The Persian Gulf is replete with such island disputes and land-border disputes. The delimitation of the boundary between Saudi Arabia and Bahrain was complicated by conflicting claims to the islands of Lubaynah al-Kabirah and Lubaynah al-Saghirah, and to the Fasht Bu Saafa. The Saudi Arabia-Qatar boundary delimitation was complicated by land-border disputes. The delimitation of the Saudi Arabia-Iran offshore boundary was complicated by conflicting claims to the islands of al-Arabiyah and Farsi. A long-standing dispute between Saudi Arabia and Kuwait over the status of the islands of Qaru and Umm al-Maradim has been a major problem in the delimitation of the offshore boundary between the Neutral Zone and Kuwait. In the lower Persian Gulf the disputes over Abu Musa and the two Tumbs have represented major obstacles to the delimitation of the continental shelf boundary between Iran and the United Arab Emirates. Similarly, disputes among the various sheikhdoms of the United Arab Emirates have complicated offshore boundary delimitations in the area. Also, Iran's claim to Bahrain, until relinquished in May 1970, had no small effect on boundary delimitation considerations in the Persian Gulf.[117] The potential renewal of Iran's claim to Bahrain under the Ayatollah Khomeini suggests new controversy in the future.

Given disputes have also had a visible effect on agreements delimiting offshore resource boundaries by requiring that certain terminal points remain undefined until such time as adjoining boundaries are delimited. For example, the two terminal points of the Iran-Oman continental shelf boundary will not be determined until the Oman-Ras al-Khaimah offshore boundary and the Oman-Sharjah offshore boundary are agreed upon. Similarly, the eastern terminal point of the Iran-Qatar continental shelf boundary is indefinite, pending the delimitation of a Bahrain-Qatar offshore boundary. The Bahrain-Qatar delimitation is hampered by the territorial dispute over Zubarah[118] and the dispute over the island of Hawar.

The effect of territorial disputes and island disputes on the delimitation of offshore resource boundaries is especially significant in the upper Persian Gulf. This is indicated by the fact that offshore boundaries have not been delimited between the following: Iran and Iraq, Iran and Kuwait, Iraq and Kuwait, Kuwait and the Neutral Zone, and Iran and the Neutral Zone. The boundary problems in each case are dependent upon, *inter alia*, the Iraq-Kuwait dispute over land borders and the islands of Bubiyan and Warbah.

Specific national interests represent a third major influence on the delimitation of offshore boundaries in the Persian Gulf. In particular, economic considerations and interest in the avoidance of conflict have surfaced in areas of overlapping concessions and have been instrumental in inducing states to seek agreements on equitable delimitations. Examples of overlapping concessions and concessions extending into areas claimed by other states have not been uncommon in the Persian Gulf and have underlined the necessity for boundary agreements. For example, the 1961 Kuwait-Shell concession overlapped the Iranian concessions granted to Iran-Pan

American Oil Company (IPAC) in 1958 and to Société Irano-Italienne des Pétrole (SIRIP) in 1957.[119] Also, Saudi Arabia protested that the Kuwait-Shell concession of 1961 overlapped with the concession Saudi Arabia granted to the Arabian Oil Company (AOC) in 1957. Similarly, Saudi Arabia claimed that the IPAC concession granted by Iran in 1958 infringed upon the Saudi AOC concession of 1957 and the Saudi Aramco concession of 1948.[120] In April 1963 a statement published in *Platt's Oilgram* that Iran would open new areas of the continental shelf for international bidding brought diplomatic protests from Iraq, Kuwait, and Saudi Arabia because of apparent overlaps.

The potential danger of such overlapping concessions became evident in an incident involving concessions granted by Iran and Saudi Arabia. On 1 February 1968 "an Iranian gunboat approached an Aramco rig, briefly arrested its American and Saudi Arabian crew, and ordered the removal of the rig."[121] The Aramco rig had been drilling in the Fereidoon area for approximately four days, and the location was on the Saudi side of a tentative boundary line established in a preliminary agreement between Iran and Saudi Arabia in December 1965. Meanwhile, Iranian naval forces had been sent to patrol the area in which its concessionaire continued drilling—an area on the Saudi side of the proposed 1965 boundary line. The "Fereidoon incident" thus represented a dangerous precedent that illustrates the seriousness of overlapping concessions. It also exemplified the importance attached to areas of previously discovered resources, and the nature of the economic interests involved.

In addition to the immediate interests of states there are wider political interests that involve broad national objectives and relationships with other states. Such political interests represent the fourth major influence on agreements delimiting offshore resource boundaries in the Persian Gulf. In light of such political interests, Iran and Saudi Arabia might pursue policies that would be based on such national objectives as regional stability. In such cases, various boundary agreements might represent, in part, a broader concern to improve relations with neighboring states. Saudi Arabia and Iran might also pursue policies that would be closely associated with changing political relationships. Such fluctuations could explain, in part, why some agreements are signed or initialed, but not concluded and ratified.

An additional consideration influencing the boundary agreements of Iran and Saudi Arabia involves changing power relationships and interests in regional stability as affected by the action of a third state. For example, Iran and Saudi Arabia had been negotiating for years on the delimitation of their offshore boundary, but agreement had not been reached. Following the announcement of the pending British withdrawal from the gulf, agreement was soon reached. The timing of the agreement was influenced by, *inter alia*, the action of a third state—Great Britain.

CONCLUSIONS

From the preceding analysis of the claims of Saudi Arabia and Iran to authority over offshore resources and their agreements based upon such claims, the following conclusions pertaining to the approaches of Iran and Saudi Arabia to international law and to the roles of the two developing states in the development of the law of the sea may be made.

First, concerning the approaches of Iran and Saudi Arabia to international law, it is apparent that although there was no clearly developed community standard on the extension of coastal state authority over offshore resources, Saudi Arabia and Iran adopted claims patterned on earlier claims of other states. In the case of claims to the resources of the seabed and subsoil of those areas contiguous to the coasts, both based their claims on the Truman Proclamation on the Continental Shelf. However, their claims were adapted to meet the needs of the Persian Gulf context, as evidenced by the Saudi emphasis on the principle of contiguity. The Iranian claim to exclusive authority over living resources was similarly made in a legal environment in which international standards were uncertain. Nevertheless, the Iranian Proclamation of 30 October 1973 was similar to previous claims of other states and is in accord with the developing preferences indicated at the Third United Nations Conference on the Law of the Sea.

Since the claims of Iran and Saudi Arabia were based on widely accepted claims or developing community preferences, it is evident that Iran and Saudi Arabia recognized the principles set forth in the international precedents as restraints on their actions. However, by making their claims in the first place and by establishing agreements with other states based on such claims, Iran and Saudi Arabia, in effect, used international law as an instrument to promote their respective economic interests and broader national objectives. Thus international law was both a restraint and an instrument for Iran and Saudi Arabia.

Second, the roles of the two developing states in the development of the law of the sea can be seen as they have affected the development of the continental shelf concept and the provisions for the delimitation of offshore resource boundaries. The emphasis on the concept of contiguity by Saudi Arabia in acknowledging the character of the Persian Gulf context (its lack of continental shelf) led the International Law Commission to broaden the concept of the continental shelf so that it would be applicable to the Persian Gulf. Furthermore, the emphasis on the use of "equitable principles" by Iran and Saudi Arabia in the delimitation of offshore resource boundaries sets an important international precedent by emphasizing the importance of context. In this instance, the practice of Iran and Saudi Arabia differed fundamentally from the preference of the International Law Commission and the emphasis of the Convention on the Continental Shelf to use the principle of equidistance as a "general rule." However, the practice of Iran and Saudi Arabia was exonerated by (and probably contributed to) the findings of the International Court of Justice in the North Sea continental shelf cases and the Court of Arbitration on the delimitation of the continental shelf.

As has been seen, the development of the law of the sea in the Persian Gulf, as indicated by the claims to authority over offshore resources and resultant agreements, has not only been in agreement with developing community preferences but also has fundamentally contributed to the development of such preferences.

NOTES

1. While some claims are phrased in terms of the resources extending seaward from the coasts, the authority over the resources of the territorial sea is considered an aspect of the juridical status of the territorial sea; the

resources are therefore subject to coastal state sovereignty.

2. Although the Persian Gulf has no continental shelf in the strict sense of the word, the use of the term to refer to submarine areas in the Persian Gulf has become common.

3. For text, *see* 43 *Supplement to the American Journal of International Law* 156 (1949).

4. For the text of the Iranian Bill relating to Persian Gulf Subsea Resources, *see* 5 *Revue Egyptienne de Droit International* 347 (1949). For the text of the Iranian Law of 19 June 1955, *see New Directions in the Law of the Sea*, 10 vols., ed. Robin Churchill, Myron Nordquist, and S. Houston Lay (Dobbs Ferry, N. Y.: Oceana, 1973), 1:307-8.

5. *See* Law of 19 June 1955, article 2.

6. Ibid., articles 3 and 5.

7. For text, *see* U. S., Department of State, *International Boundary Study, Series A—Limits in the Seas,* no. 12, "Continental Shelf Boundary: Bahrain-Saudi Arabia," 10 March 1970. The Saudi Arabia-Bahrain Continental Shelf Boundary Agreement was signed six days after Saudi Arabia "redefined" its territorial sea in Decree No. 33 and two days before the opening of the 1958 United Nations Conference on the Law of the Sea.

8. There appears to be some question whether the Saudi Arabia-Qatar agreement is still in force. *See New Directions in the Law of the Sea,* 2:869, n. 108.

9. For text, *see* 8 *International Legal Materials* 493 (1969). Iran and Saudi Arabia had initialed an agreement on 13 December 1965, but it was never concluded. For background on the Iran-Saudi Arabia negotiations on their offshore boundary, *see* Richard Young, "Equitable Solutions for Offshore Boundaries: The 1968 Saudi Arabia-Iran Agreement," 64 *American Journal of International Law* 152 (1970).

10. For text, *see* 60 *American Journal of International Law* 744 (1966).

11. For text of Royal Decree No. M-27, *see* 8 *International Legal Materials* 606 (1969).

12. *See* Royal Decree No. M-27, section 3.

13. Ibid., section 6.

14. For text, *see* U. S., Department of State, *International Boundary Study, Series A—Limits in the Seas,* no. 25, "Continental Shelf Boundary: Iran-Qatar," 9 July 1970.

15. For text, *see* U. S., Department of State, *International Boundary Study, Series A—Limits in the Seas,* no. 58, "Continental Shelf Boundary: Bahrain-Iran" 13 September 1974.

16. For text, *see* U. S., Department of State, *International Boundary Study, Series A—Limits in the Seas,* no. 67, "Continental Shelf Boundary:

Iran-Oman," 1 January 1976.

17. The agreement was ratified by Iran on 15 March 1975, but has not been ratified by the United Arab Emirates. For text, *see* U. S., Department of State, *International Boundary Study, Series A—Limits in the Seas*, no. 63, "Continental Shelf Boundary: Iran-United Arab Emirates (Dubai), 30 September 1975.

18. For press report, *see Arab Report and Record* (London), 1-15 September 1971, p. 470.

19. For "Documents on the Abu Musa Affair," including the "Memorandum of Understanding between Iran and Sharjah," *see Middle East Economic Survey* (Beirut), 15 (5 May 1972): 1-5 (Supplement).

20. For press reports of a joint communiqué announcing a final agreement, *see Arab Report and Record* (London), 1-15 January 1968, p. 4. In an interview with Ahmed Jarollah, publisher of the Kuwait weekly *As-Siyassa*, the Shah of Iran, speaking on the question of a continental shelf delineation agreement with Kuwait, stated: "We [Iran] are ready to carry out what we have agreed with you [Kuwait]. Whenever you feel the time is opportune, we will stand by our understanding." *See Kayhan* (Tehran; Weekly International Edition), 24 January 1976.

21. On 16 May 1974 Saudi Arabia also signed an agreement with Sudan for the joint exploitation of natural resources in the Red Sea. For report, *see Arab Report and Record* (London), 16-31 May 1974, pp. 202-3.

22. For details of the Iranian Proclamation of 30 October 1973, *see* Iran's general statement made by Mr. Kazemi at the Third United Nations Conference on the Law of the Sea in U. N., *Third United Nations Conference of the Law of the Sea*, 1:72, (A/CONF. 62/SR1-51).

23. The Saudi proclamation was mentioned in ibid.

24. *See* Royal Pronouncement of 28 May 1949.

25. Richard Young emphasized that the Saudi claim represented "a somewhat different approach based upon the concept of contiguity" and was not based on "some theory of jurisdiction over the continental shelf." *See* Richard Young, "Saudi Arabian Offshore Legislation," 43 *American Journal of International Law* 531 (1949); and Richard Young, "Further Claims to Areas Beneath the High Seas," 43 *American Journal of International Law* 790 (1949).

26. *See* Royal Decree No. M-27, section 1.

27. The phrase "adjacent to the shelf" is explained according to context. *See* below, pp. 145-46.

28. *See* Bill relating to Persian Gulf Subsea Resources, article 1. A continental shelf in the strict sense of the word does exist in the Gulf of Oman, but Iran's use of "continental shelf" for its claim in the Persian Gulf

in its 1949 bill was sharply criticized. Richard Young suggested that

the absence of the shelf edge makes meaningless a claim to the 'continental shelf' in such waters, and this is the obvious objection to the proposed Iranian legislation of 1949 which would have claimed the continental shelf in the Persian Gulf.

See Richard Young, "The Legal Status of Submarine Areas beneath the High Seas," 45 *American Journal of International Law* 236 (1951).

29. Law of 19 June 1955, article 2.

30. Ibid., article 1.

31. For a background report on the continental shelf, *see* "Document A/CN.4/17: Rapport de J. P. A. François, rapporteur spécial," in U. N., *Yearbook of the International Law Commission 1950*, 2 vols., 2:49-52 (A/CN.4/SER.A/1950/- Add.1).

32. The Truman Proclamation on the Continental Shelf should be distinguished from the Truman "Fisheries" Proclamation of the same date.

33. For an examination of the Persian Gulf developments in light of the Truman Proclamation, *see* Jasper Y. Brinton, "Jurisdiction over Sea-Bed Resources and Recent Developments in the Persian Gulf Area," *Revue Egyptienne de Droit International* 5:131 (1949).

34. *See* text in Marjorie M. Whiteman, *Digest of International Law*, 15 vols. (Washington, D. C.: Government Printing Office, 1965), 4:756-57.

35. For text of the White House Press Release of 28 September 1945 pertaining to the Truman Proclamation on the Continental Shelf, *see* ibid., 4:757-58.

36. Often noted in this regard is the common use of the word "appertain." *See* Brinton, "Jurisdiction Over Sea-Bed Resources," p. 133; and Herbert J. Liebesny, "Legislation on the Sea Bed and Territorial Waters of the Persian Gulf," *Middle East Journal* 4 (January 1950): 94-96.

37. Richard Young said that just about everyone was using the Truman Proclamation as a model, and that it was closely followed in the Saudi claim, except for the term "continental shelf," which was not used because there was no "edge" in the Persian Gulf. Richard Young, private interview, Washington, D. C., 23 April 1976.

38. It might also be noted that the definition for the "continental shelf" that accompanied the Truman Proclamation could be applied to the subsea area in the Persian Gulf.

39. *See Yearbook of the International Law Commission 1950*, 1:214 (A/CN.4/SER.A/1950).

40. Ibid.

41. Ibid.

42. *See* "Document A / CN.4 / 32: Memorandum présenté par le Secrétariat," in *Yearbook of the International Law Commission 1950*, 2:67-113 (A/CN.4/SER.A/1950/Add.1).

43. *Yearbook of the International Law Commission 1950*, 1:218-19 (A/CN.4/SER.A/1950/Add.1).

44. *Yearbook of the International Law Commission 1950*, 2:384 (A / CN.4/SER.A/1950/Add.1).

45. *See* Convention on the Continental Shelf (U. N. Doc. A / CONF.13 / L.55).

46. Richard Young points out this difference. *See* Young, "Saudi Arabian Offshore Legislation," p. 531.

47. *See* Royal Pronouncement of 28 May 1949. Also in the subsequent Saudi Red Sea claim, Saudi Arabia specifically claimed ownership of the "resources." *See* Royal Decree No. M-27, section 1.

48. *See* Barry B. L. Auguste, *The Continental Shelf: The Practice and Policy of the Latin American States with Special Reference to Chile, Ecuador and Peru* (Geneva: Librairie E. Droz, 1960), pp. 79, 95.

49. *See* Royal Pronouncement of 28 May 1949.

50. *See* Royal Decree No. M-27, section 6.

51. *See* Law of 19 June 1955, article 2.

52. Ibid., article 5. Also to be noted as affecting the Iranian approach to the continental shelf are the draft articles on the continental shelf, as adopted by the International Law Commission. *See* "Report of the International Law Commission covering the Work of its Fifth Session, June 1 - August 14, 1953," in *Yearbook of the International Law Commission 1953*, 2:212-17 (A/CN.4/SER.A/1953/Add.1).

53. Iran did make a reservation to article 4, indicating that the "Iranian Government reserves the right to allow or not to allow the laying or maintenance of submarine cables or pipelines on its continental shelf."

54. Saudi Arabia called for its territorial sea boundaries to be determined in a like manner.

55. *See* Royal Decree No. M-27, section 3.

56. Bill relating to Persian Gulf Subsea Resources, article 2.

57. Law of 19 June 1955, article 3. Iran did not provide for a boundary in cases in which no agreement was reached, as it did in its subsequent Act of 12 April 1959 on the territorial sea. In article 4 of the Act of 12 April 1959, Iran provided that "in the absence of agreement to the contrary, the boundary of the Iranian territorial sea with that (proximate) State is the median line." Such disparate Iranian actions reflect the fundamental difference that exists between resource boundaries and territorial sea boundaries.

58. Law of 19 June 1955, article 3.

59. "Sufficiently general" is used here to indicate that neither state chose to be limited in its possible application of equitable principles.

60. Royal Pronouncement of 28 May 1949.

61. Law of 19 June 1955, article 3.

62. Article 7 of the Draft Articles on the Continental Shelf included the following:

1. Where the same continental shelf is contiguous to the territories of two or more States whose coasts are opposite to each other, the boundary of the continental shelf appertaining to such States is, in the absence of agreement between those states or unless another boundary line is justified by special circumstances, the median line every point of which is equidistant from the base lines from which the width of the territorial sea of each country is measured.

2. Where the same continental shelf is contiguous to the territories of two adjacent States, the boundary of the continental shelf appertaining to such States is, in the absence of agreement between those States or unless another boundary line is justified by special circumstances, determined by the application of the principle of equidistance from the base lines from which the width of the territorial sea of each of the two countries is measured.

See Yearbook of the International Law Commission 1953, 2:213 (A/CN.4/SER.A/1953/Add.1).

63. Agreements that have not been published, such as the agreement between Saudi Arabia and Qatar of 27 June 1965, cannot be considered.

64. For a background of the negotiations leading to the agreements, *see* Husain M. Albaharna, *The Arabian Gulf States*, 2nd ed. (Beirut: Librairie du Liban, 1975), pp. 306-9.

65. It should be noted that English translations of the agreement vary. For example, in the translation that appeared in the United Nations Legislative Series, the agreement did not mention the term "continental shelf"; it was divided according to "clauses"; and the words "middle line" were used to refer to the boundary line in Clause 1. On the other hand, in the *Limits in the Seas*, a series of the United States Department of State, the agreement is entitled "Continental Shelf Boundary Agreement," is divided into "articles," and in the first article refers to the boundary line as being drawn on the basis of the "median line."

66. The Department of State analysis of the agreement suggested that the agreement employed "a variation of the equidistance principle." *See Limits in the Seas*, no. 12, "Bahrain-Saudi Arabia," p. 3. Richard Young

indicated that he had prepared the draft of the agreement. He described the agreement as "ad hoc" and "pragmatic," and indicated that it was signed to enable the oil exploitation from the Fasht Bu Saafa Hexagon to proceed. He also said that the Boggs method of delimitation was basically followed, but that for practicality, points were selected on the two shores, and a line approximating a median line was drawn. Richard Young, private interview, Washington, D. C., 23 April 1976.

67. The English translation of the agreement, as authorized in article 5 of the agreement, uses the phrase "boundary line separating submarine areas" and does not refer to a continental shelf boundary.

68. Richard Young points out that "in view of the Iranian claim to Bahrain" at the time, the point from which the Saudi Arabia-Iran boundary line extends was defined in only geographical terms, without mention of Bahrain by name. *See* Young, "The 1968 Saudi Arabia-Iran Agreement," p. 153.

69. The territorial seas of the islands were given full status in the Saudi Arabia-Iran agreement, unlike the earlier provisions in the Saudi Arabia-Bahrain agreement, which avoided recognizing such territorial seas for small islands.

70. For details of the breakdown of the 1965 compromise and the resultant strained relations touched off by the use of Iranian naval vessels, *see* "Offshore Demarcation: Top Problem in the Gulf," *Middle East Economic Survey* (Beirut) 9 (16 February 1968): 1-5.

71. Richard Young pointed out that the northern segment of the boundary, as finally agreed upon, "gave only a slight net gain in seabed area to Iran, but presumably a substantial increase in Iran's share of estimated oil reserves." *See* Young, "The 1968 Saudi Arabia-Iran Agreement," p. 155.

72. *See* the introductory paragraph of the Iran-Qatar Agreement of 20 September 1969.

73. For a brief analysis of the agreement, *see Limits in the Seas*, no. 25, "Iran-Qatar," p. 2.

74. *See* the introductory paragraph of the Iran-Bahrain Agreement of 17 June 1971.

75. *See* Albaharna, *The Arabian Gulf States*, 2nd ed., pp. 355-56.

76. For other provisions and background information on the very complex situation involving Abu Musa and the two Tumbs, *see* "Iranian Offer to Buy Three Gulf Islands Reported," *Middle East Economic Survey* (Beirut) 15 (5 November 1971): 5-6; and "Storm Clouds over the Gulf," *Middle East Economic Survey* (Beirut) 15 (3 December 1971): 1-9.

77. *See* the introductory paragraph of the Iran-Oman Agreement of 25 July 1974.

78. For example, it has been pointed out that "point 21 is 4.40 nautical miles closer to Oman than to Iran." *See* analysis in *Limits in the Seas*, no. 67, "Iran-Oman," pp. 4-5.

79. *See* the introductory paragraph of the Iran-Dubai Agreement of 31 August 1974.

80. It has been pointed out that "the boundary is not based on the equidistance principle," and questions pertaining to the relationship of the boundary to other emirates in the United Arab Emirates have been raised in the analysis of the agreement in *Limits in the Seas*, no. 63, "Iran-United Arab Emirates (Dubai)," pp. 3-4.

81. It seems that a group of experts had urged the International Law Commission to adopt the use of the median line as a "general rule" for the delimitation of territorial sea boundaries, but the Commission applied the same rule to continental shelf boundaries as well. *See Yearbook of the International Law Commission 1953*, 2:77-9 (A/CN.4/SER.A/1953/Add.1). *See also* David J. Padwa, "Submarine Boundaries," 9 *International and Comparative Law Quarterly* 633 (1960).

82. Such narrow interpretations are not uncommon; various agreements are criticized for not utilizing the principle of equidistance in the strictest sense. *See* Padwa, "Submarine Boundaries," p. 630, n. 8, in which he states: "Neither treaty utilizes the principle of equidistance," referring to the Saudi Arabia-Bahrain Treaty of 1958 and the Anglo-Venezuelan Treaty of 1942.

83. *See* "I. C. J. Decision in North Sea Continental Shelf Cases," 8 *International Legal Materials* 340 (1969).

84. Ibid., p. 358.

85. Ibid., p. 384.

86. Ibid.

87. For text of the Court of Arbitration's decision, dated 30 June 1977, *see* 18 *International Legal Materials* 397 (1979).

88. Ibid., para. 249 of decision, dated 30 June 1977.

89. For a discussion of "equitable principles" and "relevant circumstances" *see* M. D. Blecher, "Equitable Delimitation of Continental Shelf," 73 *American Journal of International Law* 60 (1979).

90. For the details of the Iranian claim, *see Third Conference on the Law of the Sea*, 1:72.

91. Ibid.

92. Ibid.

93. Ibid.

94. Ibid.

95. Unofficial translation of the Saudi Communiqué on Fishing Zones,

30 April 1974, article 1.

96. Saudi Communiqué on Fishing Zones, 30 April 1974, preface.

97. Ibid., article 1.

98. Ibid., article 2.

99. Ibid., article 3.

100. For the text of the Truman "Fisheries" Proclamation, *see* Whiteman, *Digest*, 4:954-55.

101. The 200-mile fishing zones claims by certain Latin American states illustrate such applications.

102. *See* Truman "Fisheries" Proclamation of 28 September 1945.

103. For a discussion of such criteria in the Anglo-Norwegian Fisheries Case, *see* Whiteman, *Digest*, 4:164-65.

104. *See* Convention on Fishing and Conservation of the Living Resources of the High Seas (U. N. Doc. A/CONF.13/L.54).

105. *See* "International Court of Justice: Judgments in the Fisheries Jurisdiction Cases," 13 *International Legal Materials* 1059 (1974).

106. *See* "United States: Fishery Conservation and Management Act of 1976, April 13, 1976," 70 *American Journal of International Law* 624 (1976).

107. *See* ICNT / Rev. 1, part V, Exclusive Economic Zone, article 56.

108. For a discussion of the findings of each case, *see* Whiteman, *Digest*, 4:744-51.

109. In an article critical of Iran's use of the term "continental shelf" in its 1949 bill, Richard Young also noted Iran's failure to refer to the Caspian Sea in its 1949 bill. *See* Young, "Legal Status of Submarine Areas beneath the High Seas," p. 236, n. 25. In the subsequent Law of 19 June 1955, Iran included a note in the second article that indicated that "the rules of international law in respect to internal seas shall apply to the Caspian Sea."

110. *See* Eugenie Clark, "The Strangest Sea," *National Geographic* 148 (September 1975): 338.

111. *See* "Iran Extends Fishing Zone," *Middle East Monitor* (15 November 1973): 3.

112. Ibid.

113. To be noted in this regard is the Soviet-Iraqi agreement establishing a joint fishing company. *See* report in *Arab Report and Record* (London), 15-29 February 1976, p. 112.

114. The status of islands has represented major obstacles in agreements yet to be reached. For example, the relative effect of the islands of Kharg off the Iranian coast and Failaka off the Kuwaiti coast has been a major obstacle to the delimitation of the offshore boundary between Iran and Kuwait.

115. Joint exploitation in the Neutral Zone was effected by Saudi Arabia and Kuwait, each granting concessions for their "undivided half interest in

the seabed and subsoil" to the Arabian Oil Company (a Japanese concern). *See* discussion in Albaharna, *The Arabian Gulf States*, 2nd ed., p. 291.

116. The provisions of the "Memorandum of Understanding" provide for the exploitation of petroleum resources to be conducted by Buttes Gas and Oil Company.

117. Iran protested the signing of the Saudi Arabia-Bahrain Agreement of 22 February 1958 because of Iran's claim to Bahrain. *See* "Iran Fights Oil Pact: Repudiates Saudi Arabia's Agreement with Bahrain," *New York Times*, 11 March 1959.

118. The Zubarah Dispute involves not only an area of land on the northern coast of Qatar, but also conflicting claims to jurisdiction over the inhabitants of the area, as determined by tribal allegiances.

119. For background material on boundary disputes and a map indicating overlapping concessions, *see* Shigeru Oda, "Boundary of the Continental Shelf," 12 *Japanese Annual of International Law* 264 (1968).

120. *See* ibid. *See also* Albaharna, *The Arabian Gulf States*, 2nd ed. pp. 290-96.

121. *See* "Offshore Demarcation: Top Problem in the Gulf," *Middle East Economic Survey* (Beirut) 9 (16 February 1968): 4.

CHAPTER 5

Claims to Regulate International Access for the Purpose of Pollution Control

FACTUAL BACKGROUND

Claims to regulate international access in the Persian Gulf primarily consist of the general provisions included in claims to the territorial sea and contiguous zone, claims to the resources of the continental shelf, and claims to exclusive fishing zones. Such general provisions include innocent passage through territorial seas and straits, access to the superjacent waters of the continental shelf for marine scientific research and the laying and maintenance of cables and pipelines, and access for fishing. In addition, however, there are claims to regulate access for the purpose of pollution control. Such environmental claims extend across the other coastal state offshore jurisdictions and purport to establish a pollution control zone in which all vessels become potentially subject to regulation.[1]

NATIONAL REGULATIONS

In the Persian Gulf the establishment of pollution control measures is in the formative stages. Iran, however, has taken the initiative to establish pollution control regulations for its territorial sea, and it has "temporarily" extended the pollution control regulations to the limits of the superjacent waters of its continental shelf.[2] These regulations enable the Iranian government not only to start legal proceedings against both nationals and foreigners who have committed violations, but they also provide for the inspection of ships suspected of technical flaws or possible leakages.[3]

MULTILATERAL AGREEMENTS

The Iranian pollution control regulations were initiated following the signing of the International Convention for the Prevention of Pollution from Ships on 2 November 1973, in London.[4] This convention provided, *inter alia*, that inspections could be made to ensure that the condition of a ship and its equipment met certain requirements and specifications.[5] If the ship did not meet the necessary requirements, it was provided that "the Party carrying out the inspection shall take such steps as will ensure that the ship shall not sail until it can proceed to sea without presenting an unreasonable threat of harm to the marine environment."[6] Moreover, the convention defined "special areas" that required more stringent protective measures for the preservation of the marine environment. The Persian Gulf was one such designated special area.[7]

In April 1978 the Kuwait Regional Conference on the Protection and Development of the Marine Environment and the Coastal Areas was convened by the Executive Director of the United Nations Environment Program.[8] At the conference an Action Plan for the Protection and Development of the Marine Environment was adopted.[9] The Kuwait Regional Convention for Cooperation on the Protection of the Marine Environment from Pollution was also signed.[10] A Protocol concerning Regional Co-operation in Combatting Pollution by Oil and Other Harmful Substances in Cases of Emergency[11] accompanied the convention. The convention identified the threats caused by pollution and the necessary action to be taken to reduce pollution. It also provided for the establishment of a regional organization for the protection of the marine environment.[12] The protocol provided for joint cooperation in marine emergencies, such as would be present in a major oil spill.

INTERNATIONAL LEGAL PERSPECTIVE

Although the international community has recognized the need to protect the marine environment, there has not been agreement on what measures should be taken. Nevertheless, states have taken unilateral actions to establish pollution control zones in response to special environmental dangers. The Canadian Arctic Waters Pollution Prevention Act is the most obvious precedent.[13] Community reactions to such measures have varied, and the measures taken have proven controversial. A major problem is the traditional principle of "flag-state responsibility." Since pollution problems often do not directly affect the flag states, they have not had sufficient motivation to act. In response to the growing danger of pollution, coastal states, such as Iran, have responded with unilateral pollution control claims. Such claims have been challenged because they tend to contradict broader community policies, such as freedom of transit or freedom of navigation. Thus Iran's claim to establish pollution control regulations is in an area of law in which community consensus has yet to develop.

The efforts at regional cooperation represent a possible solution for areas with special pollution concerns. The precedents already established in the joint efforts in the Baltic[14] and in the Mediterranean[15] support the legitimacy of the recent Kuwait agreements.

PERSIAN GULF CONTEXT

When the Iranian pollution control measures are examined in the Persian Gulf context, Iranian security interests become apparent. Iran is not only concerned with possible accidents but also with terrorist actions and subversive cargoes.

As the tanker traffic in the Persian Gulf increases, the possibility of a major oil spill in the gulf also increases. Some 60 percent of all oil carried by tankers throughout the world comes from the Persian Gulf. Writing in the *Kayhan International* in Iran, Amir Taheri noted the danger of unseaworthy tankers in the Persian Gulf, following an instance when such a tanker almost sank in a vital shipping lane. Taheri voiced the need for the coastal states in the Persian Gulf "to control and check all shipping in their waterway" in order to obviate what he termed "the risks involved in the present free-for-all."[16]

The very presence of unseaworthy ships could make such ships more vulnerable to terrorists.[17] The possibility of a terrorist attack against a supertanker has been a major consideration of Iran for some time. In 1972 the Shah pointed out the example of the Palestinian guerrilla attack on an Israeli tanker in the Strait of Bab el Mandeb as a serious precedent.[18] He indicated that such an attack in the Strait of Hormuz could close the strait and be disastrous for Iran and the other Persian Gulf states.[19]

In July 1979 world attention was given to the possibility of a terrorist attack on oil tankers in the Strait of Hormuz. Sheik Ahmed Zaki Yamani, in a *Newsweek* interview on oil and Israel, indicated that the "Palestinians are growing ever more desperate," and that he "wouldn't be surprised if one day they sank one or two supertankers in the Strait of Hormuz, to force the world to do something about their plight and Israel's obstinacy."[20] Shortly thereafter Yasir Arafat indicated that such a possibility existed. The U. S. State Department's Office of Maritime Affairs and Defense Mapping issued a warning on 19 July 1979 to crews of oil tankers and other ships to be alert for an attempt by terrorists to seize or sink one of the ships in the Persian Gulf. The possibility of such an attack was further underscored by the announcement in August 1979 by Lloyd's of London that special war-zone insurance would be required for tankers traveling through the gulf.

Rear Admiral Siamak Deyhimi, Commander of revolutionary Iran's naval fleets in the Persian Gulf and Strait of Hormuz played down the danger of a terrorist attack in the strait. He emphasized the width, depth, and current of the strait were such that "you could sink a dozen supertankers here [in the Strait of Hormuz] and traffic would still get through."[21] Nevertheless, he did accept the "threat to the Strait" as a "given."[22]

The pollution control measures implemented by Iran would enable Iranian officials to inspect foreign vessels for environmental reasons, but they would also serve to uncover arms shipments, other subversive contraband, and even terrorist groups.[23] Although former Prime Minister Hoveida remarked in a 1973 interview that Iranian actions relating to its pollution control plan had "no obvious political implications" and that Iran had encouraged other Persian Gulf states to take similar actions, Iran's security interests are served.[24] The damage to the Persian Gulf environment that could be caused by a terrorist attack presents the entire gulf community with all the more incentive to move forward toward the goals of the Kuwait Regional Conference.

CONCLUSIONS

Whereas the Iranian pollution control measures were instituted in response to a clearly recognized special environmental concern, it appears that Iran, in view of the international community uncertainty on what measures would be appropriate, adopted such legal measures as would serve Iranian interests in the Persian Gulf. Iranian environmental concerns are interrelated with Iranian security interests. Iran is using international law as a tool not only to further its interest in the preservation of the marine environment but also to support Iran's security interests in the Persian Gulf. Furthermore, the 1978 regional convention on the preservation of the marine environment represents an opportunity for increased regional cooperation and an increased monitoring of international shipping in the Persian Gulf at a time when problems in peripheral areas (for example, the Arab-Israeli conflict) could overflow into the Persian Gulf. A regional organization for the preservation of the environment could eventually result in broader types of cooperation that could implicitly or explicitly promote regional stability.

NOTES

1. All vessels could possibly carry some form of noxious cargo; all are potential polluters.

2. For explanation, *see* U. N., *Third Conference on the Law of the Sea*, 1:73 (A/CONF.62/SR1-51).

3. *See* "Oil Polluters to Get Tough Fines, Jail under Bill," *Kayhan* (Tehran: Weekly International Edition), 20 December 1975.

4. *See* "International Convention for the Prevention of Pollution from Ships, 1973," 12 *International Legal Materials* 1319 (1973).

5. "International Convention for the Prevention of Pollution from Ships, 1973," article 5.

6. Ibid.

7. Ibid., annex 1, regulation 10.

8. For conference documents, *see* 17 *International Legal Materials* 501 (1978).

9. The action plan included Bahrain, Iran, Iraq, Kuwait, Oman, Qatar, Saudi Arabia, and the United Arab Emirates. For text of the Action Plan, *see* 17 *International Legal Materials* 501 (1978).

10. The convention was signed by Bahrain, Iran, Iraq, Kuwait, Qatar, Saudi Arabia, and the United Arab Emirates on 24 April 1978. For text, *see* 17 *International Legal Materials* 511 (1978).

11. The protocol was signed by Bahrain, Iran, Iraq, Kuwait, Qatar, Saudi Arabia, and the United Arab Emirates on 24 April 1978. For text, *see* 17 *International Legal Materials* 526 (1978).

12. *See* Kuwait Regional Convention for Cooperation on the Protection of the Marine Environment from Pollution, article 16, 17 *International Legal Materials* 511, 517 (1978).

13. *See* "Canadian Legislation on Arctic Pollution and Territorial Sea and Fishing Zones," 9 *International Legal Materials* 543 (1970); Richard B. Bilder, "The Arctic Waters Pollution Prevention Act: New Stress on the Law of the Sea," 69 *Michigan Law Review* 1 (1970).

14. *See* "The Helsinki Convention on the Protection of the Marine Environment of the Baltic Sea Area," U. N., *Third Conference on the Law of the Sea*, Third Committee (A/CONF.62/C.3/L.1), 22 July 1974.

15. *See* "Convention for the Protection of the Mediterranean Sea Against Pollution," 15 *International Legal Materials* 290 (1976).

16. Amir Taheri, "The South—3: Scattered Pearls," *Kayhan International* (Tehran), 13 May 1970.

17. *See* Robert A. Friedlander, "Coping with Terrorism: What is to be Done," 5 *Ohio Northern Law Review* 432 (1978); "Terrorism in the Middle East: A Symposium," 7 *Akron Law Review* 373 (1974); "Controlling International Terrorism: An Analysis of Unilateral Force and Proposals for Multilateral Cooperation," 8 *University of Toledo Law Review* 209 (1976).

18. *See* Ruth Lapidoth, "Passage Through the Strait of Bab el Mandeb," 13 *Israel Law Review* 180, 182 (1978).

19. *See* "Shah's Press Interview, January 1972," in R. Ramazani, *The Persian Gulf: Iran's Role* 143 (1972).

20. *See* "Yamani on Oil—and Israel," in *Newsweek*, 9 July 1979, p. 21.

21. *See* "No terrorists able to block Hormuz, says Iran admiral," *Iran Times* (Washington, D. C.), 24 August 1979, p. 13.

22. Ibid.

23. The danger of terrorist mines and limpet bombs perhaps represents the major threat. *See* Arnaud de Borchgrave, "Oman: In Dire Straits," *Newsweek*, 24 September 1979, pp. 56, 61.

24. For remarks concerning Iran's pollution control action, *see* S. Lynton, "Iran Moves Toward a 50-Mile Limit in the Gulf," *Baltimore Sun*, 30 September 1973.

CHAPTER **6**

Claims in Transition

As illustrated by the Iranian pollution control regulations, certain claims concerning the law of the sea, especially if international community standards are uncertain, are fundamentally affected by the outcomes of international forums, such as the various United Nations conferences on the law of the sea. It follows that the direction of national policies and basic community policies are often shaped in such conferences whether or not the conferences reach a general agreement on the issues. This suggests that an examination of any state's participation in such conferences would provide an insight not only into its primary concerns, but also the general policy directions it might assume following the termination of the conferences.

Accordingly, the respective actions of Saudi Arabia and Iran in the 1958 and 1960 United Nations conferences are examined. Then their participation at the Third United Nations Conference on the Law of the Sea[1] is considered with a view to determining changes that might be forthcoming in the Persian Gulf.

UNITED NATIONS CONFERENCES ON THE LAW OF THE SEA, 1958 AND 1960: SAUDI PARTICIPATION

The participation of Saudi Arabia at the first United Nations Conference on the Law of the Sea was dominated by its security interests, as indicated by its efforts to establish a twelve-mile limit for territorial seas and its refusal to recognize any "right of innocent passage" that would apply to Israeli passage through the Strait of Tiran.

The attempt to establish a maximum breadth for territorial seas, together with the controversy over the right of innocent passage, represented focal points for the First Committee, as well as for Saudi Arabia, with the disagreements extending into the plenary meetings. First, the question of breadth of the territorial sea resulted in three main proposals: the American, the eight-power (including Saudi Arabia), and the Soviet proposals. The United States proposed a six-mile limit for the territorial sea, with an adjoining six-mile contiguous zone for fishing.[2] Saudi Arabia was steadfast in its denial of the proposed six-mile limit. Mr. Shukairi, the Saudi representative, went so far as to state that if the conference approved the American proposal and embodied it in a convention, his government would not become party to such convention.[3]

Saudi Arabia cosponsored the eight-power proposal, which provided that "every State is entitled to fix the breadth of its territorial sea up to a limit of twelve nautical miles."[4] The Soviet proposal suggested that the limit be set from three to twelve miles.[5] All of the proposals were rejected, with Saudi Arabia voting against the American proposal and for the other two.[6]

It should also be noted that a Saudi "compromise" proposal had been presented earlier in committee.[7] This draft resolution on the breadth of the territorial sea advocated the acceptance of four principles. These were as follows:

(1) International practice is not uniform as regards the delimitation of the territorial sea;
(2) International law does not permit an extension of the territorial sea beyond twelve miles;
(3) The extension by a State of its territorial sea to a twelve-mile limit is not a breach of international law;
(4) The three-mile limit, as a minimum, is recognized as a rule of existing international law.[8]

The proposal was withdrawn in committee because the Saudi representative believed that an agreement on a delimitation of territorial sea might be reached.[9]

The second focal point of the Saudi participation involved the "right of innocent passage," especially, "innocent passage through international straits."[10] Saudi Arabia maintained that such a right "could only be determined in light of the breadth of the territorial sea" and that the "conditions to which a State would subject the right of innocent passage would naturally depend on whether the territorial sea was wide or narrow."[11] Furthermore, Saudi Arabia proposed an amendment that provided the following:

Passage is innocent, unless it is prejudicial to the security of the coastal State. Such passage is not innocent when it is contrary to the present rules or to other rules of international law.[12]

Here the Saudi emphasis was on the words "contrary to the present rules or to other rules of international law."[13] This emphasis, based upon Saudi security interests, was closely related to the Saudi stand vis-à-vis the "illegal" presence of Israel in the Gulf of Aqaba.

The intensity of the Saudi concern over the question of innocent passage was shown in its response to the "three-power" amendment to draft article 17. The amendment provided the following:

There shall be no suspension of the innocent passage of foreign ships through straits or other sealanes which are used for international navigation between a part of the high seas and another part of the high seas or the territorial waters of a foreign state.[14]

Shukairi, the Saudi representative, strongly objected to the three-power amendment and stated that his "government's participation in the final act of the conference would be conditioned, among other things, on the rejection of the amendments to article 17 at present before the Committee."[15] Saudi Arabia further protested that "the amended text no longer dealt with the general principles of international law, but had been carefully tailored to promote the claims of one State."[16]

A related issue concerned the "innocent passage of warships." The Saudi position succinctly pointed out that "it would be unthinkable to permit warships to traverse such areas (territorial straits and national waters) without authorization."[17] The Saudi representative further argued that "warships should not enjoy complete freedom of passage." He cited Jessup, who had "compared the transit of such vessels through the territorial sea with the movement of an army across a foreign State's land territory."[18]

After extended debate on whether warships should require "prior notification" or "prior authorization," the references to a "right of innocent passage for warships" were finally omitted. However, the three-power amendment on the right of innocent passage through straits—which Saudi Arabia so emphatically opposed—was adopted 62 to 1, with 9 abstentions,[19] among them Saudi Arabia. Shukairi explained that he had abstained from voting on article 17 because he considered that paragraph 4 (the three-power amendment) was a "mutilation of international law" and had nothing to do with the principle of free navigation, which had been the pretext used to introduce "ideas foreign to the principles of international law."[20] He reiterated that he "believed paragraph 4 had been drafted with one particular case in view;" he went on to state that Saudi Arabia would take the necessary steps to protect its national interests against the interpretation and application of paragraph 4.[21]

The final results of the first United Nations Conference on the Law of the Sea were not to Saudi Arabia's liking. The Saudi proposal for a twelve-mile limit had not been adopted. In fact, no limit had been agreed upon. Furthermore, in respect to the right of innocent passage, Saudi Arabia saw an article adopted that, in effect, recognized a right of innocent passage for Israel through the Gulf of Aqaba and its straits. Saudi Arabia responded by not only refusing to sign the Convention on the Territorial Sea and Contiguous Zone, but also refusing to be a party to any of the conventions of the conference.

At the Second United Nations Conference on the Law of the Sea, the controversy over the proper limit for the territorial sea continued, with proposals remaining relatively unchanged. The United States again proposed a maximum limit of six nautical miles, with a six-mile contiguous fishing zone. The Soviet Union proposed that the limit for territorial seas be fixed at up to twelve miles. Saudi Arabia again cosponsored a draft resolution, called the ten-power draft resolution, that also fixed the limit of the territorial seas at up to twelve miles.[22] The result of the second conference was the same as that of the first; no agreement on the territorial sea was reached.

Saudi participation in the 1958 and 1960 United Nations conferences on the law of the sea, in addition to illustrating specific Saudi concerns, also suggested the general manner in which Saudi Arabia approached the law of the sea. The Saudi statements indicated that Saudi Arabia believed that certain rules of international law were outmoded and generally reflected the interests of one or two states. For example, the Saudi representative, Shukairi, stated:

The law of the sea to be drafted by the 1958 Conference should reflect the collective will of States participating as sovereign States possessing sovereign equality, and should not depend on the will of one or two nations, as had been the case in the past . . . it was only after the remnants of the antiquated rules of international law had been swept away that progressive development of that law could take place.[23]

He further indicated that "not only the maritime powers but all States . . . should have an equal voice in discussing every aspect of the law of the sea."[24] Shukairi went on to remind the First Committee that "the international community consisted of some ninety States whose vital interests must be reflected in whatever code" was adopted.[25] Saudi Arabia maintained that progressive development should be based on the vital interests of all states, not just those of the maritime powers.

Although Saudi Arabia saw itself as a newly developing state and felt that some laws were "antiquated" and based on the "customs and usage of one or two states," it did not challenge the basis of international law. Rather, it suggested that the foundations of international law be considered and that the origin of such terms as territorial sea be reviewed.[26] Moreover, the Saudi representative went to great lengths to indicate that his country's actions were "in conformity with modern trends and practice as well as with the [International Law] Commission's conclusions."[27]

These arguments are informative as they relate to the Saudi use of law. At the conferences Saudi Arabia repeatedly challenged the positions of the United States and Britain, the two major maritme powers. Saudi Arabia did not challenge Western law as such, but rather the American and British interpretations of it. On point after point Saudi Arabia challenged the American and British positions by citing Western precedents. For example, Saudi Arabia cited in great detail numerous American and British precedents in which the territorial sea was considered to extend beyond three miles.[28] In a similar manner Saudi Arabia quoted well-known Western jurists, such as Phillip Jessup, to support its position.[29] Even in Saudi Arabia's harshest criticism of the American position at the first law of the sea conference, it used an American frame of reference in considering the United States proposal "an insult to the intelligence of those who knew United States jurisprudence."[30]

In the 1960 conference Saudi Arabia continued its strong opposition to the American position, and did so in a significantly Western manner. Saudi Arabia again cited both American precedents and the works of American legal scholars, and even quoted Thomas Jefferson at length.[31] After quoting Jefferson, the Saudi Arabian representative asserted the following:

Thomas Jefferson seems to live, to argue, to advocate with us in this Conference, pleading for all draft resolutions based on twelve miles. The position he explained in 1793 is the same position that prevails in the Conference now in 1960. Thomas Jefferson spoke of a friendly conference. We are now in a Conference—friendly we wish it to be. He spoke of law being unsettled, and that is why we met in the past at The Hague, why we meet at present in Geneva, and why we might perhaps meet in the future. Thomas Jefferson enumerated the extent of territorial sea to be three miles, nine miles and twenty miles, and the draft resolutions for a twelve-mile maximum is a modest incarnation of his calculation.[32]

At the 1960 conference Saudi Arabia also challenged the American position using American sources other than legal ones. Saudi Arabia charged that the United States six-mile formula was not based on legal considerations but was "conceived as part of the Cold War between the Major Powers" and based on "the vital interests of the U. S. Navy and the submarine strategy of the Soviet Union."[33] The Saudi representative based the accusation on an article written by the head of the American delegation, published in 1958, which explained the American motivations in terms of these strategic military implications.[34]

Significantly, the import of the Saudi charge was not to deny the importance of the security implications of the United States but to object to the lack of regard for the "equally legitimate interests and apprehensions of other States."[35] In other words, Saudi Arabia wanted it known that it and other states also had a definite concern for their security and that Saudi policy with respect to the law of the sea was based on Saudi interests and should not be viewed in terms of Cold War positions.

From the Saudi participation in the first two United Nations conferences the following observations may be made. First, Saudi Arabia, as influenced by its security interests, was primarily concerned with such issues as the breadth of the territorial sea and the right of innocent passage. Second, Saudi Arabia saw itself as a new state in opposition to certain outmoded rules of law that served the interests of the maritime powers, but Saudi Arabia did not challenge international law. Instead, it claimed that it adhered to international law and called on the maritime powers to recognize the legitimate interests of all states in the codification and progressive development of international law. Third, Saudi Arabia, although strongly opposing the positions of the United States and Britain, based its arguments on essentially Western sources and assumed a Western manner in its approach to law. Fourth, the Saudi participation at the two conferences was essentially determined by Saudi security interests arising from the presence of Israel in the Gulf of Aqaba. The Saudi actions relating to the law of the sea were primarily the result of conditions existing in Saudi Arabia's immediate environment, the Persian Gulf.

UNITED NATIONS CONFERENCES ON THE LAW OF THE SEA, 1958 AND 1960: IRANIAN PARTICIPATION

The Iranian participation at the 1958 United Nations conference was not dominated by any single issue, but certain underlying interests were apparent. First, Iran was very protective on issues pertaining to its sovereignty and to its authority in offshore areas. Closely related to this general expression of Iranian security interests were Iran's views on the breadth of the territorial sea—views which became the focus of Iranian concern at the 1960 conference. Second, Iran displayed a special interest in the median-line method of delimitation, especially as it might be applied to the continental shelf in the Persian Gulf. Iran's participation, therefore, indicated certain underlying security interests, as well as more specific economic interests. Also present in the various Iranian statements and actions at both conferences was an indication of Iran's attitudes toward the maritime powers and toward international law.

Reflecting Iranian security interests, Iran's concern for its sovereignty and its authority in offshore areas was manifest on questions pertaining to the laying and maintenance of submarine cables and pipelines, marine scientific research, land-locked states, and dispute settlement. Iran also expressed such interests on more specific issues pertaining to the breadth of the territorial sea and the right of innocent passage.

On the question of the laying and maintenance of cables and pipeline on the continental shelf, Iran felt that a distinction should be made between the bed of the high seas and that of the continental shelf. Iran pointed to an International Law Commission commentary that made a special reference to the continental shelf.[36] Expressing a specific interest in the exercise of coastal state authority over the seabed of the continental shelf, Iran subsequently made a reservation to article 4 of the Convention on the Continental Shelf, in which it declared the following:

With respect to the phrase 'the coastal State may not impede the laying or maintenance of submarine cables or pipelines on the continental shelf,' the Iranian Government reserves its right to allow or not allow the laying or maintenance of submarine cables or pipelines on its continental shelf.[37]

On the question of marine scientific research, Iran voiced a dual aim of providing for such research in the waters superjacent to the continental shelf while maintaining certain safeguards to protect the interests of the coastal states. Iran called for a compromise, suggesting that

first, that there must be no obstacle to bona fide scientific research and secondly that the coastal State must be protected against other activities that might be conducted under the guise of scientific research.[38]

In order to protect adequately the interests of the coastal states, Iran proposed an amendment to article 71 that read as follows:

In the interests of scientific progress, the coastal State shall, at the request of appropriate and qualified institutions, permit them to carry out on the continental shelf any kind of fundamental research having a purely scientific objective, provided that:

(a) The institution concerned shall in its application to the coastal State give a full description of the nature and scope of the research work contemplated, that

(b) The coastal State may choose to participate in such research work, or to nominate observers to follow such work, and that

(c) The observations made, the data obtained and all conclusions derived therefrom shall be published.[39]

Although Iran's proposal was rejected, a similar French proposal was adopted.[40]

Iran's concern for its sovereignty was expressed in its statements pertaining to the question of land-locked states. In the Fifth Committee the Iranian representative, on the question of freedom of access for land-locked states, indicated that

two intrinsically different and conflicting concepts were involved—the concept of state sovereignty which presupposed the conclusion of bilateral agreements and the concept of the access of land-locked States to the sea.[41]

He went on to state that "it would not be possible in practice to reconcile those concepts by universal declaration."[42] When the right of free access to the high seas was voted on in the plenary session, Iran abstained "because it considered the preparation of a draft convention outside the terms of reference of the Fifth Committee."[43] This Iranian posture reflected, *inter alia*, certain problems with neighboring Afghanistan.

A similar concern for Iran's sovereignty was expressed in statements pertaining to compulsory jurisdiction in dispute settlements. Iran indicated that "while compulsory jurisdiction in international law represented a noble ideal, the time was not yet ripe for the inclusion of compulsory settlement clauses in all multilateral treaties."[44] Iran then went on to support the Swiss proposal for a separate protocol on dispute settlement. Iran subsequently did not sign the optional protocol.

On the question of the breadth of the territorial sea, in the 1958 conference Iran recognized that "different representatives expressed widely divergent views" and "agreed with the International Law Commission's statement in article 3 that international practice was not uniform as regards the delimitation of the territorial sea."[45] Iran called for an "equitable and practical solution"[46] but did not speak out strongly against the notion that the breadth of the territorial sea should never exceed three miles.[47] In the plenary session Iran voted for the United States compromise proposal, which would have provided a six-mile limit.[48] After the American proposal was rejected, Iran voted for the eight-power proposal, which would have provided a twelve-mile limit.[49] Iran maintained that it voted for the American proposal "out of a desire to assist a general compromise on a breadth of six miles and thus ensure the success of the Conference."[50] Iran further explained that its vote for the eight-power proposal was to "secure its freedom of action . . . as it affected the geographical region in which Iran was situated."[51] Iran's vote for the eight-power proposal thus signaled Iran's forthcoming extension of its territorial sea to twelve miles in 1959 and Iran's staunch defense of the twelve-mile limit at the 1960 conference.

At the 1960 conference the Iranian representative claimed that

the sole solution that met the requirements of the majority of States in the matters of security, conservation of marine resources and national economy was to leave States free to fix the breadth of their territorial sea at any distance up to twelve nautical miles, on the basis of international practice as confirmed by the International Law Commission.[52]

Iran maintained that it based its twelve-mile limit on its security needs as a coastal state. However, in the voting Iran did not vote against the American proposal for a six-mile limit, citing the intention "not to obstruct those delegations which were hoping to save the prestige of the conference and to produce some tangible result."[53] Iran did vote for the twelve-mile limit as proposed in the ten-power draft resolution in the plenary session.[54]

On the question of the "right of innocent passage" at the 1958 conference, Iran did not explicitly define its position. However, concerning the right of innocent passage through straits, when the proposed three-power amendment to paragraph 4 of article 17[55] was put to a vote in the first committee, Iran voted against it.[56] The amendment did pass, 31 to 30, with 10 abstentions. It later became article 16, paragraph 4 of the Convention on the Territorial Sea and Contiguous Zone. Iran signed the convention but did not ratify it. Thus the Iranian position on the right of innocent passage through straits, as expressed by its actions at the first conference on the law of the sea, was inconclusive.

On the question of innocent passage for warships, Iran's policy was quite clear. Iran maintained that the passage of warships required prior authorization. When the words "authorization of" were deleted from the proposed article 24, the Iranian delegate indicated that he would vote against the article.[57] In the 1960 conference Iran repeated its concern about the presence of foreign warships by expressing the following:

The tragic memory of the appearance of warships in the coastal sea. . .was still unforgettable, and a breadth of six miles, insufficient as it was to keep warships out of sight would not give such countries an adequate safeguard.[58]

The Iranian participation at the 1958 and 1960 law of the sea conferences reflected a strong concern for economic interests as well as security interests. Iranian economic interests were clearly manifest in Iran's position regarding the use of the median line to delimit the continental shelf. In the Fourth Committee the Iranian delegate stated that the draft articles as proposed by the International Law Commission did not conflict with existing Iranian legislation, but they did point to potential problems in application. The Iranian delegate suggested that

some of the criteria referred to, though suitable for application to the open seas, such as the Sea of Oman and the Iranian waters west of the Straits of Ormuz [Hormuz], could not apply to shallow waters covering submerged lands, especially if they were of a deltaic type, as in the Persian Gulf.[59]

The Iranian delegate stated that amendments would be submitted "with a view to making the articles more applicable to such conditions."[60]

Iran proceeded to submit a proposed amendment to article 72 which provided that

where special circumstances . . . so warrant the median line may be measured from the high-water mark along the coastline of the State concerned.[61]

Iran went to great lengths to explain why the use of a median line measured from the low-water line would not be practical to delimit submerged lands in the Persian Gulf. Mr Rouhani, an Iranian delegate, stated that

when large bodies of water carrying sediment deposited it near the coast and formed extensive mud flats which were exposed at low-water . . . it would be almost impossible to identify the low-water line by visual observation or by photography.[62]

In addition, the Iranian delegate pointed to the problem of attempting to trace a median line in the presence of islands, and explained

that if they [islands] were taken into account, serious complications would arise and the benefit of having adopted the median line rule would be lost by the difficulty of applying it.[63]

Iran contended that the purpose of its proposed amendment "was to permit some measure of relaxation of the general rule followed in delimiting the boundary. . . where an exceptional geographical configuration or other circumstance might justify such a departure."[64]

The American delegate suggested that the Iranian proposal could be included under the provision for "special circumstances" and was therefore not necessary. The proposal was defeated, but the intensity of the Iranian concern was registered in Iran's reservation to article 6 of the Convention on the Continental Shelf. The reservation provided that "one method of determining the boundary line in special circumstances would be that of measurement from the high-water mark."[65]

Iran's concern over the determination of the median line was based on the fact that a median line drawn from low-water marks in the Persian Gulf would have been distorted to Iran's disadvantage since the waters on the Arab side are shallower than those on the

Iranian side. The problem of applying the median line method of delimitation was to be reflected in later developments in the Persian Gulf, when "equitable principles" assumed a broader application.[66]

Another Iranian economic interest was evident in Iran's support of the Icelandic proposal relating to fishing. Iceland's proposal provided the following:

Where a people is overwhelmingly dependent upon its coastal fisheries for its livelihood or economic development and it becomes necessary to limit the total catch . . . in areas adjacent to the coastal fisheries zone, the coastal State shall have preferential rights under such limitations to the extent rendered necessary by its dependence on the fishing.[67]

Iran's support for this proposal indicated the direction of later Iranian claims to an exclusive fishing zone.

While specific security and economic interests were manifest in Iranian actions at the 1958 and 1960 law of the sea conferences, an insight into Iran's attitude toward the international law of the sea can be found in Iran's general statements. First, it is apparent that Iran saw a basic cleavage between the interests of the maritime powers and the interests of developing states. Iran pointed to certain inequalities that had resulted in "obsolete customs and practices" that were "enshrined in conventions to which most of the states of Asia and Africa were not parties."[68] Iran, in voicing its opposition to certain prescriptive rights included in the American proposal on fishing, charged that the proposal "sought to perpetuate an unjust practice which many under-developed or former non-self-governing countries had been unable to combat."[69] In its opposition to the American proposal for a three-mile limit, Iran asserted that such a limit would only serve the interests of the maritime powers and that, "in fact, they were laying claim to hegemony of the high seas."[70] Iran further indicated that many states were "under-developed" as a result of the "policy of colonialism followed by the states which benefited from the freedom of the seas."[71]

However, in pointing out such inequalities, Iran indicated that "a new era had begun," and said that "the under-developed states of Asia and Africa, including all those which had recently become independent, were ready to co-operate in all honesty and without bitterness with the great maritime states if they showed understanding."[72] Iran called for the progressive development of international law to be achieved through "compromise in a spirit of progressive realism."[73] In other words, Iran recognized that there were certain inequities and that the maritime powers were pursuing their vital interests, but called for the vital interests of the underdeveloped states to be recognized as well.

Iran, though noting that certain "unjust practices and customs" existed in international law, did not condemn international law, but rather called for its progressive development. In opposing the positions of the maritime powers, Iran repeatedly cited the work of the International Law Commission. Also, in challenging the arguments of the maritime powers Iran employed traditional international legal principles and cited American precedents.[74]

From Iran's participation in the 1958 and 1960 law of the sea conferences certain observations may be made. First, Iran's participation was strongly influenced by its security and economic interests in the Persian Gulf. Some of these Iranian concerns were subsequently incorporated into Persian Gulf legal developments. Second, although Iran challenged the positions of the maritime powers and cited certain inequalities and "unjust practices," it did not denounce international law. Instead, it called for its development in a spirit of "progressive realism."

THIRD UNITED NATIONS CONFERENCE ON THE LAW OF THE SEA: IRANIAN AND SAUDI PARTICIPATION

The policy positions of Iran and Saudi Arabia at the Third United Nations Conference on the Law of the Sea have been primarily influenced by their respective security and economic interests. These national interests generally exemplify similar national interests of other developing states. In addition, special interests arising from the geographic peculiarities of the Persian Gulf are also reflected in the Iranian and Saudi policy positions.

Throughout the conference three basic tensions have confronted the participants. The first, as described by an Iranian delegate, is

the divergence of opinions derived primarily from the conflict between two basic principles: the principle of territorial sovereignty over the adjacent sea and that of freedom of the high seas.[75]

The second is the tension between the theoretical concept of "the common heritage of mankind" and the practical necessities of providing a workable regime for the exploitation of deep-sea minerals. The third is the tension between the attempt to establish general rules that would be uniformly applicable and a recognition of the particular needs of special areas, as determined by specific geographic characteristics. The antinomies resulting from these tensions pervade the policies of the participants, including those of Iran and Saudi Arabia, and point to the necessity of further accommodations before a workable, balanced international law of the sea can be established.

PRESENT POLICIES

The policies of Iran and Saudi Arabia as expressed at the Third United Nations Conference on the Law of the Sea are presented here as they relate to the central issues of the law of the sea. The various issues addressed by Iran and Saudi Arabia are considered according to the three analytical categories previously examined: claims to authority over offshore areas; claims to authority over offshore resources; and claims to regulate international access.

Authority over Offshore Areas

Two important issues considered at the conference were the breadth of the territorial sea and the degree of coastal state jurisdiction over international shipping lanes that exist within territorial seas, as in international straits and archipelagoes. Concerning the breadth of the territorial sea, Mr. Kazemi, representing Iran, indicated that his country had adopted a twelve-mile limit in its law of 12 April 1959.[76] Mr. Al-Shuhail, representing Saudi Arabia, similarly indicated that his country "had set a twelve-mile limit for its territorial sea."[77]

Regarding straits used for international navigation, Kazemi summarized Iran's position in a statement in the Second Committee:

First . . . the sovereignty of the coastal State in its territorial sea was subject only to the exercise of the right of innocent passage of ships; secondly, that passage through straits used for international navigation must not affect the legal status of the territorial sea when the straits were situated within the territorial sea of one or more States; thirdly, that rules could be devised to safeguard transit through the straits while taking into account the need to protect the security and other interests of the coastal State.[78]

Kazemi had earlier indicated in a plenary meeting that

rules could be devised which would guarantee freedom of passage for foreign vessels while taking account of such questions as the security of the coastal States, the protection of the marine environment and the regulation of the passage of vessels through sea corridors.[79]

In the Second Committee he also pointed out that the breadth of the territorial sea might vary from three to twelve miles, but the navigable channels through straits remained the same. He suggested that "any proposed rules regarding passage through those straits should be based on existing rules."[80] He contended that "the nature and scope of the coastal State's sovereignty over its territorial sea" should be taken into account, but he recognized that "certain exceptions to the sovereignty of the coastal State might be envisaged in the interest of international trade and communication," providing that "the status of the territorial sea encompassing the straits" should in no way be altered.[81]

It seems that Iran is primarily interested in ensuring that the regulations enacted for its territorial sea are also applicable in the straits. This would result in what might be termed a "regulated passage." The right of free transit or innocent passage would remain as long as pertinent regulations were complied with. To be noted in this regard are the "Draft Articles on Navigation through the Territorial Sea, including the Straits used for International Navigation" cosponsored by Malaysia, Morocco, Oman, and Yemen (Yemen Arab Republic).[82] Article 8 (1) provides the following:

1. The coastal State may regulate the passage through its territorial sea of the following:
   (a) Nuclear-powered ships or ships carrying nuclear weapons;
   (b) Marine research and Hydrographic survey ships;
   (c) Oil tankers and chemical tankers carrying harmful or noxious liquid substances in bulk;
   (d) Ships carrying nuclear substances or materials.[83]

These provisions, cosponsored by Oman, must be considered because of the accord between Iran and Oman that establishes a joint naval supervision of the Strait of Hormuz.[84]

Related to Iran's policy on the territorial sea and passage through straits was Iran's move to establish a special regime for the Persian Gulf because of its characteristics as a semi-enclosed sea. In August 1974 Mr. Kazemi, speaking in the Second Committee, called for a special status for semi-enclosed seas. He stated that

the problems raised by the semi-enclosed seas with regard to the management of their resources, international navigation and the preservation of the marine environment justified granting them a particular status constituting an exception to the general rule.[85]

Kazemi contended that a distinction be made between the coastal states and all other states with regard to international navigation. He suggested that

a different regime should apply to the navigation of other States whose ships could pass through straits connecting the oceans with the semi-enclosed seas only for the purpose of calling at one of the ports of the semi-enclosed sea.[86]

Thus, a "sea of destination" would be distinguished from a "sea of transit."[87]

Saudi Arabia assumed a more general stance on the question of straits. Mr. Al-Shuhail indicated that Saudi Arabia "supported free passage in international straits connecting different parts of the high seas."[88] Saudi Arabia, however, did contend that a distinction should be made between straits. A Kuwaiti delegate, Mr. Al-Saud Al-Sabah, indicated that he was speaking on behalf of six Arab states, including Saudi Arabia, when he said that "the term 'straits used for international navigation' should be strictly confined to straits which connected two parts of the high seas."[89] He further indicated that "the Governments on whose behalf he was speaking had not acceded to the Convention on the Territorial Sea and Contiguous Zone of 1958" because it "treated all straits alike."[90] Thus the continuing attention paid to the Israeli presence in the Gulf of Aqaba by Saudi Arabia and others is shown by their positions on the question of straits.

On the question of archipelagoes, Kazemi stated that the Iranian delegation "sympathized with the view of the archipelagic States that their territorial seas should be generally limited by rationally established baselines."[91] However, Kazemi also maintained that "foreign vessels sailing in established corridors must be guaranteed the right of passage."[92] The Saudi delegate similarly indicated that Saudi Arabia "had no objection to the claims of archipelagic States if the channels of international navigation were respected."[93]

Authority over Offshore Resources

Two major developments concerning resource jurisdiction have emerged at the conference. The concept of a 200-mile exclusive economic zone is generally agreed upon, as is the establishment of some form of international seabed authority for those areas beyond the limits of national jurisdiction. However, the details and implementation of both concepts remain to be worked out.

Iran, as indicated by Kazemi, recognizes "the vital importance of the exclusive economic zone for the coastal State," but it prefers that such a zone should be limited "so as to enable the developing countries, particularly the land-locked ones, to enjoy the benefits of the exploitation of the resources."[94] Kazemi also identified a number of questions that would arise from the establishment of an exclusive economic zone. These questions concern the continental shelf, the exclusive fishery zone, the rights of land-locked states, scientific research, and the protection of the marine environment.[95]

The Saudi delegate, Al-Shuhail, indicated that Saudi Arabia supported the establishment of an "exclusive economic zone up to 200 miles on the basis of the freedom of navigation and overflight" but did not elaborate on the possible implications of such a zone.[96]

On the question of the continental shelf, Kazemi remarked that his country had already agreed on the shelf's delimitation with several coastal states in the Persian Gulf and that it sought agreements with other coastal states.[97] He indicated that "his country's position on the possible revision of the criteria for the delimitation of the continental shelf remained flexible," but that "it considered the limits of the 1958 convention to be an absolute minimum."[98] Similarly, Al-Shuhail stated that Saudi Arabia "had delimited its offshore areas by friendly agreements with most neighbour countries."[99]

Regarding fishery resources, Kazemi maintained that a twelve-mile limit was "inadequate for guaranteeing the protection of the vital fishery interests of the coastal States;" he also recognized that "coastal States had the right of jurisdiction over the water adjacent to their coasts."[100] After explaining Iran's steps to protect its fishery resources, he suggested that it would be "desirable to establish a regional fishing commission to ensure the rational use of the coastal waters."[101] Moreover, he asserted that "the rights of coastal States over living resources of the coastal zone must be exclusive and not preferential" but said that it would be in the coastal states' interest "to permit others to exploit the surplus [fishery resources] on terms to be fixed" by the coastal states.[102] Saudi Arabia did not directly speak to the question of fishery resources.

Concerning land-locked states, Kazemi identified three concerns: "their participation in the exploitation of the sea-bed; their claims to the exclusive fishery zone; and their access to the sea."[103] He indicated that the right of land-locked states to share in the revenues arising from the exploitation of the seabed had been recognized, "provided that such revenues be allocated primarily to the developing countries, coastal or land-locked."[104] Kazemi further stated that "the land-locked countries must be suitably represented in the various bodies of the International Authority."[105] On the question of land-locked states' claims to the living resources of the exclusive fishery zone, Kazemi stated that such claims "could be met only in the form of preferential rights within the framework of bilateral or regional agreements."[106] Similarly, regarding "access to the sea," he pointed to the 1965 Convention on Transit Trade of Land-Locked Countries, which called for free access to the sea in a framework of bilateral agreements. It seems that Iran maintained that the principle of reciprocity was vital and that "no state could grant privileges that might be construed as a sort of servitude prejudicial to its territorial sovereignty."[107]

Saudi Arabia was not as detailed in its statements concerning land-locked states. Al-Shuhail stated that Saudi Arabia "recognized the land-locked countries' need for access to sea transit" and also that land-locked states should have "equal rights and privileges" in an international seabed organization.[108]

Apart from the questions arising from the emerging concept of an exclusive economic zone, there are issues surrounding the area beyond the limits of national jurisdiction and the implementation of the concept of the "common heritage of mankind." While such a concern has a plethora of issues and questions in itself, the Iranian and Saudi statements indicate certain preferences.

Kazemi indicated in July 1974 that Iran favored a strong International Sea-Bed Authority with powers "as wide as possible."[109] He also stated that Iran considered the "seabed and ocean floor, and subsoil thereof, beyond the limits of national jurisdiction" to be the common heritage of mankind and thus protected against national appropriation.[110] He further explained that

in order to preserve the marine environment, the Authority must have the right to regulate all exploration and exploitation. It must be empowered to control the research activities of States . . . the Authority should be responsible for co-ordinating all research activities and for ensuring the transfer of information and the latest technology to the developing states.[111]

Concerning the structure of such an authority, Kazemi said that "his delegation felt that the supreme power must rest with a general assembly made up of representatives of all Member States."[112] The authority envisioned by Iran would be a "real semi-commercial 'Enterprise' " capable of carrying out "technical, industrial, and trade activities related to the exploitation of the international zone."[113]

Al-Shuhail stated that Saudi Arabia supported "the declaration in General Assembly resolution 2749 (XXV) that the sea-bed and ocean floor, and the subsoil thereof, beyond the limits of national jurisdiction, as well as the resources of the area, were the common heritage of mankind,"[114] provided that a 200-mile exclusive economic zone be adopted. Saudi Arabia also supported the establishment of an international seabed organization based on the "equal rights and privileges" of all states.[115]

Authority to Regulate Access

A third major group of issues in the changing international law of the sea involves the regulation of international access. While the question of access permeates almost all law of the sea issues, especially those concerning transit through the territorial sea, special attention is given here to marine scientific research, to the broader dangers of environmental pollution and to zones of peace and security.

Iran's position on marine scientific research was clearly indicated by Kazemi in Iran's general statement in the twenty-third plenary meeting. Iran contends that "scientific research must be undertaken with the consent of the coastal State and must be compatible with the State's own research programs."[116] Iran also insists that "scientific personnel of the coastal State must be allowed to participate in the research and that the results must be made available first to the coastal State."[117] Iran maintains that coastal state consent for scientific research in the exclusive economic zone should be based upon the provisions of the 1958 Convention on the Continental Shelf.[118]

Saudi Arabia was less detailed in its statement on marine scientific research, in which Al-Shuhail said that scientific research was permissible "subject to national jurisdiction."[119]

Perhaps of greater significance is the growing concern of both countries over environmental dangers. The threat of marine pollution has loomed large before them, especially with the large amount of tanker traffic and offshore drilling in the Persian Gulf; it has been emphasized accordingly in the statements of both states at the conference.

Kazemi declared that "his delegation attached great importance to the protection of the marine environment and to the struggle against the pollution of the seas."[120] He called attention to the 1973 International Convention for the Prevention of Pollution from Ships, which recognized the Persian Gulf as a "special zone" requiring additional precautions. He explained that although his government had temporarily extended its internal pollution control regulations to the limits of its continental shelf, pending the entry into force of the 1973 International Convention, "there were no limits to pollution."[121] "Accordingly," he went on, "international and regional agreements took on a vital importance."[122] He pointed out that

the question remained, who was to define the criteria and lay down standards in the struggle against pollution caused in particular by oil tankers and other merchant vessels?[123]

He suggested that the conference or another international body might undertake to establish such regulations and that the Inter-

Governmental Maritime Consultative Organization might play an important role.[124]

As for the Persian Gulf, Mr. Sadeghi, an Iranian delegate in the Third Committee, alluded to the possibility of establishing a regional arrangement. He suggested that the 1974 Helsinki Convention on the Protection of the Marine Environment of the Baltic Area represented "a good model of a regional agreement."[125] Sadeghi also proposed that

such a regional agreement should not necessarily be confined to preservation of the marine environment and could also provide, for example, for the establishment of a regional fund to cover accidental or inadvertent damage to coastal States.[126]

He also suggested that in Iran's area the 1971 International Convention on the Establishment of an International Compensation Fund for Oil Pollution Damage might be supplemented by agreements between the Persian Gulf states.

Iran's interest in the preservation of its marine environment was also evident in its recommendation that semi-enclosed seas be granted special consideration. Mr. Parsi commented in the Second Committee that:

Enclosed or semi-enclosed seas represented more acute problems which could not be solved by global norms applicable to all oceans. . . . They formed an intrinsic geophysical and ecological entity and were vulnerable to pollution and over-fishing.[127]

Later, Kazemi, also speaking before the Second Committee, explained that

the semi-enclosed seas were highly vulnerable to pollution owing to the small volume of their waters which lowered their capacity for absorption, and the absence of currents to change waters.[128]

Relating to Iran's overlapping interests in the preservation of the marine environment and special consideration for semi-enclosed seas, Iran cosponsored with nine other states on 31 July 1974 "draft articles on a zonal approach to the preservation of the marine environment."[129] However, Sadeghi insisted in the Third Committee that the draft articles were "incomplete, especially with regard to the provision concerning special zones and regional agreements";[130] he "hoped that additional articles would be prepared."[131]

In a subsequent development Sadeghi addressed the question of the preservation of the marine environment in the Third Committee in April 1975. He stressed that "Iran, as a coastal State, was concerned with the preservation of the marine environment and continued freedom for international shipping," but he maintained that "primary jurisdiction should rest with the coastal State."[132] He reiterated that Iran favored a "balanced approach" that took into account both the needs of the coastal state and freedom of international shipping.[133] He then went on to criticize the nine-power draft articles on the preservation of the marine environment.[134] First, he was especially critical of those provisions pertaining to the setting of uniform international standards for land-based sources of pollution. Sadeghi contended that "it would be too much to expect countries in the early stages of economic and social development to apply such standards."[135] He recommended instead that "land-based sources of pollution should be controlled through national regulations that took account of international regulations."[136]

A second Iranian concern relating to the proposed nine-power draft articles involved the emphasis on "flag-State powers at the expense of coastal States' rights."[137] Sadeghi indicated that "the coastal State should have the right and power within its territorial sea to prevent pollution and should have rights and obligations in its economic zone."[138] He also stressed that the "port States' inspection and enforcement powers should not be weakened."[139] Finally, Sadeghi called attention to the draft articles' ambiguity about who had the right to establish pollution control regulations, remarking that "the provision on that subject stated that responsibility would lie with 'States, acting through the competent international organization."[140] He explained that

his delegation had some difficulty in accepting that arrangement because it believed that the residual powers should not be given entirely to the competent international organization, but rather to the coastal States, which were in a better position to establish rules and regulations through regional arrangements. In addition, they should have enforcement powers.[141]

It seems that Iran is very concerned about the danger of environmental pollution in the Persian Gulf, and it is seeking means to control pollution while preserving freedom of navigation. Iran believes that in some cases regional agreements are essential in implementing certain international standards. Moreover, it has favored a balanced approach to the problem of controlling pollution in an attempt to establish a workable arrangement that would ensure freedom of navigation and effectively control pollution.

Saudi Arabia also addressed the marine pollution problem in the Persian Gulf in its general statement. Al-Shuhail mentioned that Saudi Arabia had 122 nautical miles of coastline that were "subject to extensive marine pollution."[142] He also remarked that Saudi Arabia "had been an active member of the Inter-Governmental Maritime Consultative Organization since 1969," and, being a party to the 1954 International Convention for the Prevention of Pollution of the Sea by Oil, it "had taken fundamental steps in that respect."[143] Saudi Arabia did not initially express the detailed interest in pollution control that Iran did. In the seventh session, in 1978, Saudi Arabia, along with other Arab states, expressed a serious concern for establishing "responsibility and liability" for any damage to the marine environment caused by pollution or "resulting from scientific research."[144]

Another topic that involves regulation of access is the proposed establishment of zones of peace and security. Speaking for Iran at the fourth session, in 1976, Mr. Bavand indicated that the Treaty on the Prohibition of the Emplacement of Nuclear Weapons should be reviewed and updated "with a view to widening the scope of the prohibitions contained in it to cover more weapon systems than merely fixed weapons of mass destruction."[145] He maintained that since the treaty "did not restrict the operations of ballistic missile submarines, nor prohibit manned military underwater stations and anti-submarine-warfare detection systems," it "would be no obstacle to the development of a nuclear arms race in the whole of the ocean environment."[146] After calling attention to Iran's "participation in the preparation and adoption of the Declaration" of the Indian

Ocean as a zone of peace (General Assembly Resolution 2832), he indicated that a collective effort was necessary to realize the objectives of the Declaration.[147] He went on to propose six steps to be taken to uphold the principle of the peaceful uses of ocean space. These were as follows:

(1) The passage of foreign ships, particularly warships, through territorial waters, including those of straits, should be subject to the principle of innocent passage and conducive to the development of international commerce and communications.

(2) All foreign military installations should be excluded from the economic zones and continental shelves of the coastal states and any activities in that connexion should be subject to their consent.

(3) The convention should include a mandatory article stipulating that the non-civilian aspect of the principle of the peaceful uses of ocean space would be considered in an appropriate international forum.

(4) Negotiations on further demilitarization of the sea-bed in accordance with article V of the Treaty on the Prohibition of the Emplacement of Nuclear Weapons should begin as soon as possible, and the review conference should closely consider the relationship between the Treaty and the future convention on the international regime for peaceful uses. In that connexion, the International Sea-bed Authority should assume verification responsibilities.

(5) To lessen suspicion about the offensive purpose of military and scientific research on the sea-bed and ocean floor, such research might be internationalized under the auspices of the International Sea-bed Authority.

(6) The International Sea-bed Authority, in co-operation with the International Atomic Energy Agency, should regulate and control the dumping of nuclear waste and biological and chemical agents on the sea-bed, with a view to reducing the danger of leakage.[148]

FUTURE POSSIBILITIES

The actions of Iran and Saudi Arabia at the Third United Nations Conference on the Law of the Sea suggest several likely developments. Iran, along with others, had called for a regional agreement on pollution control. The results of the Kuwait Regional Conference represent the realization of a regional agreement and possibly the beginning of a permanent regional organization. Iran also called for a regional fishery regime. Saudi Arabia followed Iran's lead and established an exclusive fishing zone extending to the limits of its continental shelf. Similar actions by other gulf states would suggest the eventuality of a regional fishery regime. Furthermore, with the broad community acceptance of a 200-mile exclusive economic zone—an action that would enclose the Persian Gulf for resource jurisdiction—it seems likely that the gulf states will move toward the establishment of a special regional regime. In such case, the Persian Gulf could lose its previous status as part of the high seas and, in effect, become a closed sea. Such an action might be tied to questions concerning the status of the Persian Gulf as a zone of peace and security, especially with expressed desire of the gulf states to avoid a superpower presence.

NOTES

1. The ongoing Third United Nations Conference on the Law of the Sea is considered only through April 1979.

2. The United States had initially proposed a three-mile limit, but offered a six-mile limit as a compromise. For the American proposal, *see* U. N., *United Nations Conference on the Law of the Sea*, 2:126 (A/CONF. 13/38).

3. *See* ibid., 3:36 (A/CONF.13/39).

4. Ibid., 2:128.

5. Ibid., p. 126.

6. For the voting on the three proposals, *see* ibid., pp. 39-40.

7. Ibid., 3:251.

8. Ibid.

9. Ibid., p. 180.

10. Generally speaking, the maritime powers were more interested in the right of innocent passage; the weaker coastal states were more concerned with their security interests. Saudi Arabia was in the second category.

11. *Conference on the Law of the Sea*, 3:71.

12. Ibid., p. 230.

13. Ibid., p. 85.

14. Ibid., p. 231.

15. Ibid., p. 94.

16. Ibid., p. 96. Max Sorensen, the recorder, pointed out that "although never officially stated, the Strait of Tiran at the entrance to the Gulf of Aqaba, giving access from the Red Sea to Israel's port of Eilath," was "in everybody's mind." Sorensen, "The Law of the Sea," *International Concili-*

ation, no. 520 (November 1958), p. 236.

17. *Conference on the Law of the Sea*, 3:129.

18. Ibid., p. 130.

19. Ibid., 2:65.

20. Ibid.

21. Ibid.

22. For the text of the ten-power draft resolution, *see* U. N., *Second United Nations Conference on the Law of the Sea: Summary Records of Plenary Meetings and Meetings of the Committee of the Whole* (A/CONF. 19/9), p. 172.

23. *See Conference on the Law of the Sea*, 3:3.

24. Ibid.

25. Ibid.

26. Ibid., p. 36.

27. Ibid.

28. Ibid., pp. 134-36.

29. Ibid., p. 130.

30. Ibid., 2:36.

31. *See Second United Nations Conference on the Law of the Sea: Committee of the Whole* (A/CONF.19/9), p. 396.

32. Ibid., p. 397.

33. *See Second Conference on the Law of the Sea: Summary Records*, p. 16.

34. *See* Arthur H. Dean, "Freedom of the Seas," *Foreign Affairs*, 37 (October 1958): 83-94.

35. *Second Conference on the Law of the Sea: Summary Records*, p. 16.

36. *Conference on the Law of the Sea*, 6:80 (A/CONF.13/52).

37. For the Iranian reservation, *see* U. N., *Multilateral Treaties in Respect of which the Secretary General Performs Depository Functions* (ST/LEG/SER.D/8), 1975, p. 453.

38. *Conference on the Law of the Sea*, 6:87.

39. Ibid., p. 139.

40. Ibid., p. 141.

41. Ibid., 7:26 (A/CONF.13/43).

42. Ibid.

43. Ibid., 2:29.

44. Ibid., p. 33.

45. Ibid., 3:65.

46. Ibid.

47. Ibid., 4:23 (A/CONF.13/40).

48. Ibid., 2:39.
49. Ibid., p. 40.
50. Ibid., p. 41.
51. Ibid.
52. *Second Conference on the Law of the Sea: Summary Records*, p. 103.
53. Ibid., pp. 13, 30.
54. Ibid., p. 31.
55. *See* above, p. 170.
56. *Conference on the Law of the Sea*, 3:100.
57. Ibid., 2:67.
58. *Second Conference on the Law of the Sea: Summary Records*, p. 104.
59. *Conference on the Law of the Sea*, 6:14.
60. Ibid.
61. Ibid., p. 142.
62. Ibid., p. 92.
63. Ibid., p. 96.
64. Ibid., p. 94.
65. Ibid., p. 119.
66. *See* above, pp. 128–31.
67. *Conference on the Law of the Sea*, 2:109.
68. Ibid., 4:23-24.
69. Ibid., 2:41.
70. Ibid., 4:23.
71. Ibid.
72. Ibid.
73. Ibid., p. 24.
74. *See Second Conference on the Law of the Sea: Summary Records*, p. 103.
75. U. N., *Third United Nations Conference on the Law of the Sea*, 2:115 (A/CONF.62/SRL-51).
76. Ibid., 1:71.
77. Ibid., p. 144.
78. Ibid., 2:123.
79. Ibid., 1:71-72.
80. Ibid., 2:124.
81. Ibid.
82. *See* "Document A / CONF.62 / C.2 / L.16," in ibid., 3:192-95 (A / CONF.62/SRL-51/Add.).
83. Ibid., p. 193.
84. The accord provides Iran with the main responsibility for a joint naval supervision of the strait and is aimed at ensuring that the waters on

both sides of the strait remain "secure and free." For a report of the Iran-Oman accord, *see* "Iran: Accord with Oman on Naval Presence," *Asian Recorder,* 21 (29 January - 4 February 1975): 12418.

85. *Third Conference on the Law of the Sea,* 2:273.

86. Ibid.

87. Ibid.

88. Ibid., 1:144.

89. Ibid., 2:139.

90. Ibid.

91. Ibid., 1:71.

92. Ibid.

93. Ibid., p. 144.

94. Ibid., p. 72.

95. Iran's policy on marine scientific research and the protection of the marine environment will be considered in the next section under claims to regulate international access.

96. *Third Conference on the Law of the Sea,* 1:144.

97. Ibid., p. 72.

98. Ibid.

99. Ibid., p. 144.

100. Ibid., p. 72.

101. Ibid.

102. Ibid.

103. Ibid. (Questions concerning land-locked states are included here even though the issues overlap.)

104. Ibid., p. 73.

105. Ibid.

106. Ibid.

107. Ibid.

108. Ibid., p. 144.

109. Ibid., p. 72.

110. Ibid.

111. Ibid.

112. Ibid.

113. Ibid.

114. Ibid., p. 144.

115. Ibid.

116. Ibid., p. 72.

117. Ibid.

118. *See* the statement of Mr. Momtaz in the third committee, in ibid., 2:347.

119. Ibid., 1:144.

120. Ibid., p. 73.

121. Ibid. *See also* statement of Mr. Sadeghi in the third committee, in *Third Conference on the Law of the Sea*, 2:329.

122. *Third Conference on the Law of the Sea*, 1:73.

123. Ibid.

124. Ibid.

125. Ibid., 2:239.

126. Ibid.

127. Ibid., pp. 115-16.

128. Ibid., p. 273.

129. *See* "Document A / CONF.62 / C.3 / L.6," in ibid., 3:249-50. Iran had earlier cosponsored a proposal in the Seabed Committee that reflected its belief that "more stringent rules should be established for special areas adjacent to coasts." *See Third Conference on the Law of the Sea*, 2:329.

130. *Third Conference on the Law of the Sea*, 2:360.

131. Ibid.

132. Ibid., 4:90 (A/CONF.62/SR52-56).

133. Ibid.

134. *See* "Document A/CONF.62/C.3/L.24," ibid., pp. 210-11.

135. Ibid., p. 90.

136. Ibid.

137. Ibid.

138. Ibid.

139. Ibid.

140. Ibid.

141. Ibid.

142. Ibid., 1:144.

143. Ibid.

144. *See* the Informal Proposals for article 236 and article 264 as put forth by Saudi Arabia and other states in *Third Conference on the Law of the Sea*, 10:185-86, 188.

145. *Third Conference on the Law of the Sea*, 5:65-66.

146. Ibid., p. 65.

147. Ibid., p. 66.

148. Ibid.

CHAPTER **7**

The Roles of Iran and Saudi Arabia in the Development of the Law of the Sea

The implications of the Iranian and Saudi law of the sea claims, agreements, and policy statements not only offer insights into the nature of the development of the law of the sea, but also suggest future developments and possible actions that could lead to the resolution of current disputes. Here the trends in the development of the law of the sea in the Persian Gulf are evaluated in terms of their effects on the basic community policies within the gulf, their contributions to the development of the international law of the sea, and their insights into the role of the developing state in international law.

BASIC COMMUNITY POLICIES IN THE PERSIAN GULF

In examining the current law of the sea in the Persian Gulf the effect of the Iranian and Saudi precedents is evident, as is the continuing tendency of the other littoral states to follow their lead. The claims and agreements of Iran and Saudi Arabia in the gulf have effectively established certain international legal norms that are not only complied with by the other littoral states but are also reflected in their respective claims.

Iran's claim to six-mile territorial waters in 1934 established the first precedent by a modern Persian Gulf state. Saudi Arabia, on the advice of American legal experts, followed Iran's example in its 1949 claim. In February 1958 Saudi Arabia was the first gulf state to extend the breadth of its territorial sea to twelve nautical miles. Iraq followed the Saudi precedent and claimed a twelve-mile territorial sea in November 1958. Iran extended its territorial sea to twelve miles in April 1959, as did Kuwait in December 1967. Sharjah claimed a twelve-mile territorial sea in 1970. Oman defined its claim to a twelve-mile territorial sea in 1972. The twelve-mile territorial sea has become the accepted standard in the Persian Gulf; in practice, it has been adopted by all the littoral states, even though Bahrain, Qatar, and the United Arab Emirates (with the exception of Sharjah) have not yet declared twelve-mile limits through explicit governmental actions.[1]

Coastal state claims to the resources of the seabed and subsoil beyond the territorial sea—continental shelf claims as they are commonly called—represent the second major area of legal development in the Persian Gulf. Moreover, bilateral treaties based on such claims have led to the demarcation of continental shelf boundaries, the "equitable" allocation of subsea resources, and a clarification of resource jurisdiction in much of the Persian Gulf.

In May 1949 Saudi Arabia, basing its claim on the Truman Proclamation on the Continental Shelf, promulgated the first Persian Gulf claim to authority over the resources of the seabed and subsoil extending beyond the "coastal sea". The British-protected states in the Persian Gulf all followed the Saudi precedent: Bahrain, Qatar, Kuwait, Abu Dhabi, Ajman, Dubai, Ras al-Khaimah, Sharjah, and Umm al-Qaiwain all defined their respective claims to the resources of the seabed and subsoil contiguous to their "territorial waters" in June 1949. Iran defined its continental shelf claim in June 1955. Iraq established its claim in November 1957. With Oman's claim to the resources of its continental shelf in July 1972, all of the littoral states have made such claims.

Saudi Arabia and Bahrain signed the first agreement delimiting subsea boundaries in the Persian Gulf in February 1958. Saudi Arabia next signed an agreement on marine boundaries with Qatar in June 1965. In July 1965 Saudi Arabia signed an agreement with Kuwait on the partition of the Neutral Zone that included provisions relating to offshore resources. The demarcation of offshore boundaries in the Persian Gulf received a major impetus with the signing of the Saudi Arabia-Iran offshore boundary agreement of 24 October

1968. Subsequently Iran signed agreements demarcating continental shelf boundaries with Qatar in September 1969, with Bahrain in June 1971, and with Oman in July 1974. Iran had reached an agreement with Kuwait in January 1968, but the agreement has yet to become final. Iran also initialed an agreement with Abu Dhabi in September 1971 and signed an agreement with Dubai in September 1975, but there remains some question about the legal status of agreements entered into by individual sheikhdoms. The "Memorandum of Understanding" of November 1971 between Iran and Sharjah includes provisions on authority over offshore resources and has been implemented, but the arrangement continues to be disputed. In addition to the agreements entered into by Iran and Saudi Arabia, other offshore boundary agreements have been signed in the Persian Gulf. For example, Abu Dhabi and Dubai delimited their offshore boundaries in February 1968, and Abu Dhabi and Qatar signed an agreement in March 1969.

Despite the numerous bilateral agreements in the Persian Gulf, multilateral and regional agreements pertaining to offshore resources have not materialized, and a number of offshore disputes remain. The continuing island and boundary disputes between Kuwait and Iraq in the north and the dispute over Abu Musa and the two Tumbs in the south remain, among others, as major obstacles to the complete demarcation of submarine boundaries in the Persian Gulf. Nevertheless, the number of continental shelf boundary agreements in the gulf is significant, and the delimiation of the continental shelf is considerably advanced.

Iran set a new course in resource claims in the Persian Gulf in October 1973 when it claimed an exclusive fishing zone extending to the limits of its continental shelf. The Iranian precedent was followed by Saudi Arabia and Qatar. Such actions represent, in effect, the establishment of exclusive economic zones in the Persian Gulf, and they parallel the developments at the Third United Nations Conference on the Law of the Sea.

A second development still in its formative stages concerns pollution control measures in the gulf. In extending its domestic pollution control regulations to the limits of the continental shelf and advocating regional pollution control measures, Iran has been instrumental in bringing about a community recognition of the growing danger facing the marine environment in the Persian Gulf. The recognition of the Persian Gulf as a "special zone" in the 1973 International Convention for the Prevention of Pollution from Ships and the actions taken at the Kuwait Regional Conference on the Protection and Development of the Marine Environment and Coastal Areas in 1978 indicate a growing awareness on the part of the gulf states for the necessity of concerted action.[2]

While all of the states in the Persian Gulf have participated in the development of the law of the sea, the actions of Iran and Saudi Arabia have significantly contributed to the establishment of basic community policies in the area. The effects of Iranian and Saudi precedents are visible and are reflected in the actions of other littoral states. Although some disputes remain, and despite the fact that none of the Persian Gulf states have acceded to any of the 1958 Geneva conventions on the law of the sea, a sophisticated international law of the sea has been established in the Persian Gulf.

THE CONTRIBUTIONS OF IRAN AND SAUDI ARABIA TO THE DEVELOPMENTS OF THE INTERNATIONAL LAW OF THE SEA

While Saudi Arabia and Iran have been in the forefront of legal development in the Persian Gulf, they have also contributed to the development of the international law of the sea and have established precedents that are applicable elsewhere. Although many of their actions effectuating change in the Persian Gulf were based on previously accepted or suggested claims of other states in the international community, several of their adaptations and applications of specific legal concepts have contributed to ongoing international legal development.

Concerning claims to authority over offshore areas, the contribution of Iran and Saudi Arabia might be considered as simply participation. Each adopted the use of straight baselines in the delimitation of its territorial waters. In addition, Iran and Saudi Arabia were early advocates of six-mile and twelve-mile territorial sea limits.

Concerning the claims to authority over offshore resources, Iran and Saudi Arabia have significantly contributed to the development of the continental shelf concept and to a broad interpretation of "equitable principles" in the delimitation of continental shelf boundaries. First, the Saudi claim to the resources of the seabed and subsoil of the area extending beyond its territorial waters was based on the Truman Proclamation, but it was also adapted to the physical characteristics of the Persian Gulf. Since the gulf represents a basin that has "no edge," the Saudi claim—as recommended by Manley O. Hudson and Richard Young—was based on the concept of contiguity rather than on the geological formation known as a continental shelf. When the International Law Commission initially considered the emerging concept of the continental shelf, Judge Hudson, then a member of the Commission, specifically pointed to the case of the Persian Gulf, which had no shelf. In order to provide for such a case as the Persian Gulf, which was shallow enough to permit the exploitation of the resources of the seabed and subsoil, the International Law Commission eventually adopted the concept of exploitability. While the Saudi offshore claim was not responsible for the subsequent use of the concept of exploitability to extend the limits of the continental shelf to greater depths, it was responsible for its emergence.

The most significant contribution of the Persian Gulf practice of Iran and Saudi Arabia has been their imaginative and pragmatic application of "equitable principles" in the delimitation of continental shelf boundaries. Politically sensitive disputes involving conflicting claims to offshore petroleum resources have been resolved in the Persian Gulf by such methods as granting authority over a disputed area containing valuable resources to one state but providing for an equal distribution of the profits from the exploitation of the area's resources between two states (Saudi Arabia-Bahrain); diverting the boundary line between two states so as to divide previously discovered resources in place equitably (Saudi Arabia-Iran); and granting half-effect to an island in the determination of the baseline from which the boundary line is to be determined (Saudi Arabia-Iran). Such examples as these represent an expansion of the equitable principles concept beyond the principle of equidistance to include a consideration of the irregular geographic configurations and the principle of proportionality in the allocation of continental shelf resources.

The widely accepted Truman Proclamation provided that continental shelf boundaries between proximate states would be determined "in accordance with equitable principles." However, the concept of equitable principles, as influenced by the recommendation of the International Law Commission and as included in the 1958 Geneva Convention on the Continental Shelf, came to be equated with the principle of equidistance and the use of the median line. It was not until the judgment of the International Court of Justice in the North Sea Continental Shelf Cases that the emphasis on the principle of equidistance was reduced and the "importance of all relevant circumstances" acknowledged by the international community. The practice of Iran and Saudi Arabia preceded, and probably contributed to, the findings of the Court in the North Sea continental shelf cases and the cases involving the delimitation of the continental shelf between Britain and France.

The broader application of equitable principles is more conducive to agreement than a rigid application of the principle of equidistance. Thus it is not inconceivable that other offshore disputes, such as the dispute between Greece and Turkey over offshore petroleum resources, could be resolved in the same manner as those in the Persian Gulf. Moreover, as the search for offshore petroleum resources expands, and as conflicting claims multiply, the significance of Persian Gulf precedents could increase accordingly.

Concerning claims to regulate international access, the contributions of Iran and Saudi Arabia are yet to be realized. However, the Persian Gulf practice appears to be poised on the precipice of change, awaiting, among other things, the outcome of the Third United Nations Conference on the Law of the Sea. The current developments in the Persian Gulf and the recommendations of Iran at the Third United Nations Conference could lead to a new regional precedent that could be of major importance to the developing law of the sea. Iran and other states have called attention to the special problems of semi-enclosed seas—problems that cannot be solved by broad global norms but require regional cooperation. To deal with the growing problems of pollution, overfishing, and regional security, Iran and other gulf states have advocated special regional arrangements. Considering the growing vulnerability of semi-enclosed seas to increased usage, the necessity of establishing a special regime for the Persian Gulf continues to be cited. The success of such regional cooperation as envisioned at the Kuwait Regional Conference in 1978 would have major implications for the many other semi-enclosed seas that are yet to experience the degree of usage of the Persian Gulf. In view of the desire of the gulf states to avoid the presence of foreign powers in the gulf and to prevent the increase of destabilizing elements, as well as their growing concern for the problems of marine pollution and overfishing, the establishment of a special regime and the closing of the gulf to nonregulated passage appear in the offing.

INSIGHTS INTO THE ROLE OF THE DEVELOPING STATE IN INTERNATIONAL LAW

The approaches to international law of two developing states, Iran and Saudi Arabia, shed light on the role of the developing state in international law. The Persian Gulf practice reflects not only the Iranian and Saudi use of law but also their general orientation to international law.

The Iranian and Saudi use of law, as expressed by their claims and agreements in the Persian Gulf, has generally been in accord with previously established international community standards. However, where no clear community consensus exists, Iran and Saudi Arabia have adopted those legal principles that have best suited their interests as determined by the Persian Gulf context. As international practice has developed, and as accepted usages have crystallized, Iran and Saudi Arabia have amended their claims to reflect international community preferences.

Iran and Saudi Arabia have used international law as an instrument to support their respective interests in a given context, and they have recognized international law as a constraint on what actions would be appropriate. In establishing an initial six-mile claim to its territorial waters in 1934, Iran was using law as an instrument to further certain national interests in the Persian Gulf. Similarly, the Saudi extension of its territorial sea to twelve nautical miles in 1958 represented the use of law as a tool to support Saudi interests in response to the presence of Israel in the Gulf of Aqaba. The broad application of "equitable principles" in the delimitation of offshore boundaries by Iran and Saudi Arabia represented the use of law as an instrument of policy while recognizing certain overriding principles upon which law is based.

The general orientation to international law, while exemplified in part by the empirical use of law, is also expressed by the legal style and the manner in which international law is conceptually approached. Of special significance in this regard is the reliance of Iran and Saudi Arabia on Western sources and precedents to support their claims and to challenge the claims of others, including those of the advanced states. In questioning the applicability of certain previously accepted community standards, Iran and Saudi Arabia have suggested the reapplication of the basic principles upon which the standards were based in view of the changing circumstances, rather than questioning the applicability of international law itself. Although at times conflicting with advanced states on given legal questions, Iran and Saudi Arabia have not failed to recognize the interests of the advanced states, but they have called for the interests of the emerging developing states to be considered as well. In addition, as illustrated by Saudi Arabia, Western legal expertise has been an important component in the approach of developing states to international law.

The reliance on Western sources and precedents and the use of Western legal experts suggest, contrary to some prevailing generalizations, that the approaches of developing states to international law are similar to those of advanced states. The use of law by Iran and Saudi Arabia illustrates that the role of the developing state in international law is not unlike that of advanced states, since it is based upon specific interests as determined by the nature of the context in which they are situated.

NOTES

1. *See* Husain M. Albaharna, *The Arabian Gulf States*, 2d ed. (Beirut: Librairie du Liban, 1975), p. 359.

2. Kuwait, especially, has been a leader in calling for joint action for the preservation of the marine environment in the gulf. *See* U. N., *Third United Nations Conference on the Law of the Sea*, 1:156.

Bibliography

AGREEMENTS AND NATIONAL ENACTMENTS

Iran. 19 July 1934. "Act of July 19, 1934 relating to the Breadth of the Territorial Waters and Zone of Supervision." In United Nations, *Law and Regulations on the Regime of the Territorial Sea*. United Nations Legislative Series (ST/LEG/SER.B/6), 1957.

_____. 19 May 1949. "Bill relating to Persian Gulf Subsea Resources, May 19, 1949." 5 *Revue Egyptienne de Droit International* 346 (1949).

_____. 19 June 1955. "Law of June 19, 1955 concerning the Continental Shelf." In *New Directions in the Law of the Sea*, vol. 1: *Documents*. Ed. Robin Churchill, S. Houston Lay, and Myron Nordquist. Dobbs Ferry, N. Y.: Oceana, 1973.

_____. 12 April 1959. "Act of April 12, 1959 Amending Act relating to the Breadth of the Territorial Sea and Contiguous Zone of Iran dated July 19, 1934." In United Nations, *Second United Nations Conference on the Law of the Sea*, A/CONF.19/5.

_____. 24 October 1968. Iran-Saudi Arabia. "Agreement concerning Sovereignty over Al-Arabiyah and Farsi Islands and Delimitation of Boundary Line Separating Submarine Areas between the Kingdom of Saudi Arabia and Iran." 8 *International Legal Materials* 493 (1969).

_____. 20 September 1969. Iran-Qatar. U. S. Department of State. *International Boundary Study, Series A—Limits in the Seas*, no. 25. "Continental Shelf Boundary: Iran-Qatar." 9 July 1970.

_____. 17 June 1971. Iran-Bahrain. U. S. Department of State. *International Boundary Study, Series A—Limits in the Seas*, no. 58. "Continental Shelf Boundary: Bahrain-Iran." 13 September 1974.

_____. November 1971. Iran-Sharjah. "Memorandum of Understanding between Iran and Sharjah." *Middle East Economic Survey* (Supplement, 15 (5 May 1972):2.

_____. 30 October 1973. "Proclamation of 30 October 1973 concerning the Outer Limit of the Exclusive Fishing Zone of Iran in the Persian Gulf and the Sea of Oman." *National Legislation and Treaties Relating to the Law of the Sea*. United Nations Legislative Series (ST / LEG / SER.B/18), 1976.

_____. 25 July 1974. Iran-Oman. U. S. Department of State. *International Boundary Study, Series A—Limits in the Seas*, no. 67. "Continental Shelf Boundary: Iran-Oman." 1 January 1976.

_____. 31 August 1974. Iran-Dubai. U. S. Department of State. *International Boundary Study, Series A—Limits in the Seas*, no. 63. "Continental Shelf Boundary: Iran-United Arab Emirates (Dubai)." 30 September 1975.

Saudi Arabia. 28 May 1949. "Decree No. 6/4/5/3711 (Territorial Waters of Saudi Arabia), 28 May 1949." 43 *American Journal of International Law* (Supplement) 154 (1949).

_____. 28 May 1949. "Royal Pronouncement concerning the Policy of the Kingdom of Saudi Arabia with Respect to the Subsoil and Sea Bed of Areas in the Persian Gulf contiguous to the Coasts of the Kingdom of Saudi Arabia, May 28, 1949." 43 *American Journal of International Law* (Supplement) 156 (1949).

_____. 16 February 1958. "Decree No. 33 Defining the Territorial Waters of the Kingdom, February 16, 1958." In United Nations, *Supplement to Laws and Regulations on the Regime of the High Seas (Vols. I & II) and Concerning the Nationality of Ships*. United Nations Legislative Series (ST/LEG/SER.B/-Suppl.), 1959.

_____. 22 February 1958. Saudi Arabia-Bahrain. U. S. Department of State. *International Boundary Study, Series A—Limits in the Seas*, no. 12. "Continental Shelf Boundary: Bahrain-Saudi Arabia." 10 March 1970.

_____. 7 July 1965. Saudi Arabia-Kuwait. "Agreement between the State of Kuwait and the Kingdom of Saudi Arabia relating to the Partition of the Neutral Zone, July 7, 1965." 60 *American Journal of International Law* 744 (1966).

_____. 7 September 1968. "Royal Decree No. M-27 relating to Ownership of Red Sea Resources, September 7, 1968." 8 *International Legal Materials* 606 (1969).

_____. 24 October 1968. Saudi Arabia-Iran. U. S. Department of State. *International Boundary Study, Series A—Limits in the Seas*, no. 24. "Continental Shelf Boundary: Iran-Saudi Arabia." 6 July 1970.

_____. 30 April 1974. Saudi Arab Regulations on Fishing Zones, 30 April 1974. (Unofficial translation courtesy of Richard Young.)

_____. 16 May 1974. "Agreement between Sudan and Saudi Arabia relating to the Joint Exploitation of the Natural Resources of the Sea-Bed and Sub-Soil of the Red Sea in the Common Zone, done at Khartoum on 16 May 1974." *National Legislation and Treaties relating to the Law of the Sea.* United Nations Legislative Series (ST/LEG/SER.B/18), 1976.

DOCUMENTS AND OFFICIAL PUBLICATIONS

Aitchison, C. U., compiler. *A Collection of Treaties, Engagements and Sanads relating to India and Neighboring Countries containing the Treaties, and etc., relating to Aden and the South Western Coast of Arabia, the Arab Principalities in the Persian Gulf, Muscat (Oman), Baluchistan and the North-West Frontier Province.* Vol 11. Delhi: Government of India, 1933.

"Bahrain-Iran-Iraq-Kuwait-Oman-Qatar-Saudi Arabia-United Arab Emirates: Agreements from the Kuwait Regional Conference on the Protection and Development of the Marine Environment and the Coastal Areas [Held in Kuwait 15-23 April 1978]." 17 *International Legal Materials* 501 (1978).

"Canadian Legislation on Arctic Pollution and Territorial Sea and Fishing Zones." 9 *International Legal Materials* 543 (1970).

"Circulaire Note Verbale of 1ᵉʳ Octobre 1914 (of the Sublime Porte defining the Territorial Waters of the Ottoman Empire)." In G. FR. de Martens, *Nouveau Recueil Géneral des traités et autres actes retatifs aux rapports de droit international.* Vol. 10. Ed. Heinrich Triepel. Leipzig: Librairie Theodor Weicher, 1920. pp. 101-2.

"Convention for the Protection of the Mediterranean Sea Against Pollution." 15 *International Legal Materials* 290 (1976).

"Convention on Supervision of International Trade in Arms and Ammunition and in Implements of War signed at Geneva on June 17, 1925." In *International Legislation.* Vol. 3: *1925-27.* Ed. Manley O. Hudson. Washington, D. C.: Carnegie Endowment for International Peace, 1931. pp. 1634-38.

"Curzon's Analysis of British Policy and Interests in Persia and the Persian Gulf, September 21, 1899." In *Diplomacy in the Near and Middle East.* Vol. 1: *A Documentary Record: 1535-1914.* Ed. J. C. Hurewitz. Princeton, N. J.: D. Van Nostrand Co., 1956.

Food and Agricultural Organization. *F. A. O. Commodity Review and*

Outlook 1973-1974. Rome: Food and Agricultural Organization, 1974 (FAO1/C73/973-74).

_____. *The Fish Resources of the Ocean.* Ed. J. A. Gulland. Surrey, England: Fishing New, 1971.

_____. *Yearbook of Fishery Statistics 1973.* Vol. 34 (FAO1/F52/34).

"France-United Kingdom: Arbitration on the Delimitation of the Continental Shelf." 18 *International Legal Materials* 397 (1979).

"International Convention for the Prevention of Pollution from Ships, 1973." 12 *International Legal Materials* 1319 (1973).

"International Court of Justice Decision in North Sea Continental Shelf Cases." 8 *International Legal Materials* 340 (1969).

"International Court of Justice: Judgments in the Fisheries Jurisdiction Cases." 13 *International Legal Materials* 1049 (1974).

League of Nations. *"Proceedings of the Conference for the Supervision of International Trade in Arms and Ammunition and in Implements of War."* Geneva (4 May - 17 June 1925). A.13.1925.IX.

"Madison's War Message, June 1, 1812." In *Ideas and Diplomacy.* Ed. Norman A. Graebner. New York: Oxford University Press, 1964.

"Speech by President Nasser on Closing of the Gulf of Aqaba, 22 May 1967." In *The Arab-Israeli Conflict*, Vol. 3: *Documents.* Princeton, N. J.: Princeton University Press, 1974.

United Nations. *Convention on the Continental Shelf,* A/CONF.13/L.55.

_____. *Convention on Fishing and Conservation of the Living Resources of the High Seas,* A/CONF.13/L.54.

_____. *Convention on the High Seas,* A/CONF.13/L.53.

_____. *Convention on the Territorial Sea and Contiguous Zone,* A/CONF. 13/L.52.

_____. Department of Economic and Social Affairs. *Monthly Bulletin of Statistics,* 29 (June 1975): 230-31 (ST / ESA / STAT / SER.Q / 30).

_____. Department of Economic and Social Affairs. *Statistical Yearbook 1973.* Vol. 25 (ST/ESA/STAT/SER.S/1).

_____. Department of Economic and Social Affairs. *World Energy Supplies 1950-1974,* 1976 (ST/ESA/STAT/SER.J/19).

_____. General Assembly, 9th Session, 2 October 1957. *Official Records,* A/PV697.

_____. *Informal Composite Negotiating Text* / Revision 1, A / CONF.62 / WP.10/Rev.1 of 28 April 1979.

_____. *Letter dated April 12, 1957 from the Permanent Representative of Saudi Arabia to the United Nations, addressed to the Secretary General,* A/3575.

_____. *Multilateral Treaties in Respect of which the Secretary General Performs Depository Functions,* 1975 (ST/LEG/SER.D/8).

_____. *Second United Nations Conference on the Law of the Sea: Committee of the Whole,* A/CONF.19/9.

_____. *Second United Nations Conference on the Law of the Sea: Summary Records of the Plenary Meetings and Meetings of the Committee of the Whole,* A/CONF.19/9.

_____. Secretariat of the Third United Nations Conference on the Law of the Sea. *Problems of Acquisition and Transfer of Marine Technology* (A/CONF.62/C.3/L.3), 25 July 1974 (mimeographed).

_____. *Third United Nations Conference on the Law of the Sea.* Vols. 1-8, 10.

_____. *United Nations Conference on the Law of the Sea.* Vols. 1-8, A/CONF.13/37-A/CONF.13/43.

_____. *Yearbook of the International Law Commission 1950.* Vols. 1 and 2.

_____. *Yearbook of the International Law Commission 1951.* Vol. 1.

_____. *Yearbook of the International Law Commission 1953.* Vols. 1 and 2.

_____. *Yearbook of the International Law Commission 1956.* Vol. 2.

United States. *Area Handbook for Iran.* Washington, D. C.: Government Printing Office, 1971.

_____. *Area Handbook for Saudi Arabia.* Washington, D. C.: Government Printing Office, 1971.

_____. Congress. House of Representatives, Committee on International Relations. *Oil Fields as Military Objectives: A Feasibility Study.* Washington, D. C.: Government Printing Office, 1975.

_____. Congress. Senate, Committee on Energy and Natural Resources. *Access to Oil—The United States Relationships with Saudi Arabia and Iran.* Washington, D. C.: Government Printing Office, 1977.

_____. Defense Mapping Agency, Hydrographic Center. *Sailing Directions for the Persian Gulf.* Pub. 62. 5th ed., rev. 1975.

_____. Department of Interior. *Summary of 1972 Oil and Gas Statistics for Onshore and Offshore Areas of 151 Countries,* by Sherwood E. Frezon. Geological Survey Professional Paper no. 885. Washington, D. C.: Government Printing Office, 1974.

_____. Department of State. Bureau of Intelligence and Research. Office of the Geographer. *International Boundary Study, Series A—Limits in the Seas,* no. 36. "National Claims to Maritime Jurisdictions." rev. 1 March 1973.

_____. Department of State. Bureau of Intelligence and Research. Office of the Geographer. *Sovereignty of the Sea.* Geographical Bulletin no. 3 rev. ed. Washington, D. C.: Government Printing Office, 1969.

_____. Department of Treasury. *Summary of Saudi Arabian Five Year Development Plan 1975-1980.* 23 October 1975.

_____. "Fishery Conservation and Management Act of 1976, April 13, 1976." 70 *American Journal of International Law* 624 (1976).

BOOKS, MONOGRAPHS, PAMPHLETS, AND PROCEEDINGS

Albaharna, Husain M. *The Arabian Gulf States: Their Legal and Political Status and Their International Problems.* 2nd rev. ed. Beirut: Librairie du Liban, 1975.

_____. *The Legal Status of the Arabian Gulf States.* Dobbs Ferry, N. Y.: Oceana, 1968.

Amuzegar, Jahangir. *Iran: An Economic Profile.* Washington, D. C.: Middle East Institute, 1977.

Anthony, John Duke. *Arab States of the Lower Gulf: People, Politics, Petroleum.* James Terry Duce Memorial Series, Vol. 3. Washington, D. C.: Middle East Institute, 1975.

Auguste, Barry B. L. *The Continental Shelf: The Practice and Policy of the Latin American States with Special Reference to Chile, Ecuador, and Peru.* Geneva: Librairie E. Droz, 1960.

Bynkershoek, Cornelius Van. *De Dominio Maris Dissertatio.* Ed. James Brown Scott. New York: Oxford University Press, 1923.

Center for Mediterranean Studies. *The Changing Balance of Power in the Persian Gulf.* Ed. Elizabeth Monroe. New York: American Universities Field Staff, 1972.

Cline, Ray. *World Power Assessment.* Boulder, Colo.: Westview Press, 1975.

D'Amato, Anthony, and Hargrove, John Lawrence. *Environment and the Law of the Sea.* Studies in Transnational Legal Policy, no. 5. Washington, D. C.: American Society of International Law, 1974.

Friedmann, Wolfgang. *The Future of the Oceans.* New York: Braziller, 1971.

Grotius, Hugo. *The Freedom of the Seas.* Ed. James Brown Scott. New York: Oxford University Press, 1916.

Hagen, Everett E. *The Economics of Development.* Homewood, Ill.: Richard D. Irwin, 1968.

Hay, Sir Rupert. *Persian Gulf States.* Washington, D. C.: Middle East Institute, 1959.

Hoffman, Stanley. *Gulliver's Troubles, or the Setting of American Foreign Policy.* New York: McGraw-Hill, 1968.

Hollick, Ann L., and Osgood, Robert E. *New Era of Ocean Politics.* Studies in International Affairs, no. 22. Baltimore: John Hopkins University Press, 1974.

Ingrams, William Harold. *The Yemen: Imams, Rulers, and Revolutionaries.* New York: Praeger, 1964.

International Institute for Strategic Studies. *The Military Balance, 1970-71;
1975-76; 1977-78; 1978-79.* London: Chatto & Windus, 1970-79.
International Petroleum Encyclopedia, 1975; 1977. Tulsa, Okla.: Petroleum
Publishing, 1975–77.
Kashmeeri, Bakor Omar. "The Role of Saudi Arabia in the Arab League."
Master's Thesis, University of Virginia, 1971.
Kunz, George Frederick, and Stevenson, Charles Hugh. *The Book of the
Pearl.* New York: Century, 1908.
Law of the Sea Institute. *The Law of the Sea: Needs and Interests of Devel-
oping Countries.* Proceedings of the Seventh Annual Conference of
the Law of the Sea Institute. Ed. Lewis M. Alexander. Kingston,
R. I.: University of Rhode Island, 1973.
Lissitzyn, Oliver J. *International Law Today and Tomorrow.* Dobbs Ferry,
N. Y.: Oceana, 1965.
McDougal, Myres S., and Burke, William T. *The Public Order of the
Oceans.* New Haven, Conn.: Yale University Press, 1962.
_____, and Feliciano, Florentino P. *Law and Minimum World Public
Order.* New Haven, Conn.: Yale University Press, 1961.
The Middle East 1953. 3rd ed. London: Europa Publications, 1953.
The Middle East 1955. 4th ed. London: Europa Publications, 1955.
Middle East Institute. *The Arabian Peninsula, Iran and the Gulf States:
New Wealth, New Power.* Proceedings of the 27th Annual Confer-
ence of the Middle East Institute. Washington, D.C.: Middle East
Institute, 1973.
_____. *World Energy Demands and the Middle East.* Proceedings of the
26th Annual Conference of the Middle East Institute. Washington,
D. C.: Middle East Institute, 1972.
The Middle East and North Africa 1964-1965. 11th ed. London: Europa
Publications, 1964.
The Middle East and North Africa 1972-1973. 19th ed. London: Europa
Publications, 1972.
The Middle East and North Africa 1978-1979. 25th ed. London: Europa
Publications, 1978.
Mohammed Reza Shah Pahlavi, Shahanshah of Iran. *Mission for My
Country.* New York: McGraw-Hill, 1961.
Nakhleh, Emile A. *Arab-American Relations in the Persian Gulf.* Washing-
ton, D. C.: American Enterprise Institute, 1975.
O'Connell, D. P. *The Influence of Law on Sea Power.* Manchester, England:
Manchester University Press, 1975.
Page, Stephen. *The U. S. S. R. and Arabia: The Development of Soviet
Policies and Attitudes towards the Countries of the Arabian Peninsula.*

London: Central Asian Research Center, 1971.

Philby, H. St. John. *Saudi Arabia*. New York: Praeger, 1955.

Ramazani, Rouhollah K. *The Foreign Policy of Iran, 1500-1941: A Developing Nation in World Affairs*. Charlottesville, Va.: University Press of Virginia, 1966.

_____. *Iran's Foreign Policy, 1941-1973: A Study of Foreign Policy in Modernizing Nations*. Charlottesville, Va.: University Press of Virginia, 1975.

_____. *The Persian Gulf: Iran's Role*. Charlottesville, Va.: University Press of Virginia, 1972.

Rovine, Arthur W. *Digest of United States Practice of International Law 1973*. Washington, D. C.: Government Printing Office, 1973.

Shwadran, Benjamin. *The Middle East, Oil and the Great Powers*. New York: Wiley, 1974.

Stockholm International Peace Research Institute. *Arms Trade Registers: The Arms Trade with the Third World*. Stockholm: Almqvist and Wiksell, 1975.

_____. *The Arms Trade with the Third World*. Stockholm: Almqvist & Wiksell, 1971.

_____. *World Armaments and Disarmament. SIPRI Yearbook 1978*. London: Taylor and Francis, 1978.

Swarztrauber, Sayre A. *The Three-Mile Limit of Territorial Seas*. Annapolis, Md.: Naval Institute Press, 1972.

Tahtinen, Dale R. *Arms in the Persian Gulf*. Washington, D. C.: American Enterprise Institute, 1974.

To Use the Sea: Readings in Seapower and Maritime Affairs. Annapolis, Md.: Naval Institute Press, 1973.

Vattel, Emerich de. *Le droit des gens, ou principes de la loi naturelle appliques à la conduite et aux affaires des nations et de souverains*. Vol. 3: *Translation of the Edition of 1758*. Trans. Charles G. Fenwick. The Classics of International Law. Ed. James Brown Scott. Washington, D. C.: Carnegie Institution of Washington, 1916.

Wenner, Manfred. *Modern Yemen, 1918-1966*. Baltimore, Md.: Johns Hopkins University Press, 1967.

Whiteman, Marjorie M. *Digest of International Law*. Vol. 4. Washington, D. C.: Government Printing Office, 1965.

PERIODICAL ARTICLES AND PARTS OF BOOKS

Bowen, Richard LeBaron, Jr. "The Pearl Fisheries of the Persian Gulf." *Middle East Journal* 5 (Spring 1951): 161-81.

Castañeda, Jorge. "The Underdeveloped Countries and the Development of International Law." *International Organization* 15 (Winter 1961): 34-48.

Clark, Eugenie. "The Strangest Sea." *National Geographic* 148 (September 1975): 338-43.

Dawisha, A. I. "Intervention in the Yemen: An Analysis of Egyptian Perceptions and Policies." *Middle East Journal* 29 (Winter 1975): 47-63.

De Borchgrave, Arnaud. "Colossus of the Oil Lane." *Newsweek* (21 May 1973): 40.

_____. "Oman: In Dire Straits." *Newsweek* (24 September 1979): 56-61.

Dean, Arthur H. "Freedom of the Seas." *Foreign Affairs* 38 (October 1958): 83-94.

Enders, Thomas O. "O. P. E. C. and the Industrial Countries: The Next Ten Years." *Foreign Affairs* 53 (July 1975): 625-37.

Farmanfarmaian, Khodadad, et al. "How Can the World Afford O. P. E. C. Oil." *Foreign Affairs* 53 (January 1975): 201–22.

Fatouros, A. A. "Participation of the 'New' States in the International Legal Order of the Future." In *The Future of the International Legal Order*. Vol. 1: *Trends and Patterns*. Ed. Richard Falk and Cyril E. Black. Princeton, N. J.: Princeton University Press, 1969.

Hassner, Pierre. "Le système international et les nouveaux états." In *La communauté international face aux jeunes états*. Ed. Jean-Baptiste Duroselle and Jean Meyriat. Paris: Librairie Armand Colin, 1964.

Hay, Sir Rupert. "The Persian Gulf States and Their Boundary Problems." *Geographical Journal* 120 (December 1954): 433-45.

Heller, Charles A. "The Strait of Hormuz—Critical in Oil's Future." *World Petroleum* 40 (October 1967): 24-26.

Henkin, Louis. "Politics and the Changing Law of the Sea." *Political Science Quarterly* 89 (March 1974): 46-67.

Hollick, Ann L. "Seabeds Make Strange Politics." *Foreign Policy* 9 (Winter 1972-73): 148-70.

Landen, Robert G. "The Modernization of the Persian Gulf: The Period of British Dominance." In *Middle East Focus: The Persian Gulf*. Proceedings of the Twentieth Annual Near East Conference. Ed. T. Cuyler Young. Princeton, N. J.: Princeton University Conference, 1969.

Liebesny, Herbert J. "Legislation on the Sea Bed and Territorial Waters of the Persian Gulf." *Middle East Journal* 4 (January 1950): 94-96.

Maechling, Charles, Jr. "The Politics of the Ocean." *Virginia Quarterly Review* 48 (Autumn 1971): 505-17.

Marlowe, John. "Arab-Persian Rivalry in the Persian Gulf." *Journal of the Royal Central Asian Society* 51 (January 1964): 23-31.

Meister, Jurg. "Iran's Naval Buildup." *Swiss Review of World Affairs* 23 (July 1973): 14-6.

Ramazani, Rouhollah K. "Emerging Patterns of Regional Relations in Iranian Foreign Policy." *Orbis* 18 (Winter 1975): 1043-69.

———. "Iran's Changing Foreign Policy: A Preliminary Discussion." *Middle East Journal* 24 (Autumn 1970): 421-37.

———. "Iran's White Revolution: A Study in Political Development." *International Journal of Middle Eastern Studies* 5 (April 1974): 124-39.

———. "Security in the Persian Gulf." *Foreign Affairs* 58 (Spring 1979): 821-35.

Salons, Carl F. "Gulf of Aqaba and Strait of Tiran: Troubled Waters." *U. S. Naval Institute Proceedings* 44 (December 1968): 54-62.

Smolansky, Oles M. "Moscow and the Persian Gulf: An Analysis of Soviet Ambitions and Potential." *Orbis* 14 (Spring 1970): 92-108.

Sorenson, Max. "The Law of the Sea." *International Conciliation* 520 (November 1958): 1–256.

Tucker, Robert W. "Oil: The Issue of American Intervention." *Commentary* 59 (January 1975): 21-31.

Wylie, J. C. "The Sixth Fleet and American Diplomacy." In *Soviet-American Rivalry in the Middle East*. Ed. J. C. Hurewitz. New York: Praeger, 1969.

Young, Richard. "The Law of the Sea in the Persian Gulf: Problems and Progress." In *New Directions in the Law of the Sea*. Vol. 3: *Collected Papers*. Ed. Robin Churchill, K. R. Simmonds, and Jane Welch. Dobbs Ferry, N. Y.: Oceana, 1973.

LEGAL ARTICLES

Abi-Saab, Georges, "The Newly Independent States and the Rules of International Law: An Outline." 8 *Howard Law Journal* 95 (1962).

Alexander, Lewis M. "Regionalism and the Law of the Sea: The Case of Semi-Enclosed Seas." 2 *Ocean Development and International Law* 180 (1974).

Bilder, Richard B. "The Anglo-Icelandic Fisheries Dispute." 1973 *Wisconsin Law Review* 37 (1973).

———. "The Arctic Waters Pollution Prevention Act: New Stress on the Law of the Sea." 69 *Michigan Law Review* 1 (1970).

Brinton, J. Y. "Jurisdiction over Sea-Bed Resources and Recent Developments in the Persian Gulf Area." 5 *Revue Egyptienne de Droit International*

Falk, Richard A. "The New States and International Legal Order." 118 *Recueil des cours* 1 (1966).

Friedlander, Robert A. "Controlling International Terrorism: An Analysis of Unilateral Force and Proposals for Multilateral Cooperation." 8 *University of Toledo Law Review* 209 (1976).

_____. "Coping with Terrorism: What is to be Done." 5 *Ohio Northern Law Review* 432 (1978).

_____. "Terrorism in the Middle East: A Symposium," 7 *Akron Law Review* 373 (1974).

Kassim, Anis F. "The Law of the Sea: Conflicting Claims in the Persian Gulf." 4 *Journal of Law and Economic Development* 282 (1969).

Lapidoth, Ruth. "Passage through the Strait of Bab Al-Mandeb." 13 *Israel Law Review* 180 (1978).

Moore, John Norton. "The Control of Foreign Intervention in Internal Conflict." 9 *Virginia Journal of International Law* 205 (1969).

_____. "Prolegomenon to the Jurisprudence of Myres McDougal and Harold Lasswell." 54 *Virginia Law Review* 662 (1968).

Oda, Shigeru. "Boundary of the Continental Shelf." 12 *Japanese Annual of International Law* 264 (1968).

Padwa, David J. "Submarine Boundaries." 9 *International and Comparative Law Quarterly* 633 (1960).

Ramazani, Rouhollah K. "The Settlement of the Bahrain Dispute." 12 *Indian Journal of International Law* 1 (1972).

Selak, Charles B., Jr. "Recent Developments in the High Seas Fisheries Jurisdiction under the Presidential Proclamation of 1945." 44 *American Journal of International Law* 675 (1950).

Waldock, Sir Humphrey. "The Anglo-Norwegian Fisheries Case." 28 *British Yearbook of International Law* 144 (1951).

Young, Richard. "Equitable Solutions for Offshore Boundaries: The 1968 Saudi-Iran Agreement." 64 *American Journal of International Law* 152 (1970).

_____. "Further Claims to Areas beneath the High Seas." 43 *American Journal of International Law* 790 (1949).

_____. "The Legal Status of Submarine Areas beneath the High Seas." 45 *American Journal of International Law* 236 (1951).

_____. "Lord Asquith and the Continental Shelf." 46 *American Journal of International Law* 512 (1952).

_____. "Saudi Arabian Offshore Legislation." 43 *American Journal of International Law* 530 (1949).

NEWSPAPERS AND NEWS SUMMARIES

Arab News (Jeddah), 1979.
Arab Report and Record (London), 1968-79.
Asian Recorder (New Delhi), 1975-79.
Baltimore Sun, 1973.
Iran Times (Washington, D.C.), 1979.
Kayhan (Tehran; Weekly International Edition), 1974-78.
Kayhan International (Tehran), 1970.
Middle East Economic Survey (Beirut), 1968-71; 1978-79.
Middle East Monitor, 1973-76.
New York Times, 1958, 1974-79.
Washington Post, 1974-79.

OTHER SOURCE

Richard Young. Personal Interview. Washington, D. C. 23 April 1976.

Index

ABOUT THE AUTHOR

CHARLES G. MacDONALD is Visiting Assistant Professor in the
Woodrow Wilson Department of Government and Foreign Affairs
at the University of Virginia, while on leave from Florida International University. He has contributed to the *Journal of South Asian
and Middle Eastern Studies*.